A CALCULATED RESTRAINT

A CALCULATED RESTRAINT

WHAT ALLIED LEADERS SAID
ABOUT THE HOLOCAUST

RICHARD BREITMAN

Harvard University Press

Cambridge, Massachusetts & London, England

2025

Publication of this book has been supported through the generous provisions
of the Maurice and Lula Bradley Smith Memorial Fund.

First printing

Cataloging-in-Publication Data available from the Library of Congress

ISBN: 978-0-674-29364-9 (alk. paper)

To Carol Breitman and Judy Bittel

The historian who wishes faithfully to record and judge the struggle of those involved has first of all to explain people's behavior on the basis of what they themselves knew at the time; whether a particular decision was rational, judicious, moral, must be determined by whatever yardstick the participants themselves would have been ready to submit to. Naturally, people will be found to have acted on different levels of rationality, and where moral considerations are involved, they will be found to have possessed different degrees of courage and character. But moral judgment can only be pronounced on individuals when we have fully imagined the plight they were in, and that is why any such moral judgment has to be preceded by a reconstruction of the situation as exact as the historical sources will permit.

—Jacob Katz, "Was the Holocaust Predictable?"

CONTENTS

A CALCULATED RESTRAINT

INTRODUCTION

O n September 22, 1942, Franklin Roosevelt's personal representative to the Vatican gave Pope Pius XII a report on Nazi atrocities. Myron Taylor, a retired chief executive of U.S. Steel turned diplomat and refugee policy official, suggested to the pontiff that if he condemned these barbaric acts publicly, it would hearten those working to save thousands from suffering and death. In addition, Taylor gave Cardinal Luigi Maglioni, the Vatican secretary of state, a long memorandum describing the massacre of Poland's Jews, including the partial liquidation of the Warsaw Ghetto and the killing of Jews from several other countries. According to this second document, deportations of Jews from various countries to the East for "work" were a ruse to hide Nazi mass murder from the outside world. Taylor asked whether the Vatican could confirm such reports and whether the pope could help suggest ways to mobilize "the forces of civilized public opinion" to stop these barbarities.[1] Civilized public opinion was a clever phrase that suggested that the pope take a broad view of his moral responsibilities and his immense moral authority.

Taylor then exchanged information with other people gathering evidence about Nazi mass murder. Stopping in London on his way back to Washington, he met with leaders of the

British Section of the World Jewish Congress. They presented him with a copy of a report originating from a secret German informant that Hitler's headquarters was considering a plan to exterminate 3.5 to 4 million Jews to resolve the Jewish question once and for all. A few weeks later, in the United States, Taylor told Rabbi Stephen Wise and Nahum Goldmann of the World Jewish Congress that the reported atrocities in France, Poland, and Yugoslavia had been confirmed. He then took to the White House the documents and information he had gathered for the president and the secretary of state. They, too, were still only partly informed about what was later to be called the Holocaust.[2]

While Taylor was traveling, his assistant Harold Tittmann, who was resident in Vatican City, went to the Apostolic Palace "to pray that a response be given, even at any hour, to the memo left by His Excellency Myron Taylor on the killings of the Jews." The pope's adviser on Jewish matters, Monsignor Dell'Acqua, a member of the secretariat of state, discerned a political purpose behind the American inquiries. He warned Pius XII that Allied publicity about any Vatican confirmation of Nazi mass killings of Jews could have unpleasant consequences for the Vatican and also for the Jews themselves. Vatican officials then told Tittmann that although reports of severe measures against "non-Aryans" had reached them, it was impossible to confirm them, and that the Vatican had no practical suggestions to make, apparently believing that only military force, not moral suasion, could end Nazi barbarities.[3]

The Vatican received reports from clergy throughout Europe. The extent of the Vatican's own information about the Holocaust, in contrast with the reluctance of Pope Pius XII to condemn it publicly, has fueled decades of intense curiosity and controversy. Only in 2020 did the Vatican open the records of Pius XII's tenure to outside researchers.

The contrast between what Allied leaders knew and what they said publicly about the Holocaust remains murky and is still largely unexplored. My aim in this book is to connect analysis of what Churchill, Stalin, and Roosevelt *knew* about the Holocaust to what they *said* about it in their most important statements on the subject. First, I examine the extent to which they sought to create and mobilize an international imagined community, based on an asserted common morality, in which the fate of Jews mattered in a war that had to be won. Second, I examine the critical question of how Allied leaders understood the relationship between the Holocaust and the war itself during the war's different stages. In this comparative analysis I have drawn on my own selective archival research, key published primary sources, including the correspondence between Churchill and Stalin and between Roosevelt and Stalin, numerous biographies of these leaders, and relevant scholarly monographs.

Government records related to the Holocaust became available to researchers, some soon after the war, others according to existing declassification schedules, and still others from special laws or public pressure related to interest in the Holocaust. Western governments have now declassified most World War II intelligence and war crimes records, and the former Soviet Union had at least begun to do so before again restricting access. Partly for this reason, scholars have made major advances in understanding what, and when, Allied government agencies knew about the Nazi persecution and extermination of Jews.

Nonetheless, relevant sources on Allied leaders—none of whom kept regular diaries—are sketchy. Roosevelt refused to permit cabinet minutes, nor did he did allow visitors to take notes during conversations with him. Roosevelt, Churchill, and Stalin never corresponded among themselves about the Holocaust; Churchill and FDR exchanged few words about it.[4] Although Churchill and FDR may have talked privately about

Nazi mass killings of Jews during the prime minister's visits to the United Sates or on transatlantic phone calls, no proof of such conversations has emerged; thus, direct evidence of their reactions is limited. That makes it all the more important to study the occasions when they *did* speak publicly about the Nazi campaign against the Jews.

While two of the leaders discussed here—Stalin is the outlier— frequently gave radio addresses to large audiences, they also depended on print media to convey their priorities and to educate their citizenry. Individual journalists accumulated and published their own information about Nazi killings of Jews, and I have integrated some of their efforts into my narrative and analysis. Though their reporting on the Holocaust lagged behind events, the media still played an important role in spreading its awareness in Europe and America. Media reports, which sometimes forced Allied leaders to react, offer some sense of the connections between the war and the Holocaust.

This book begins with Adolf Hitler's own public pronouncements. His speeches in the months before World War II set the stage for genocide, and they were a warning to outsiders of his future plans for the Jews. In his January 30, 1939, speech to the German Reichstag, Hitler threatened to annihilate the Jews of Europe. What Hitler, and other Germans, called his "prophecy" reinforced other signs of the impending mass murder of German Jews. Drawing on some new evidence, Chapter 1 analyzes his full speech—and not just the most infamous portion. Here the views of then Associated Press bureau chief in Berlin, Louis P. Lochner, are important in deciphering Hitler's intentions. Lochner understood the Nazi regime well. He kept a diary during 1939 that few historians have made use of, and his contemporaneous published articles contained valuable nuggets of information. My analysis here challenges the common interpretation that Hitler at this time was merely trying to force or induce Western countries to assist German and European Jews to immigrate elsewhere. Instead, I claim that he already hoped to physically eliminate the Jews of Europe. He meant what he said.

In Chapter 1, I also investigate the ways in which Hitler's speeches were heard outside of Germany. In early 1939, statesmen and observers were most concerned about the danger of war in Europe and not about what they perceived as empty rhetorical threats to foreign Jews. Winston Churchill and Franklin Roosevelt were exceptions in recognizing the danger that Hitler posed. For years while Churchill was out of power, he warned his country that Hitler threatened all of Europe. Roosevelt concluded that Hitler's territorial ambitions were essentially boundless and that they directly menaced the United States. Roosevelt's perception of Hitler's goals was a key link in the chain of political, diplomatic, and military moves—the actions and reactions among the leaders of the Soviet Union, the UK, and United States, and, of course, Germany—that continued until the war's end and the collapse of the Nazi regime.

In responding to Hitler's threats and Nazi actions against Jews, Churchill and Roosevelt shared a similar problem: they viewed the Nazi war against the Jews as a politically—and sometimes militarily—sensitive issue. Hitler and Nazi propagandists frequently declared that the Allies were fighting a war on behalf of the Jews and that Jews were also the puppet masters behind the Communist regime in the USSR.[5] If Churchill and FDR criticized Nazi persecution of the Jews, many Europeans, and some Americans, would have taken their words as evidence supporting Nazi accusations of Jewish influence over their governments. Both leaders had to gauge the impact of their words at a time when antisemitism was prevalent throughout much of the world. But their complete silence about Nazi atrocities might also have prompted accusations from liberal and pro-Jewish sources in various countries that Allied leaders were condoning the Nazis' behavior.[6] Churchill and Roosevelt usually finessed this dilemma by denouncing Nazi atrocities *in general*, as we shall see beginning in Chapter 2.

Stalin had his own unique reasons to overlook Nazi killings of Jews, as Chapter 3 shows. Communist ideology held that Nazism was an extreme form of capitalism, but not a racial ideology or movement. Soviet propaganda also tried to mask national, ethnic, and religious identities among its population, even if the regime usually favored those of Russian nationality.[7] As a totalitarian dictatorship, the Soviet Union had more in common with Nazi Germany than with the Western Allies, and Stalin's internal politics and policies before the war were more lethal than Hitler's. These similarities may have helped make Stalin willing to bargain with Hitler over territorial expansion and to sign a nonaggression treaty with Germany in late August 1939.

During the last months of 1939 and up to June 1941—the period of the German-Soviet Nonaggression Pact—Stalin avoided explicitly criticizing Nazi persecution of the Jews. However, after Germany invaded the USSR, he sought opportunities to strengthen his relationship with Churchill and Roosevelt so as to help stave off military defeat and also to serve postwar Soviet interests. Like many outsiders, he assumed that Jews had more influence in the West than they did. Stalin's diplomatic and military concerns influenced his own willingness to mention publicly Nazi persecution and mass murder of Jews; he hoped to attract Jewish resources and mobilize Jewish influence in the West. But for internal political reasons, Stalin wanted to focus his public statements primarily on the Nazi threat to the state and the people of the Soviet Union. By comparison, the fate of Soviet Jews meant virtually nothing to him.

The practice of generalizing the threat of Nazi atrocities, thus subsuming Nazi policy to exterminate the Jews among broader atrocities, was not simply the personal preference of the three leaders. The United States, the UK, and the USSR all conducted what they called psychological warfare (today's information warfare) against Germany and its allies and satellites. As I discuss in Chapter 4 and Chapter 5, Allied governments learned to guide the media toward perceived Axis weaknesses, and well-informed journalists had some influence on their governments. Speeches by the Allied leaders, usually keeping psychological warfare calculations in mind, avoided subjects that experts thought might make them vulnerable to counterattack by Nazi propaganda. For Roosevelt and Churchill, this meant limiting their explicit rhetorical attacks on the Holocaust.

Whether this restraint produced the desired results is something we can best judge today after detailed study of the interaction between their decisions about the war and their awareness of the Holocaust, a major theme of this book. As Chapter 5 ultimately suggests, they could have gone further than they did in sponsoring an Allied declaration on December 17, 1942, denouncing the Nazi policy of mass murder.

What Churchill, Stalin, and Roosevelt said publicly about the Nazi murder of Jews would have mattered at the time. A public speech or statement would have shown solidarity with the most important ideological enemy of the Nazi regime. It would have offered confirmation of rumors and stories circulating about what Nazi "resettlement" of Jews really involved. If any of the Allied leaders had spoken out clearly enough and early enough, such warning might have convinced more Jews to flee, and it might have encouraged others, like Anne Frank's family, to go into hiding where that was possible. As Myron Taylor told Pope Pius XII, it would have encouraged those gentiles who were willing to take serious risks to help save Jews. It might have influenced some neutral governments to do more.

The constraints of the war, and of politics, usually prevented Churchill and Roosevelt from acting according to civilized opinion. Nor did they have the time or energy to become caught up in the detailed implementation of refugee policies, which was usually handled by lower-level government officials. The president and prime minister focused their time and energy primarily on mobilization, war strategy, and military operations. But the two democratic Allied leaders could at least have spoken out on occasion. A leader's speech could have suggested to their own government officials that they consider measures to alleviate the plight of those trying to escape their Nazi executioners.

Since the end of World War II, the idea of an international legal standard of behavior, marked by key milestones such as the International Military Tribunals at Nuremberg and Tokyo, the UN Genocide Convention, and the establishment of the International Criminal Court at The Hague, has substantially expanded interest in exposing and punishing extreme violations of human rights. The belief that the Western Allies could have taken greater account of moral concerns during the Holocaust is now widely held.

Some twenty-first-century observers have argued, retrospectively, that there should have been targeted Allied military responses to Nazi crimes against Jews and other civilians. For example, BBC-2 TV called wartime proposals to bomb the gas chambers and crematoria at Auschwitz one of the greatest moral questions of the twentieth century.[8] Israeli Prime Minister Benjamin Netanyahu has said that the Allies could have saved millions of Jews by bombing the Nazi extermination camps.[9] This gulf between the wartime decisions and actions of the democratic Allied leaders and some current moral sensibilities is a sign that, in some quarters, the new weight given to moral standards has eclipsed Churchill and Roosevelt's successes and failures in managing the war. But only victory in the war could end the Holocaust.

Recent popular discussion of the Allied leaders' reactions to the Holocaust has often narrowed to an assessment of character: Churchill, a self-professed Zionist, was good for the Jews, while Stalin was bloodthirsty and antisemitic, with Roosevelt somewhere in between. Some writers on the subject suggest that it might have been easy for the two democratic leaders to recognize the proper moral course and to act accordingly. But such blanket judgments fail to take sufficient account of the wartime pressures on each leader. We need to reconstruct their motives based on both their context and on the surviving evidence. The Allied leaders did not live in a twenty-first-century world. Today's moral condemnation or praise should not obviate what we can learn from settled history—placing their actions in the context of their time. After that, we can suggest what present-day perspectives reveal about the limitations of their priorities and their judgment.

Much literature on wartime Britain follows or parallels Churchill's official biographer, Martin Gilbert, who credits Churchill with speaking out early and forcefully against the Holocaust.[10] In Chapter 2, I closely examine his key August 1941 speech, in which he famously decried "a crime without a name," to seriously undermine that claim. Churchill may or may not have understood then that Jews were the primary target of Nazi executioners. In any case, he tried to improve relations with Stalin by describing Soviet popular resistance as provoking Nazi executions. Stalin is often ignored because he does not fit easily into today's moral universe, but he was the only Allied leader to briefly mention Nazi killings of Jews relatively early in the Holocaust. As I show in Chapter 3, his one speech, delivered in November 1941, seems to have had some practical effect in freeing some subordinates to publicize systematic Nazi killings of Jews in occupied areas. Finally, some have condemned Roosevelt for silence and inaction until late in the Holocaust, even though he was the only Allied leader to authorize a rescue effort during the war.

Chapters 6 through 8 show that FDR gradually accumulated information about the Holocaust and that he paid some attention to rescue and relief issues even before he established the War Refugee Board in January 1944. This evidence challenges David Wyman's monochromatic portrait of Roosevelt and US policies in his 1984 book, *The Abandonment of the Jews*, which presented him as indifferent and negligent regarding the fate of the Jews. Roosevelt's statement at a press conference on March 24, 1944, in which he denounced the continuation of the Holocaust, became the centerpiece of the War Refugee Board's campaign to oppose the Holocaust in Hungary.

Assessing Allied leaders' statements on the Holocaust amidst the military and political constraints of World War II helps to counteract extreme ex post facto judgments. Such assessment also offers important perspective and guidance today, when antisemitism has again spread widely. Other genocides, too, have taken place even as government officials and politicians have refrained from speaking out. This history remains far too relevant, if often disputed or misunderstood.

CHAPTER ONE

HITLER'S AUDIENCES

O n Monday, January 30, 1939, Adolf Hitler planned to give a speech to what he called the first Reichstag of Greater Germany. He chose not to show himself in advance to the crowd outside the Reich Chancellery that howled for the Führer to make an appearance on the sixth anniversary of his appointment as chancellor.[1] The experienced American consul and diplomat Raymond Geist had heard that Hitler intended to challenge President Franklin Roosevelt and, at the same time, to pose as the "arch-champion" against the democracies, Bolshevism, and international Jewry. Geist warned one of his high-level Nazi contacts that Hitler might further poison Germany's relations with the United States if he attacked the president.[2]

A shocking eruption of Nazi violence against German Jews had severely tarnished Germany's image in the United States. Herschel Grynszpan, a young Polish Jew, had fatally shot a German diplomat in Paris on November 7, 1938. Hitler and Propaganda Minister Joseph Goebbels then unleashed a coordinated punitive operation that morphed into a pogrom by Nazi activists and German youths. Over several days, some 1,400 synagogues across Greater Germany as well as many thousands of Jewish stores and shops were destroyed. The Gestapo rounded up about 31,000 Jewish men and dispatched them to concentration camps. Close to a hundred Jewish Germans were killed. On November 10, Hitler expressed satisfaction with the punishment and roundup, but he and Goebbels agreed to call off the destruction of property. Nonetheless, Hitler made it clear that this action was only the start of more radical, aggressive measures against the Jews.[3] The controlled German press and state radio justified this action and prepared the public for more to come with daily warnings about Jewish criminals and conspirators.[4]

Negative American media coverage of the violence called Kristallnacht (night of broken glass) outstripped any other story about Germany since Hitler came to power. Nearly one thousand US newspaper editorials denounced the Nazi regime.[5] On November 14, US ambassador to Germany Hugh R. Wilson was called home from Berlin for consultation, a diplomatic rebuke. On the evening of November 14, in a radio address that had advance White House approval, Secretary of the Interior Harold Ickes Jr. denounced Nazi attacks on Jews and Christians, calling them an assault on reason and civilization. He also tied the Jewish refugee problem to the danger of war. America had to follow its ideals to protest brutal violations of the laws of humanity and un-Christian acts in various parts of the world.[6] The next day, Franklin Roosevelt declared at a press conference that he could scarcely believe such events could occur in a twentieth-century civilization. Uncharacteristically, he allowed reporters to quote him directly.[7]

Consul Geist wrote that no condemnation of Nazi Germany for Kristallnacht could be too strong, but he also argued that further US government criticism of Germany would be ill-advised as it might lead Hitler to break off diplomatic relations, which in turn would end Jewish immigration to the United

States. It might even lead him to accelerate his timetable of escalating persecution. Geist warned that if the United States wanted to criticize Nazi persecution openly, it should be prepared to go to war in a coalition with other Western democracies; otherwise, it was better to handle criticism privately and let immigration to the United States continue.[8] Sometime in January, however, Geist warned Hitler's military adjutant Fritz Wiedemann that another Nazi "performance" like that of November 10 would lead the United States to break off relations with Berlin.[9] Although Geist had no authorization for this move, he did grasp the likely consequences of another Kristallnacht, and he hoped that his warning might help to prevent one.

In his State of the Union address on January 4, 1939, President Roosevelt obliquely attacked Germany, declaring that unnamed foreign dictatorships threatened the United States through their aggression and disruptive actions. FDR observed that the elimination of democracy and religion was spreading strident ambition and brute force in international affairs, and that the United States had to defend "the very tenets of faith and humanity on which their churches, their governments and their very civilization are founded. The defense of religion, of democracy and of good faith among nations is all the same fight. . . . We have learned that long before any overt military act, aggression begins with preliminaries of propaganda, subsidized penetration [subversion], the loosening of ties of good will," the president explained.[10]

Fearing embarrassment if Hitler responded by attacking FDR, Prentiss Gilbert, the highest-ranking US diplomat still in Germany, chose not to attend the dictator's January 30 address. Instead, Gilbert sent "certain Embassy secretaries" to get their firsthand impressions.[11] High Nazi officials sat on the stage of the Kroll Opera House behind Hitler, and on the back wall above them all was a mounted casting of a huge eagle clutching a large swastika. Following the quick election of Hermann Göring as president of the Reichstag, Hitler began speaking at 8:15 p.m.[12]

In six years, Hitler boasted, the Nazis had achieved the dreams of centuries by bringing Germans together, a success achieved by the grace of God. He paid tribute to two decades of "fanatical struggle on behalf of a political idea" by hundreds of thousands of Nazi activists.

He did not discuss the seminal events of 1933, when a group of conservatives led by former chancellor Franz von Papen had persuaded aged President Paul von Hindenburg that they would be able to control Hitler if he became chancellor. On January 30 of that year, amidst parliamentary gridlock, Hindenburg legally appointed Hitler head of a coalition government. Afterward, with Nazi paramilitary forces dominating the streets, Hitler and his key subordinates forced through a series of semilegal measures that in effect ripped out the heart of Germany's democratic constitution and eviscerated the coalition government. The nation then became a one-party state. When President Hindenburg died in August 1934, Hitler assumed his office as well, and now Nazi Germany became a totalitarian system guided by a Führer whose will was turned into written and unwritten law.

In his speech, Hitler tossed verbal barbs at the pessimists, the skeptics, and the indifferent who, he said, had contributed the least to the achievement of German unity. He implied that many Germans had much to learn and later stressed that obedience and full commitment were not just for soldiers—and that character and leadership ability mattered far more than education. It would be necessary for Germans to abandon outmoded class prejudices and tenets of social morality, and instead fully dedicate themselves to whatever would improve the collective national body (*Volkskörper*). He left future internal goals vague.

Welcoming new parliamentary representatives from now-annexed Austria and the former Czech border region known as the Sudetenland, Hitler professed to be overwhelmed by recent foreign policy events. He said that he had simply acted to prevent turmoil when he took over Austria in March 1938. He castigated Czechoslovakian President Edvard Beneš for seeking to provoke Germany and for blackening Germany's reputation in the summer and fall of 1938 during disputes over the Sudetenland. Only then, he said, did he decide to resolve the Sudeten German question once and for all. That had brought Britain, France, Italy, and Germany to the Munich Conference at the end of September. He politely recognized British Prime Minister Neville Chamberlain and French Premier Edouard Daladier for agreeing to the German annexation of the Sudetenland, and he paid tribute to his friend Benito Mussolini for his effective "mediation" at Munich. Gullible Germans and foreigners sympathetic to Germany may have bought Hitler's rhetorical version of these events.

The real sequence of events was quite different. Hitler had planned to attack and destroy Czechoslovakia, and if Britain and France came to its defense, he believed that broader fight was bound to come later anyway. He knew that the German military was better prepared than its rivals; he was not impressed with British and French leadership, and he believed in the inherent superiority of the German race. Though Hitler had settled for a diplomatic victory at the Munich Conference, it left him with a sour aftertaste. He had no intention of respecting the sovereignty of what was left of Czechoslovakia. He resented signs that the German public celebrated the avoidance of war after Munich.[13]

Aware of how many Germans still hated the terms of the 1919 Treaty of Versailles, Hitler used his January 30 speech to offer German listeners a mixture of grievances and pride: despite

outside plundering of Germany and the imposition of huge
debts upon it, despite the loss of its colonies, Germany had now
fed and clothed its people and eliminated unemployment.
Which of the "great democracies" had done as much? he asked.
Hitler identified Germany's basic problem as overcrowding.
Either Germany had to both import and export more, which
he believed was a vicious circle, or it needed more land for its
population—what he termed living space. He did not state explicitly that the solution would require war, let alone that he
expected to go to war soon. But it was inescapable: Germany
could not reduce the density of its population and displace
non-German inhabitants from their lands without a major
war. And Hitler, approaching his fiftieth birthday, believed he
would die young. He might not have all that much time.[14]

With very few exceptions, the nearly six hundred deputies of
the Reichstag in the auditorium on January 30 knew nothing of
his plans. In a secret November 1937 meeting at the Reich
Chancellery with the commanders of the armed services, the
war minister, and the foreign minister, Hitler had set forth part
of his agenda for a major war no later than 1943–1945—
Germany would wage war against both Britain and France
while seeking more land elsewhere, presumably in the east. (His
military adjutant Friedrich Hossbach wrote a summary after
the meeting that survived the war and would be used as evidence of German war-planning at the International Military
Tribunal at Nuremberg.[15]) Fulminating against foreign warmongers, Hitler projected his own desires even as he tried to
obtain tactical advantage. Raymond Geist knew enough to be
worried; he had reported in early January 1939 that Hitler and
the radical Nazi elements would soon launch aggression that
would give the world a series of grave shocks in 1939.[16] Only
days before his speech to the Reichstag, Hitler privately told an
audience of 217 senior officers, including top generals and

admirals, that the Roman Empire served as a precedent; one day, the Aryan race would conquer the world. According to rumors Lochner heard later, Hitler also declared that Britain was decadent, and that Germany would dominate for 5,000 years.[17]

In his Reichstag speech, however, Hitler kept alive the option of increasing German exports and using the income to buy sufficient food for the nation. He warned that if foreign statesmen blocked German access to their markets, it would initiate a desperate economic struggle that Germany could bear better than others. He would do whatever was necessary to prevail. He declared it the duty of every German to support his economic policy.

Through his reading, Hitler had come to believe that Germany had been cheated by history.[18] Here he attacked those who had once thrown the world into "the firestorm of war" and who were again trying to heighten animosities to the point of combustion. He blamed certain democracies for poisoning international opinion against so-called totalitarian countries that had no harmful intentions. He denounced several apostles of war (*Kriegsapostel*), none of whom was currently in power in the democracies, but they could become leaders within months. Germany would not let their distortions go unanswered; it would preserve its sovereignty through the weapons it forged and through acquisition of friendly allies.

Hitler's British apostles of war began with former First Lord of the Admiralty Duff Cooper, who had resigned in protest shortly after the Munich Conference. In Parliament he explained that Chamberlain believed in addressing Hitler with the "language of sweet reasonableness." Cooper said he believed in the use of the language of the mailed fist.[19] Next came former Foreign Secretary Anthony Eden, who had resigned in February 1938 after Chamberlain tried to improve British relations with Mussolini. There was some irony in Hitler's depiction of Eden as an enemy. Until his resignation, Eden had been a half-hearted supporter of Chamberlain's appeasement policy toward Germany, and he had been indecisive about how to deal with Italy.[20]

Winston Churchill had a long, consistent record of warning about the threat from Nazi Germany. Hitler had first attacked Churchill at a November 1938 rally just before Kristallnacht. After Churchill responded in (for him) mild tones that, regretfully, success had not mellowed Hitler, Hitler asked whether the Almighty had handed the key to democracy to such people as Churchill. As Churchill biographer Andrew Roberts observes, this was a remarkable broadside on an MP who held no cabinet position at the time and who had only negligible influence on the government.[21] Hitler included Churchill as a known enemy and a future threat to his plans.[22]

The lone American "apostle" Hitler mentioned was Harold Ickes, perhaps the sharpest US government critic of Germany after the events of Kristallnacht. He had no responsibility for US foreign policy, only modest standing in the Democratic Party, and hardly looked like a future president.[23] But for Hitler, he was a less risky target than Roosevelt. Hitler may well have heeded Geist's warning not to alienate the United States with a direct attack on the president.[24]

Hitler claimed that Jewish or non-Jewish agitators were continuously stirring up antagonism against Germany and its people. From now on, he announced, German propaganda and the press would expose these self-interested politicians, unconscionable profiteers, and, above all, international Jewry. Their lies about Germany represented outrageous slander. He then cited examples of what he considered falsehoods.

Germany had never attacked America, he said, but during the Great War, America had attacked Germany. An investigative committee of the House of Representatives determined that the United States had no good cause for war in 1917, but that

capitalistic motivations were the prime reason, he said. Hitler
was referring to the Nye Committee, led by Senator George Nye,
Republican of North Dakota. From 1934 to 1936, this Senate
committee had held hearings and written an exaggerated report
about the influence of Wall Street and the armaments industry
on US entrance and involvement in the war in 1917–1918. This
report had some influence on Congress's passage of Neutrality
Acts in the mid-1930s, and it became a touchstone for US isolationists in the late 1930s. Of course, Hitler omitted any mention
of Germany's unrestricted submarine warfare in the Atlantic,
the catalyst for US entrance into the war in 1917. In his address
he also avoided any broadside against the American public.

About an hour into his speech, Hitler suddenly declared that
foreign attempts to intervene in Germany would not influence
him in any way, especially on the resolution of the Jewish question. The entire democratic world oozed with sympathy for
"poor tormented Jewish people" but was unwilling to do anything to help them, he told the applauding deputies. How could
Western countries with large, thinly settled world empires claim
they were unable to receive Jews, when Germany, with its dense
population, was forced to accommodate them? German Jews
never belonged in Germany, Hitler suggested; they were para-
sitic carriers of political and actual diseases. Whatever wealth or
positions they had acquired came at the expense of naïve Germans, particularly during the years after the Great War when so
many Germans had died, suffered, or were forced to live in new
countries bordering a Germany shrunk by the Versailles peace
settlement. Foreign countries had no right to speak of humanity
and no right to demand that German Jews receive capital for
immigration elsewhere. Germany would no longer allow its affairs to be determined by foreign nations, Hitler announced.

Hitler at least partly grasped the real emigration situation:
the US immigration quota for Germany was currently filled.

The Roosevelt administration was pressing Latin American countries to take in Jewish refugees, but an international effort to resettle German and other European Jews had fallen into a diplomatic swamp.[25] An Intergovernmental Committee on Refugees (IGCR), a product of the July 1938 refugee conference sponsored by President Roosevelt, often called the Évian Conference, struggled both to find viable outlets for large numbers of European Jews and to conduct direct negotiations with Nazi Germany.

A rational antisemitic leader might have welcomed the IGCR, spelled out general terms for releasing German Jews, and challenged the West to meet them. Instead, Geist said that the Nazi regime viewed the IGCR as a tool designed to place Germany in an unfavorable light, that it was a part of "international Jewry's" campaign against Germany.[26]

Reichsbank president Hjalmar Schacht was the only high German official initially willing to talk with a small refugee delegation headed by IGCR director George Rublee that arrived in Berlin in January 1939. After Hitler dismissed Schacht, Geist convinced Göring, who headed the Office of the Four-Year Plan and who valued commercial relations with the United States, that President Roosevelt would resent any snub of the refugee committee. As a result, Göring arranged for one of his men, Helmut Wohlthat, to carry on negotiations. At the time, Geist thought that continued talks might stave off a massacre of German Jews.[27]

In his January 30 speech Hitler sarcastically told his foreign critics that instead of complaining about the "barbaric expulsion" of a culturally valuable element, they should be grateful to Germany for making the Jews available to them. But he was not trying to convince Western countries to welcome German Jews. Rather, Hitler's broadsides aimed to convince foreigners as well as Germans that Jews were a worldwide pestilence. His foreign policy was designed to divide and weaken Germany's enemies, even as his domestic policy priorities were to prepare for war and more extreme anti-Jewish persecution.

Some two weeks after Kristallnacht, during a conversation with South African Defense Minister Oswald Pirow, Hitler had mentioned the need to make all Jews disappear from Europe, and in the weeks before January 30, he privately discussed different possibilities for removing them. On January 5, he told Polish Foreign Minister Josef Beck that he would have sent Jews to some distant colony if the Western powers had shown more understanding of Germany's colonial objectives. The implication, however, was that Germany had to control colonial territory. On January 21, he told Czech Foreign Minister Frantisek Chvalkovsky that the Jews of Germany should be "annihilated," but he also mentioned shipping them off to some distant place, and if the Anglo-Saxon countries did not cooperate, they would be responsible for their deaths.[28] These threats encompassed a range of possibilities, but they veered toward the radical.

Hitler linked the Jews to the ridicule he often faced during his struggle for power: chiefly that the Jewish people had laughed at his prophecy that he would one day lead the state and Volk. Now they were choking on that laughter, he said.

Past the midpoint of his two and one-quarter hour address, Hitler thundered that he now wished to be a prophet once again. If "international finance Jewry"—Jews inside and outside Europe—once again plunged the nations into a world war, they would regret it. Gesticulating forcefully with his right arm and right index finger, he exclaimed: *"The result will not be the bolshevization of the earth and thereby the victory of Jewry, but the annihilation of the Jewish race in Europe"* (emphasis in printed text). The Nazi deputies applauded wildly at what has become the most quoted section of Hitler's most infamous speech.[29] Even though a head of government rarely threatened the extinction of another people, it was not obvious that Hitler meant this to be the highlight of his speech. Antisemitic language by the Nazis was so common that by this time it anesthetized many listeners.

In a nod to Mussolini's enactment of a new Italian racial law in November 1938 that restricted the civil rights of Jews and excluded them from public offices and education, Hitler lauded Italy for joining Germany's campaign to enlighten the world about the poisonous nature of the Jews. Then, once again linking Jews to the prospect of war, Hitler argued that all nations that wished to avoid battlefield deaths had an interest in recognizing their common enemy. The "Jewish slogan . . . proletarians of all nations, unite" will give way to "working members of all nations, recognize your common enemy," he predicted.

He went on to rebut Roosevelt's criticism that Nazi Germany was an enemy of religion. He mentioned generous German government subsidies given to the churches, while baldly maintaining that no one in Germany had been persecuted for their religious beliefs. However, he warned that the government would crack down harshly on priests who insulted the government or its leaders, as well as on those who endangered the biological health of the German people. Hitler again accused Western democratic politicians of a double standard because they had allegedly remained silent while many tens of thousands of priests were slaughtered in Russia and in Spain. It was fortunate, Hitler noted, that Germany and Italy had supported General Francisco Franco in the Spanish Civil War to prevent Bolshevism from spreading across Europe. Normally a primary target of Nazi propaganda, Bolshevism made a late entrance in Hitler's address.

Continuing, Hitler dressed up Germany's relations with various European countries. Particularly in the case of Eastern European states such as Poland, his positive remarks were simply duplicitous. Then he again raised the specter of Bolshevism while praising the treaty initiated by Germany against the Communist International (the Anti-Comintern Pact with Japan, Italy, and Hungary). The expansion of this treaty signified world resistance against the "Jewish-international Bolshevist threat."

Hitler used much of his speech to attack critics in the Western democracies, because he understood that those countries could potentially interfere with Germany's coming expansion. But toward the end of his speech—and for tactical reasons—Hitler struck a conciliatory pose. He renounced territorial claims except for the return of German colonies in Africa taken under the Treaty of Versailles. This colonial issue was not one that by itself could initiate war, he reassured foreigners. He argued that the Jewish press was largely responsible for Western criticism of Germany. Although German relations with the United States were suffering from this slander campaign, "none of us believe that these efforts reflect the will of the American people. . . ."

Hitler avoided direct attacks on leaders of the Western democracies. He especially avoided any attack on FDR. Even though he had just told the German military attaché to the United States that he thought FDR might be Jewish,[30] he did not mention the president even once in his speech. It was a striking—and calculated—omission in a speech that was partly a rebuttal to Roosevelt's State of the Union Address.

In Hitler's audience was fifty-one-year-old Louis Lochner, chief Associated Press correspondent in Berlin, an American who had lived and worked in Germany for a third of his life. Lochner had pressed Karl Bömer, the Propaganda Ministry official who handled the foreign press, to give him a translation of Hitler's speech in advance.[31] Lochner's German was excellent, but he did not have much time to write. The time difference between Berlin and New York was six hours, which made it tight but not impossible to publish an article in the January 30 evening papers. Using the draft translation, Lochner succeeded, but at the cost of some key omissions.

Lochner described Hitler standing in his car cheered by large crowds on his way to the Kroll Opera House; he also mentioned the SS guards at the building. He even identified the recently dismissed Reichsbank president Schacht in the audience. Lochner showed readers that he had witnessed the event. The headline to his article also hit the mark: "Hitler Warns Against Interference of Other Powers in Nazi Aims." His lead paragraph had Hitler warning against interference "in matters concerning us alone with the purpose of preventing natural and sensible solutions." Hitler had applied this phrase to German foreign policy, and he similarly argued against foreign interference with Nazi persecution of the Jews. But there was no mention of Jews whatsoever in Lochner's article. The subtitle of Lochner's article in a Colorado newspaper—"Bolshevists Get Strong Lashing; Franco is Upheld"—probably gives a sense of the translated draft's emphasis.[32] Whether the draft translation entirely omitted Hitler's discussion of the Jewish question or simply failed to emphasize it is unclear. Lochner's article, datelined January 30, offers the only glimpse of a near-final draft of Hitler's speech in what another AP reporter called a semi-official translation.[33]

The next day Lochner drew upon what he had heard and on the final German text of Hitler's speech to write a longer and more accurate article. In his diary he noted that people were still talking about the speech, wondering which part to emphasize. Presumably, he was referring to other journalists still writing their stories. Lochner called attention to the fact that Hitler made last-minute changes but identified only one of them—his avowal that he believed in a long peace. But Lochner now included Hitler's statement that Europe would not find peace until it had resolved the Jewish question, and the AP journalist quoted Hitler's now-famous threat to annihilate the Jewish race in Europe.

Did Hitler's speech signal war or peace? Lochner's lead paragraph cited diplomats taking heart because Hitler did not see the return of Germany's lost colonies as grounds for war.[34] The noted American columnist Walter Lippmann, in a February 4 article, thought Hitler's speech had clarified the European situation and that Germany was now hoping for a Munich-type settlement for its former colonies.[35] It was a colossal misreading of the speech and the man. The Nazi propaganda on colonies represented a feint. Hitler certainly wanted to exploit German resentment over the loss of colonies dictated by the Treaty of Versailles, and perhaps he wanted to distract foreigners from his objectives in Eastern Europe. The return of colonies, not the resettlement of Jews, was the message amplified by the German press and received by diplomats, most Western commentators, and Western governments.

Some Jewish newspapers also played down Hitler's threat of extermination. The New York Yiddish newspaper *Forverts* put it into the headline on January 31, but the article concentrated on the chance of war and Hitler's professed allegiance to Italy and Japan. The Yiddish daily *Haynt* in Warsaw summarized Hitler's main points without including his prophecy. Only a day later did it mention in a subtitle that "Hitler threatened the Jews with annihilation." *Haynt*'s editorial on February 3 found Chamberlain's approval of the speech more shocking and astonishing than the speech itself.[36]

Some contemporaries located the essence of the speech. In a February 5, 1939, appearance at a Hadassah meeting in New York, James G. McDonald, chair of Roosevelt's Advisory Committee on Political Refugees, called Hitler's declarations on the Jewish situation and on international relations "the most threatening he had ever made."[37] But McDonald, having talked privately with Hitler about the "Jewish question" in April 1933, was unusually well-informed, and his reaction was atypical. A German Jew named Luise Solmitz wrote in her diary on January 30, "Führer's speech in the Reichstag. Colonial demands."[38]

On February 2, Göring's man Helmut Wohlthat proposed that Germany allow the emigration of 150,000 adult Jews under strictly circumscribed, economically ruinous conditions, leaving about 250,000 Jews who would have to remain in Germany indefinitely.[39] Raymond Geist was unhappy about last-minute "monkey wrenches" in the offer—probably Hitler's doing, he said. He urged his friend Lochner to write a dispatch pressing the Nazis hard if they made things impossible for George Rublee. Because there was a Nazi offer of sorts, Lochner wrote an article quoting the two main negotiators Rublee and Wohlthat (who had to profess optimism) and suggesting that the negotiations had made progress toward mass emigration. Lochner did not spell out the still-secret terms of Wohlthat's offer, but he did specify that they did not involve any outside loan to Germany or any increase in German exports, both anathema to the State Department. Lochner wrote that any deal rested on the foundation that Germany was irrevocably determined to become "free of Jews" within a reasonable time, but also that there would be no further incidents like that of November 9. Geist's blunt warning to Fritz Wiedemann found its way into these negotiations.

Much of Lochner's story (and its headline) seemed optimistic about German-Jewish emigration, but the ending was a rude awakening. Anonymous German sources "emphatically insisted" there had been no official negotiations and that Wohlthat did not represent the government's position. The document from the negotiations was entirely Rublee's work, and Göring's private representative Helmut Wohlthat had no role in shaping it, the unnamed Germans declared.[40]

Only high SS officials would have dared to repudiate Wohlthat and potentially Göring. Lochner had met and interviewed Reinhard Heydrich, head of the Security Police, about two weeks earlier, and it is likely that Heydrich was one source.[41] Geist later wrote that the Gestapo (part of the Security Police) did not favor the concessions Göring made.[42]

Lochner and Geist both knew that Nazi Germany rejected the less punitive options to remove Jews from Germany. Hitler wanted to remove all the Jews from Europe and to recruit other countries to participate. Resettling all the Jews of Europe was impossible for European countries and potential receiving countries alike.

Hitler moved toward annihilation of Jews shortly after Kristallnacht. The number two man in the Gestapo, Werner Best, secretly spoke to Geist about it. In early December 1938, Geist wrote: "The Germans are determined to resolve the Jewish problem without the assistance of other countries, and that means eventual annihilation."[43]

If Hitler wanted to send a message to Western countries that they should admit large numbers of German Jews—or else—he did a poor job of it. He apparently did not include his threats against the Jews in his translated draft; that draft and his speech signaled to the West that he wanted the return of Germany's colonies. Hitler apparently added the apocalyptic threat against international Jewry at the last minute, or someone decided not to include it in the translation given to Lochner.

Hitler's first intended audience for the threat of annihilation was Western Jewry, which he now perceived as the power base of international Jewry. He believed that only Jewish influence could drive Western governments to declare war against Germany. Thus, if he could silence the Jews, he could postpone Western countries' entrance into the war he intended to launch. And if a broader war did come, it would make sense—at least in

Hitler's mind—to take vengeance against the Jews of Europe.[44] The fact that Jews lacked major political influence in any of the Western democracies did not penetrate Hitler's fantasy world. Because (as has been stated) the Western democracies were bound to actively intervene against German expansion sooner or later, the coming war made the Holocaust nigh inevitable. In this sense, Hitler's ideology led directly to the Holocaust.

Hitler's second audience was ordinary Germans, whom he wanted to prepare for racial war. Early in his speech, Hitler called upon Germans to dedicate themselves to whatever improved the Volk as a whole, abandoning what he considered outmoded ethics. But this section of his speech has been forgotten, as has his demand for obedience. Hitler would need millions of Germans to collaborate in ever-intensifying anti-Jewish persecution, and now he began to prepare the way. He spoke beyond those deputies and visitors assembled in the Kroll Opera House: millions of Germans listened to him on radio.[45] The Nazi Party also published the text of his speech to reach others.[46]

The third audience for his threat against the Jews was Hitler himself. On February 1, Lochner wrote that the German press, taking its signal from Hitler's speech, was pressing for colonies, while Hitler's lieutenants were now seeking to increase Germany's exports. Hitler allegedly "sat back, well pleased with the echo to his Reichstag speech."[47] Here Hitler was able to express himself frankly and passionately without incurring serious damage to Germany's foreign policy.

Hitler's fourth audience was Western supporters of appeasement and isolationism, some of whom were also antisemitic. He hoped to at least make things politically difficult for Western government officials allegedly beholden to the Jews, and here Roosevelt was a prime target.

Hitler made it clear that anti-Jewish policy was an arena for subordinates competing for his favor, which explains some subsequent inconsistencies in the first half of 1939. Wohlthat was allowed to continue meeting with an IGCR representative but was ordered not to take any further steps unless and until the IGCR came up with a specific plan for resettlement. Within Hitler's framework, this "moderate" option had some immediate benefits. The resettlement negotiations at least gave hope to Western Jews and their supporters who would supposedly restrain the United States from openly siding with Germany's enemies in the event of war. But Hermann Göring by no means staked all his chips on a negotiated agreement; in March 1939, he also quietly established his authority to draft Jewish labor—not exactly a step toward large-scale emigration.[48]

Meanwhile, the Gestapo told Jews released from concentration camps to leave the country soon if they valued their lives. After release from camps, desperate Central and Eastern European Jews slipped across France's porous borders, for example, adding tens of thousands of illegal refugees to those who had entered legally. The Gestapo itself dumped some groups of German Jews into France. In high-level negotiations French officials asked Germany to prevent additional Jews from entering their country. Over time, more and more French officials also became concerned that they were harboring a dangerous enemy within. The term Fifth Column was in the air.[49] Hitler apparently calculated that foreign reaction to these practices would diminish opposition to Germany and bolster support for a comprehensive solution to the Jewish question. Only he could determine when such initiatives clashed with his ultimate goals. Nonetheless, in April 1939, Geist was able to predict the future course favored by the SS and Gestapo: placing all the able-bodied German Jews in work camps, confiscating all Jewish wealth, isolating the Jews and putting additional pressures on them, and getting rid of as many as they could by force.[50]

By February 1939, Hitler already had plans to destroy what
was left of Czechoslovakia.[51] After that, he intended to move
against Poland. Not knowing when a broader war might break
out, as part of his preparations, he decided to give a series of
lectures to military audiences to ensure that they had a proper
sense of their coming role.[52] On February 10, Hitler returned
to the Kroll Opera House to speak on "Tasks and Duties of
Officers in the National Socialist State," to hundreds of army
officers (commanders from the rank of captain up). Hitler said
that he proposed to explain his political objectives so that his
officers would fight for them more convincingly. He told them
that, since January 30, 1933, he had pursued a step-by-step
plan to rearm and to expand Germany in which only the timing
of the stages was uncertain. After reviewing some specific
moves, he said, in effect, that he had planned them all along,
and his plan had brought success. He then indicated that this
process was only beginning, and that he would take every opportunity to continue his mission to expand Germany's living
space: his goal was to establish the German people as the strongest in the world. He urged them to trust and obey him without
hesitation. One of Hitler's military adjutants noted, however,
that only part of the military audience was enthusiastic; others
were skeptical.[53]

With this group, Hitler only alluded vaguely to the projected
mass murder of Jews. He told the army officers that the next
war would be a purely ideological war, "a conscious war of peoples and races."[54]

A month later, Hitler *may* have given a candid foreign policy
presentation to a small audience of supportive industrialists,
some top military men, and select Nazi Party subordinates. He
held several different gatherings during the second week in
March 1939, and he likely continued his campaign to explain
and convince subordinates. But very little information about

these meetings surfaced. There are questions about the quality of the evidence of Hitler's statements on March 8, the most plausible date for what follows.[55] The nominal purpose of this meeting was to discuss economic and labor problems with some businessmen, military officers, and party officials, including Gauleiter Josef Bürckel of Austria.[56] It was a group loyal enough for Hitler to reveal his objectives and to unleash his emotions.

The first of two related US diplomatic-intelligence reports on this event mistakenly locates Hitler at Berchtesgaden, listing two alleged attendees, Nazi businessman Wilhelm Keppler and another industrialist, whose name is garbled. Leaving for Vienna soon afterward, they discussed Hitler's comments with others they met with there just before Germany occupied the remainder of Czech territory.[57]

According to the first (March 1939) report, Hitler announced that he would seize Czechoslovakia on March 14, that he would take control of the rest of Central and Eastern Europe in the summer, and that in 1940 he would "wipe France and the French race from the map and would reduce Great Britain to serfdom." In 1941 he would, as part of a joint attack with Japan on North and South America, conquer the United States. The second (September 1939) report offers more detail: after again stressing Germany's need for raw materials and more land, Hitler said that to secure its well-being, Germany would have to radically exterminate its enemies—the Jews, the democracies, and the international powers. He warned that if these groups held power anywhere in the world, they would be a menace to the German people.

Hitler said that Czechoslovakia would be occupied (which had already happened by the time of this report), and that Poland would soon follow. These steps would bring Hungary, Romania, and Yugoslavia into Germany's orbit, giving it access to their large agricultural resources and petroleum. In 1940,

France would be obliterated from the map of Europe. Then Germany would easily dominate an England weakened by democracy, taking control of its world empire. After unifying the continent, Germany would use British and French possessions in the Western Hemisphere to settle accounts with the "Jews of the dollar" in the United States: "We will exterminate this Jewish democracy and Jewish blood will mix itself with the dollars." Once again, Hitler attributed opposition to Germany's expansion to Jewish influence, and once again, his rhetoric suggested mass murder.

Despite some errors of detail characteristic of thirdhand sources, this evidence is worthy of consideration because it fits into the context of Hitler's speeches in January and February. Hitler's comments about foreign policy and the "Jewish question" were an extension of his Kroll Opera House speeches even though Hitler did not and could not reveal such specific goals and such raw emotions there.

Independent sources confirm that Keppler went to Vienna just before Germany took over Czech territory in mid-March.[58] Otto von Habsburg, a key member of the former imperial family of Austro-Hungary—the pretender to the throne of an empire that no longer existed—obtained the information about Hitler's plan from trusted sources in Vienna. Then he spoke with US ambassador (to France) William Bullitt. Marking his cable personal and secret, Bullitt fully endorsed Otto's reports and directed them to Secretary of State Cordell Hull and President Roosevelt. Whether or not Hitler gave this speech in the second week of March 1939, an ambassador, the secretary of state, and the president probably thought he did. And Hitler's reported comments were consistent with previous US assessments of Hitler's intentions.

Franklin Roosevelt could be excused if he did not listen to Hitler's January 30, 1939, speech, for it was the president's fifty-seventh birthday. He had a full workday, followed by a birthday dinner with a couple of dozen guests, followed by a recorded broadcast for the infantile paralysis campaign close to his heart and a late evening meeting with fundraisers in this campaign. And if his banter at the press conference the next day is accurate, there was celebrating late into that evening.[59]

The next day, FDR told reporters at a press conference that he had not listened to Hitler's speech. Still, he clearly found time to read about it or receive a briefing on it because he called one portion of Hitler's statements to the attention of the seventeen senators on the Senate Military Affairs Committee at a White House meeting before the press conference.[60]

The purpose of that meeting was to explain the administration's recent, secret sale of the advanced Douglas DB-7 bombers to France and Britain. After one of the new planes crashed outside Los Angeles, a French pilot who accompanied the American pilots in training on the new planes was among the injured. The sale of these planes arguably violated the spirit, if not the letter, of neutrality laws designed to keep the United States out of any potential European conflict. To dampen congressional criticism, the president decided to give key senators a broader assessment of foreign threats to the United States. The chair of the Senate Military Affairs Committee, Morris Sheppard of Texas, recommended that Roosevelt brief all seventeen senators on the committee, which included five fervent isolationists: two Republicans, Gerald Nye of North Dakota and Robert Reynolds of North Carolina; one Farmer-Labor Party representative, Ernest Lundeen of Minnesota; and two Democrats, Joel Bennett Clark of Missouri and J. Hamilton Lewis of Illinois. Unbeknownst at the time, Lundeen was working with a propagandist on the payroll of the German Embassy trying to prevent US intervention in Europe. FDR requested that they all keep their discussion secret. The president met with the senators early in the afternoon of January 31. By the time he spoke to the press three hours later, there was a flood of leaks.[61]

Roosevelt colored in dangers that he had sketched in his State of the Union Address. Since 1936, Germany, Italy, and Japan had begun to coalesce into a deadly threat to dominate the world, he said. Germany had already compromised the independence of four of the eighteen European nations, and the president expressed doubt that any of the others would remain independent if France and Britain fell. Then Germany would move into the African colonies of France and Britain, and from there it would move against Central and South American countries. At this point FDR mentioned Hitler's speech—the section where he expressed interest in the Western Hemisphere. The president mentioned some 250,000 German immigrants living in Brazil who could pose a threat to the government. In Central America there was not one country immune to a foreign power willing to invest heavily in arranging revolution. American strategy toward Germany and Italy involved strengthening Britain and France, Roosevelt summed up. He also had some choice words for Hitler, calling him "a wild man" and "a nut."[62]

This was the general context, FDR said, in which the United States decided to sell planes to France, so long as they paid "cash on the barrel head." He hoped that the French and the British would buy the fastest planes the United States could turn out, so long as that did not delay the buildup of US forces. He concluded: "I cannot overemphasize the seriousness of the situation."[63] In the words of eminent historian Gerhard Weinberg, "Roosevelt saw . . . large-scale sales of planes to France and a revision of the neutrality laws to permit the sale of weapons in time of war the most likely deterrent to future adventures by Germany leading to a new world war."[64]

Starting the seventh year of his presidency, FDR was presumably a lame duck. He had failed badly to purge some anti-New Deal Democrats through primaries in 1938.[65] Then a coalition of Republicans and conservative Democrats took control of the Senate in the November elections. Roosevelt had lost "the aura of invincibility," in the words of one biographer.[66] The president, however, believed that he could handle the international dangers better than anyone else, and his self-confidence would ultimately fuel his decision to run for an unprecedented third term in 1940. The two-term presidency then was a custom, not a constitutional limit.

There was good intelligence about the vast scope of Hitler's intentions. Six months earlier, Raymond Geist had warned that there could be no peace with the dictators, and the United States should rid itself of the illusion that it could stay out of any European conflict.[67] And Hitler's January 30 speech in the Kroll Opera House, though tempered by tactical consideration, nevertheless gave additional support to that intelligence. The Soviet Union had spies in Poland and Japan, who, around this time, supplied a similar picture of Hitler's step-by-step plans for expansion, including a war against the Western Powers and then an attack on the USSR.[68]

After a sharp exchange with the president, several isolationist senators decided to violate the off-the-record status of the meeting in the hope of arousing public opinion against Roosevelt's foreign policy. Some of what the isolationists attributed to the president appeared in the American and the German press on the evening of January 31. According to one leak, the president went beyond the notion that the United States had to support other democracies in Europe: Roosevelt allegedly declared that America's effective frontier was on the Rhine, the border between France and Germany.[69] At the January 31 press conference FDR explicitly denied making this politically toxic statement, calling the leak a deliberate lie and the leaker a "boob."[70]

Reporters asked whether the sale of planes was part of a secret military alliance, something that an isolationist had apparently charged. FDR cast the sale of the new bombers as a measure to stimulate production in the aircraft industry, which could benefit from economies of scale. Early French orders of US bombers did fuel the rapid expansion of the American aircraft industry in the months before World War II. By late 1939, the industry had a backlog of $640 million of orders for bombers, of which about $400 million came from outside the United States.[71]

At the press conference Roosevelt denied that US foreign policy had changed. More convincingly, he explained that the United States received intelligence reports from various foreign sources, and though he might believe intelligence to be accurate, he could not make that information public without exposing the sources and cutting off the future flow of intelligence. He said that he had good reason to maintain some secrets.[72]

Roosevelt's 1939 campaign to dilute and ultimately nullify the neutrality laws began with his State of the Union Address on January 4, and then advanced with these clashes on January 31, 1939. Hitler's speech in the Kroll Opera House and more general US intelligence about Nazi intentions supplied ammunition for this effort. But it took the outbreak of war and many months of battles with the isolationists until the president succeeded with Congress in October.[73]

At Roosevelt's press conferences on January 31 and February 3, not a single reporter asked about Hitler's threat to annihilate the Jews of Europe. Nor did FDR raise this subject with the seventeen senators. Doing so would only have raised the temperature of the isolationists among them, suggesting that US opposition to Germany and potential assistance to the democracies in Europe were linked with the administration's concerns about the fate of German Jews. For most Americans, these were separate matters. Hitler, on the other hand, viewed war and genocide as part of the same campaign to establish German domination.

Hitler never forgot his prophecy to the Reichstag on January 30, 1939. He referred publicly to this speech at least four times during the war, along with other references in private conversations and secret party speeches, doing so in a matter reinforcing his belief in the connection between the war and the Final Solution of the Jewish question. Intentionally or subconsciously, he misdated his prophecy: instead of January 30, 1939, he said September 1—the date World War II started with Germany's invasion of Poland.[74]

Louis Lochner, too, saw a direct link between Hitler's January 30 speech and later events. After the Nazis began to deport German Jews in the fall of 1941 to unknown destinations in the east, Lochner, still in Berlin, wrote a column describing some of what he knew without going so far as to provoke Nazi censors and to threaten his own standing. He began with the assertion that complete elimination of Jews from European life appeared to be fixed German policy. And he repeated Hitler's January 30 quote about the annihilation of the Jewish race in Europe.[75]

CHAPTER TWO

CHURCHILL'S ALLIES

D uring a thirty-minute radio broadcast on August 24, 1941, British Prime Minister Winston Churchill denounced massive Nazi police executions carried out in conquered Soviet territory. Some historians have depicted this portion of Churchill's speech as a warning about the Holocaust, which was just then unfolding.[1] Churchill actually wanted to recruit and placate allies in the war. He apparently did not yet grasp that the Nazis were waging a war of extermination against the Jews.

In this speech Churchill spoke only briefly about the killing of civilians in the East. He did not raise his voice or slow his pace for emphasis when he declared:

The aggressor is surprised, startled, staggered. For the first time in his experience mass murder has become unprofitable. He retaliates by the most frightful cruelties. As his armies advance, whole districts are being exterminated. Scores of thousands, literally scores of thousands of executions in cold blood are being perpetrated by the German police troops upon the Russian patriots who defend their native soil. Since the

Mongol invasions of Europe in the sixteenth century [sic]
there has never been methodical, merciless butchery on such
a scale or approaching such a scale. And this is but the beginning. Famine and pestilence have yet to follow in the bloody
ruts of Hitler's tanks. We are in the presence of a crime
without a name.²

His last line has become famous, but what Churchill meant by it
is still disputed.

Churchill began this speech with a report to the world on his
secret shipboard meetings with President Franklin Roosevelt
held on August 8–12 in Placentia Bay, off Newfoundland. He
said that the undisclosed location reminded him of the west
coast of Scotland. He then offered a paean to Anglo-American
cultural and political solidarity: "Fortunately for the progress of
mankind [the British Empire and the United States] happen to
speak the same language and very largely think the same
thoughts, or anyhow, think a lot of the same thoughts. . . . It
[this meeting with Roosevelt] symbolizes something even more
majestic, namely, the marshalling of the good forces of the world
against the evil forces." This bond helped the two governments
to agree on a declaration of principles known as the Atlantic
Charter, which Churchill summarized. It was the first official
statement of war aims and of their outline of the postwar world.³

In his speech Churchill also sought to create a more favorable
public view of the Soviet Union. He called Germany's August
1939 nonaggression treaty with Soviet Russia a cynical move to
inactivate the Soviets until Hitler was ready to attack them.
Then Churchill sympathized with the latest Nazi victim: "Here
is a devil [Hitler] who, in a mere spasm of his pride and lust for
domination, can condemn two or three millions, perhaps it may
be many more, of human beings to speedy and violent death.
Let Russia be blotted out. Let Russia be destroyed." Churchill

praised the Russian will to fight, their efficient organization, and their excellent equipment.

Continuing, on August 24, 1941, Churchill condemned Japanese aggression in China, with Japanese military factions supposedly emulating Hitler and Mussolini. The prime minister did not dismiss negotiations between the Japanese and the Americans but said that if such talks failed and war broke out between them, Britain would side with the United States.

Churchill portrayed the Nazi New Order for Europe as one based on the rule of an alleged master race and on the elimination of democracy, freedom, and decency. He appealed to the peoples of subjugated lands to avoid collaboration. He claimed that Hitler's plan was to dispatch his enemies one by one. Thus, the German assault on Russia was designed to eliminate it from the war so that Hitler could turn all his forces on Britain. After that, he would move against the United States and the Western Hemisphere. Churchill expressed gratitude that Roosevelt recognized the extreme dangers now facing the American people as well as the British. Churchill flattered both of his potential major partners, helping to bring about what he later called the Grand Alliance. That was his main goal in this speech.

The *Manchester Guardian*, which published the full text of this speech, stressed its key points in an editorial: the leadership of the English-speaking peoples of broad toiling masses in all the continents; a message of hope and deliverance to the oppressed and attacked peoples; and a warning to Japan. It would be welcomed in Russia, the editorialist wrote, to whose "people's struggle" Churchill paid tribute. The editorial made no mention of Nazi executions in the USSR. It praised Churchill for avoiding an explicit appeal to the United States to enter the war, allowing Americans to draw their own conclusions about Nazi Germany's strategy of overcoming enemies one by one. The *Manchester Guardian* called it one of Churchill's greatest wartime speeches.[4]

Also publishing the text of Churchill's speech, the *New York Times* added an article focused narrowly on Churchill's warning to Japan and its impact on the battle between the supporters of the Roosevelt administration and the isolationists.[5] The AP's feature article bore an extensive sub-headline: "British Prime Minister Pledges Support If America is Attacked by Japan; Says Tokyo Grab 'Must Stop'; Lauds Soviet." It quoted a portion of Churchill's comment about the war in the East, but not the word exterminated, the executions, or a crime without a name.[6] This brief sample of press coverage suggests that if Churchill wanted to send a sharp message about Nazi killing of civilians in the East, it was buried.

CHURCHILL'S EXPERIENCE

Churchill was no stranger to warfare: he was the first prime minister in more than a century who had been a soldier and had fought in battle.[7] He attended Sandhurst Royal Military Academy, served in India, fought in colonial wars in Afghanistan and Sudan, acted as a journalist during the Boer War, and served as First Lord of the Admiralty before and during World War I and again during the early part of World War II. He also fought for several months at the front during World War I. His record contained evidence for both his admirers and his detractors. He had some spectacular failures, such as planning the disastrous Gallipoli expedition against the Ottoman Empire in 1915. Another failure was his effort as war minister in 1919 to overthrow the Bolshevik regime. He supported anti-Bolshevik (White Russian) forces after the Bolshevik Revolution and kept more than 15,000 British troops in Russia to support them. In April 1920, Churchill described Bolshevism as "that foul combination of criminality and animalism."[8] Churchill himself concluded that he had survived near-death encounters and political catastrophes to fulfill a higher purpose, which materialized when he became prime minister in May 1940.[9] Churchill was an imperialist in the traditional sense. Biographer Andrew Roberts, noting Churchill's lack of interest in formal religion, describes the British Empire as his substitute.[10] But politically, Churchill resisted categorization. A social Tory by family orientation, he deserted the Conservatives in 1905 for a two-decade political career as a Liberal, rejoining the Tories in 1925, only to depart from the Conservative leadership in 1931. Some of his zigzags were opportunistic, but on other occasions he acted because of serious political and policy disagreements, such as with his opposition to Conservative disarmament and to appeasement of Germany in the 1930s.

Alongside his political career, Churchill wrote best-selling histories, including a multivolume history of his ancestor, the Duke of Marlborough, perhaps the ablest European commander of the late seventeenth and early eighteenth centuries. The Soviet ambassador to the UK, Ivan Maisky, later wrote in his diary that Churchill in some ways resembled the swashbuckling Marlborough.[11]

Churchill contrasted Jews and Zionism with Bolshevism— although he recognized that the Bolshevik leaders in the Soviet Union contained a disproportionate number of persons of Jewish descent. In a 1920 article, he gave the Jews credit for a system of ethics essential to civilization, and he noted that most Jews themselves condemned Bolshevism. For Jews unattached to a national culture, Zionism served as a positive alternative to Bolshevism, Churchill wrote.[12] As an MP during the 1930s when he was out of the cabinet, he repeatedly condemned Hitler and stressed the threat from Nazi Germany, and he called Nazi anti-semitism irrational and foolish. His pro-Jewish stances only went so far: he generally avoided promoting German-Jewish immigration to the UK. After Kristallnacht he reportedly favored sending large numbers of German Jews to British Guiana, a prospect which Chamberlain's government slow-walked to death.[13]

Churchill's books, speeches, lectures, and from late 1938 on, radio broadcasts, brought him fame in the United Kingdom and in the United States and enough wealth to manage his aristocratic lifestyle and his multifaceted career. He possessed a rich storehouse of energy, a marvelous command of the written and spoken word, a keen sense of history as a source of guidance and of inspiration, a strong belief in the importance of good intelligence in war, and the courage to fight for what he believed in regardless of the odds. These qualities counterbalanced his impetuousness, political inconstancy, desire to micromanage, and intense devotion to preserving the fading British Empire. He alienated so many Tories along the way that he lacked a secure political base.[14]

On May 10, 1940, at the age of sixty-six, Churchill became prime minister after Neville Chamberlain found his own appeasement of Hitler discredited and Britain's war effort in chaos. Chamberlain, Churchill's political rival Lord Halifax, and the chief government whip David Margesson all agreed that Churchill, again serving as First Lord of the Admiralty, was the best choice to lead a government of national unity, and Churchill's name was sent forward to King George VI. Churchill promised those who joined his government "nothing but blood, toil, tears, and sweat," and on May 13, 1940, he repeated this vivid phrase before Parliament. He added:

> You ask, what is our policy? I will say: It is to wage war, by sea, land and air, with all our might and with all the strength that God can give us; to wage war against a monstrous tyranny never surpassed in the dark, lamentable catalogue of human crime. . . . You ask, what is our aim? I can answer in

one word: It is victory at all costs, victory in spite of all terror, victory, however long and hard the road may be; for without victory there is no survival.[15]

Churchill's finely crafted, slightly archaic vocabulary and his potent delivery inspired citizens struggling to cope with subsequent hardships, casualties, and reports of one military blow after another.[16]

Churchill's Conservative rival Lord Halifax threatened to resign as foreign secretary if he were not given freedom to pursue peace negotiations with Italy and Germany. Halifax tried to win over Churchill's cabinet several times during the dark days before British and French troops were evacuated from Dunkirk. Churchill outmaneuvered Halifax, arguing that, with the upper hand, Germany would seek to make Britain a slave state with a puppet government under someone like Oswald Mosley, leader of the British Union of Fascists. The mere start of negotiations would demoralize the country, Churchill believed.[17] He got his way, soon dispatching Halifax off to Washington to serve as ambassador there.

Then, in the summer and fall of 1940, Churchill led Britain through the German bombing campaign that has become known as the Battle of Britain or simply the Blitz, the effort by Hermann Göring's Luftwaffe to bludgeon the country into submission. Despite tens of thousands of casualties, British morale held. On September 15, Hitler decided to postpone the planned invasion of Britain codenamed Operation Sea Lion.[18]

But in the first half of 1941, Britain suffered one defeat after another in the Mediterranean and North Africa, while German submarines exacted a fearful toll of British shipping in the Atlantic. The UK could not land enough troops to fight effectively on the continent; a botched effort to send British troops to Greece to ward off a German invasion showed that all too clearly. Britain adopted a default military strategy to defeat

Germany based on strategic bombing of targets in Germany, a naval blockade of much of Europe, fomenting unrest or discontent in German-occupied lands and in Germany itself—and playing for time, lots of time. Even after he had gained allies, Churchill frequently leaned on this approach.[19]

WHAT BRITISH INTELLIGENCE KNEW

German sources and British signals intelligence declassified in the 1990s and early twenty-first century give a reasonably good picture of what Nazi SS and police forces were doing behind the battlelines in the Soviet Union in July and August 1941.[20] Immediately after the German invasion of the USSR, Reichsführer-SS Heinrich Himmler sent various SS and police units to follow the army into Soviet territory and to carry out roundups and mass executions of Jews, Communist officials, and other civilian targets perceived as Nazi enemies. He often avoided issuing written orders about mass killings of civilians, instead traveling around to meet with his Higher SS and Police Leaders in Soviet territory. Higher SS and Police Leader Hans-Adolf Prützmann told a subordinate about Himmler's verbal order to resettle "criminal elements." When the subordinate asked where, Prützmann responded, "into the next world." Resettlement and criminal elements were among common Nazi euphemisms to conceal the mass murder of enemies. Himmler preferred to have the most sensitive information from the front sent to him via air couriers, but courier service was too limited. Later, in mid-September 1941, one of his top subordinates laid down the rule that anything marked top secret (*Geheime Reichssache*) had to go by courier, but before then, company and battalion commanders as well as the regional Higher SS and Police Leaders mostly used circumlocutions in their radio messages, and frequently they did not do even that.

The two main branches of the German police, the Security Police (which included the Gestapo) and the Order Police, used differing cipher systems for their radio messages. The Security Police and the battalion-sized killing units called Einsatzgruppen used a sophisticated German machine called Enigma to encode transmissions, while the Order Police battalions used an older hand cipher.

Shortly after Churchill became prime minister in May 1940, British cryptographers operating secretly at Bletchley Park broke the Luftwaffe's Enigma code, and then decoded communications of other branches of the German military. But Bletchley managed to decode only a portion of intercepted messages, and interception was difficult and partial. The highest priority—useful military information—got the most attention. These Enigma decodes have become known as the Ultra Secret.[21] Churchill had gained experience with signals intelligence successes during World War I, while he served as First Lord of the Admiralty. He now wanted direct daily access to all Enigma materials. This quickly became impossible because of the number of decodes.

British intelligence had broken some of the older Order Police codes as early as 1937, and they began to do so more frequently during the early months of World War II. Two British intercept sites were devoted primarily to German military and police messages. These two sites could not possibly scoop up all German police messages; in effect, they sampled. German police messages were among those decrypted, translated, and analyzed in Hut 6 at Bletchley Park. A lower priority target, these decodes offered only glimpses of a rapidly evolving situation.

By the summer of 1941, Stewart Menzies, the head of MI6 known as "C," supplied the prime minister with a daily summary of important signals intelligence, which included some reports of Order Police executions. Churchill may also have received weekly English-language summaries of Order Police activities. The official history of British intelligence mentions them, although these weekly documents were not located in the archives. Still, longer reports covering irregular multi-weekly periods survive in the archives, offering a good picture of what Churchill read—and what he did not read. The British never broke the "key" they regarded as central to Gestapo operations. Therefore, British intelligence knew virtually nothing at the time about the massive killings of Jews by the Einsatzgruppen, which were closely tied to the Security Police.[22] But the Order Police battalions were quite active in mass murder as well.

In his speech on August 24, 1941, Churchill spoke of scores of thousands of executions carried out by German police troops victimizing Russian patriots defending their native soil. This formulation was simultaneously precise and misleading. It gave such a clear view of the identity of the executioners that, at a moment when outsiders knew little to nothing about both the Einsatzgruppen and Order Police battalions, Churchill endangered the secrecy of British code-breaking operations. But the identity of the victims was doubly inaccurate: if Russian patriots were defending their native soil, they were partisans or guerrillas. Churchill said nothing about the fact that most of the victims were Jewish. German casualties in systematic roundups and mass shootings of peaceful Jewish men, women, and children were miniscule. Lopsided casualty statistics in the decodes indicated that these were hardly standard after-action battlefield reports.

In the central Russian sector, the area from which most early decodes came, Higher SS and Police Leader Erich von dem Bach-Zelewski minimized or qualified his use of the word Jews, as with his phrase "Jewish plunderers." After Bach-Zelewski boasted, on August 7, of the number of executions in his sector, the British analysts wrote, "the tone of this message . . . suggests that a definite decrease in the total population of Russia would be welcome in high quarters."[23] But nothing in these British intelligence reports specified Russian patriots defending their native territory, and nothing as well suggested that executions were reprisals for effective Soviet military resistance. Those conclusions were Churchill's own: he wrote his own speeches.[24] Churchill may have believed that the police units participated in or alongside the fighting and carried out reprisals, not that they pursued the "Holocaust by bullets" that we recognize today. Early in his speech Churchill had referred to Hitler's condemning millions of people in Russia to death.

When direct evidence is not conclusive, the historian faces a dilemma. Occam's razor calls for the simplest explanation consistent with the facts. The simplest one here is that Churchill did not receive clear enough information about Nazi executions of scores of thousands of Jews before August 24, 1941, to refer to them in his broadcast. It would mean that Churchill did not project from his knowledge of Hitler's antisemitism. The more complicated alternative is that Churchill recognized that Jews were the most common victims of mass executions. Despite that conclusion, he cast these horrific events into an imprecise formulation that was less politically sensitive and more advantageous in terms of British-Soviet relations.

THE CONTEXT OF CHURCHILL'S SPEECH

Before June 22, 1941, the USSR had been friendly to Germany, willing to honor the August 1939 Nonaggression Pact and follow it up with economic agreements. Soviet raw materials sent to Germany, including grain, oil, cotton, iron ore, nickel, and platinum, helped Hitler prepare his military offensive in western Europe in the spring of 1940.[25] Meanwhile, Soviet relations with the UK were badly strained. The Nazi-Soviet treaty, the subsequent Soviet invasion and takeover of eastern Poland, and the Soviet attack on Finland in the winter of 1939–1940 had antagonized much of the British political elite. Some Britons thought the Communists in the USSR were a greater threat than Germany. To make matters worse, Stalin was deeply suspicious of Churchill as a reactionary British imperialist.[26]

Soviet entrance into the war against Germany would alter British strategic calculations. In April 1941, British ambassador Stafford Cripps passed on to Moscow information from a "trusted agent" (a disguise for Bletchley Park's intelligence) that Germany was planning to shred its pact with the USSR and to invade it. But the warning reached Stalin in diffused form, and he would not believe anything the British sent. He suspected Churchill of trying to provoke war between the Soviets and Germany. He would not credit similar, even more detailed and alarming intelligence the British passed along in June.[27]

In a May 1941 conversation with the Swedish ambassador in London, Churchill illustrated the UK's situation (and his mood) with a self-created fable about two frogs, one a pessimist, the other an optimist. The frogs smelled milk through the open window of a dairy and jumped in. Unfortunately, they landed in a large jar filled with milk. The pessimist saw that the walls of the jar were too steep and too smooth for him to climb out. He gave up, turned on his back, and sank to the bottom. The optimist decided to do whatever he could to "avoid perishing disgracefully." He swam all night and beat his legs energetically. By morning, he found that he had churned a big knob of butter, which he used to jump out. Churchill concluded, "the same will happen to the British Empire."[28]

Swedish ambassador Björn Prytz asked whether, in the event of war between Germany and the USSR, the Soviets would automatically become a UK ally. Conscious of his anti-Communist reputation, Churchill reddened, crying out, "To crush Germany

I am prepared to enter into an alliance with anyone, even the devil."[29]

Churchill later retouched this episode in his own history of the Second World War. Shortly before the German invasion of the Soviet Union, Churchill allegedly said at a dinner, "If Hitler invaded Hell I would at least make a favourable reference to the Devil in the House of Commons." Churchill did attend a dinner on June 21, the night before the German invasion of the USSR, and he did predict the invasion. But he also said that he expected Germany to be successful. He added that Britain would nonetheless try to help Russia.[30]

In the early morning hours of June 22, 1941, more than three million German troops plus 475,000 Finns, 325,000 Romanians, and about 100,000 Hungarians and Slovaks, composing 152 divisions, accompanied by 3,300 panzers, 2,250 warplanes, and more than 7,000 mobile guns and artillery pieces, demolished Soviet border defenses. Codenamed Operation Barbarossa, the German assault seized immediate control of the air and made astonishing gains—as much as six hundred square miles per hour—on the ground. On the first day, the Luftwaffe put sixty-six Soviet air bases out of action.[31]

In a broadcast on the evening of June 22, the day of the German attack, Churchill urged Britons to treat the Soviets as allies. He then began to cultivate a regular relationship with Soviet ambassador Ivan Maisky. Maisky, in turn, appreciated Churchill's focus on victory: "His fable about the optimistic frog has proved unexpectedly prescient. . . . [His] radio broadcast on 22 June [was] remarkable for its form and inner force; it also presented the case for fighting to the last and offering maximum aid to the USSR with the utmost clarity and implacability. . . ."[32]

Churchill's openness to an alliance with the Soviets departed not only from his decades of anti-Communist rhetoric, but also from his private comments to King George VI when he was appointed prime minister. Churchill had said that Nazism and Communism were roughly comparable systems. In one sense that was truer than he knew or at least would recognize publicly. In his speech to Parliament on May 13, 1940, Churchill described Nazi Germany as a monstrous tyranny never surpassed in the catalogue of human crime. But at that time, Stalin had given orders to kill more people—his own people—than Hitler had. Stalin's 1937–1938 campaign against anti-Soviet elements alone resulted in the execution of 634,000 persons. Stalin kept secret his own role in signing execution orders. Still, it was obvious that Stalin had frequently arranged to have actual and potential opponents killed. But Churchill considered Germany a mortal and immediate threat to Britain and the empire, while the USSR was at most an intermediate-term danger. Churchill told an associate that he had only one single (official) purpose—the destruction of Hitler.[33] How much he knew of Stalin's earlier atrocities, including the terror-famine in Ukraine in the early 1930s, is a question not easily answered, but at this moment in the war they did not matter to him.

THE SUMMER 1941 CRISIS

After the first week of battle, the Soviet situation looked bleak. On July 1, Churchill informed Roosevelt that he was ordering defensive preparations for a German invasion of Great Britain from September 1 on. If the Soviet Union made peace or imploded, Churchill expected Hitler to turn back to his Operation Sea Lion plan against the UK. Military experts in London and Washington expected the Soviet armies to collapse within a month or two. Churchill was less pessimistic than his military advisers about the Soviets' ability to withstand the massive German assault, but he was not an unwavering optimist.[34]

Once Stalin and Churchill began to correspond, the prime minister tread carefully, balancing praise and encouragement of the Soviets with reservations. On July 7, he wrote Stalin to commend the bravery and tenacity of the Soviet army and people, adding: "We shall do everything to help you that time, geography, and our growing resources allow. The longer the war lasts, the more help we can give."[35]

Stalin still feared that Britain might decide to make peace with Germany at the USSR's expense. Perhaps he projected from his own past collaboration with Hitler, or was influenced by Ambassador Maisky's portrayal of the British ruling classes as oriented toward compromise.[36] On July 12, Britain and the Soviet Union signed a vague commitment to mutual assistance and a binding pledge not to negotiate a separate armistice or peace with Germany. It was called an agreement, not a formal alliance. Roosevelt endorsed the move. FDR had for years felt that the USSR was abandoning the notion of world revolution, which meant that it might be induced to participate constructively in international affairs. In mid-1941, Soviet survival was vital to Britain, and perhaps also the United States. A few days later, Churchill, speaking in the House of Commons, unilaterally and unceremoniously upgraded the UK-USSR agreement to an alliance.[37]

Stalin suddenly pressed for a change in British military strategy designed to make Germany divert forces from the Eastern front. On July 18, in a personal message presented by Maisky, Stalin asked Churchill to send troops to northern France and along the Arctic Sea to open new fronts there. Churchill politely but firmly rejected this notion: "The chiefs of staff do not see any way of doing anything on a scale likely to be of the slightest use to you." He pointedly reminded Stalin that Britain had carried on the fight by itself for more than a year. In his next meeting with Maisky, Churchill was even more emphatic, calling Stalin's idea risky and bound to lead to disaster for Britain.[38]

Churchill soon decided to give the USSR two hundred fighter planes, and praised the "grand Soviet defense" of their native soil. Not swayed by small gestures, Maisky wrote that the British were fixated on their defensive strategy, which made sense when they had no allies. Now, he believed, it represented a real danger.[39] Britain's military strategy was not purely defensive, but it was more patient than the Soviets thought they could afford.

On July 28, Churchill agreed to Stalin's request to ship Moscow a large supply of rubber. Toward the end of his message, he added encouragement: "The grand resistance of the Russian armies in defense of their soil unites us all . . . Thank you very much for your comprehension, in the midst of your great fight, of our difficulties in doing more."[40] This formula of compliments in lieu of opening a second front on the continent anticipated and resembled Churchill's praise of Soviet resistance in his August 24 speech.

Maisky poured out his frustration in a meeting with British Foreign Secretary Anthony Eden just after Churchill's speech on August 24. After listing huge Soviet losses, he asked, rhetorically, what was England doing? Something, but "not enough to pinch the rabid beast's tail; it must be hit round the head with a club! The British bombers haven't forced the Germans to withdraw a single squadron from the east. . . ." At the end of August Stalin warned that if Britain did not open a second front within the next three to four weeks, the USSR might lose the war.[41] These diplomatic exchanges and Stalin's calls for British landings on the continent would continue for many months.

Churchill felt that he had to shore up Soviet morale and keep on good terms with Stalin. Therefore, in his speech on August 24, he cast German police executions of Soviet citizens into a narrative of Soviet resistance: "Russian patriots defending their native soil." He could not responsibly open a second front in the west, but he could at least compliment Stalin's forces. Having entered into an alliance with the USSR as a military necessity, he could easily justify generous rhetoric.

THE INTELLIGENCE AFTERMATH OF AUGUST 24, 1941

Churchill looked closely at later signals intelligence about executions in the USSR. After he received a report on August 28 that Police Battalion 314 of Police Regiment South had shot 367 Jews, he circled the figure. On August 31, he was sent a report that SS Infantry Regiment 10, 1 SS Brigade, Police Battalions 314 and 45, and Police Regiment South had recently shot several hundred Jews, and then the Regiment South shot 1,342. Churchill circled most of the last figure. A week later, several units shot more than 3,000 Jews, and Churchill again marked the number. The multi-weekly intelligence report covering the period August 15–31 also analyzed the trend in the individual decodes: "The execution of 'Jews' is so recurrent a feature of these reports that the figures have been omitted from the situation reports and brought under one heading. . . . Whether all those executed as 'Jews' are indeed such is of course doubtful [!]; but the figures are no less conclusive as evidence of a policy of savage intimidation if not ultimate extermination."[42] On September 1, Churchill received a brief summary of an August 26 report to Himmler about developments in the Berdichev (today Berdychiv) Korosten area: 47 prisoners taken, 1,246 Jews shot, German losses nil. The number 1,246 was circled in red, likely by an MI6 official.[43]

British decodes revealed that, between August 23 and August 30, SS units and Order Police battalions (but not the Einsatzgruppen) killed 12,361 Jews. The intelligence analysts noted that the real number was probably much larger since they only deciphered about half of the transmissions. By September 12, MI6 reached a less convoluted conclusion: the German police in Soviet territory were killing all Jews that "fell into their hands." The department did not intend to continue briefing Churchill specially on these butcheries "unless so requested."[44] It appears that MI6 took this action because the pattern was clear, this issue was not a high priority, and there were many other decrypts with substantial military information, which represented the government's highest priority. It is possible that Churchill instructed MI6 to stop sending the execution tallies, but there is no direct evidence of it.

There may well have been another reason for the cessation: Churchill had revealed too much during his speech on August 24. Perhaps MI6 did not want to tempt Churchill to denounce the execution of Jews and further endanger the secrecy of the Bletchley Park decoding operations.

On September 13, Order Police Chief Kurt Daluege instructed the Higher SS and Police Leaders in the East to cease sending execution reports by radio. The Order Police also abandoned their coding system known as Double Transposition, adopting one called Double Playfair instead. A contemporaneous British intelligence document linked Daluege's order with Churchill's speech: "[General Daluege,] alarmed perhaps by our evident awareness of the unspeakable activities of his police in Russia, sent the following message [about not sending execution totals by radio]."[45] Linking Daluege's order to Churchill's speech may or may not be correct. But Churchill's speech was very widely publicized, Daluege's actions followed soon after, and British intelligence officials perceived the connection at the time. The tie is much more likely than not. Geoffrey Wheatcroft's recent biography of Churchill accepts this cause and effect.[46]

By mid-September 1941, Nazi officials tried harder to draw a curtain over their murderous activities with tightened security and new codes. Churchill may well have had some sense of what later was called the first wave of the Holocaust, the so-called Holocaust by bullets. But Churchill had already risked too much by speaking publicly based on Ultra Secret sources. He did not request continuation of the execution totals, and most SS and police units ceased reporting them by radio. Churchill gave no follow-up speech to the world about the massacre of hundreds of thousands of Jews in conquered Soviet territory. Of course, the prime minister had bigger problems: the British-Soviet side was still losing the war.

THE GRAND ALLIANCE

An Anglo-American alliance, once it materialized, would have a more stable foundation than the UK-USSR's alignment of necessity. In 1950, Churchill the historian, writing about his meeting with FDR on August 8–12, 1941, focused on Roosevelt's suggestion of a joint declaration of principles for a peace settlement. Churchill then had subordinates create a draft of what became known as the Atlantic Charter. Other sources show that Roosevelt and Under Secretary of State Sumner Welles reworked the British version to feature a pledge of self-determination for the postwar world and the right of individuals to live without fear and want. This charter was a tacit alliance based on supposedly common ideology.[47]

Nonetheless, the two sides differed over free trade, with Churchill seeking to salvage imperial preference. He also did not see political self-determination as extending throughout the empire. But these two democracies were much closer than either was to the Soviet Union.

The most Churchill could get in August 1941 was a tacit bond because the president was not yet prepared to try to bring the

United States into the war. While Roosevelt and Churchill were wrapping up their meeting, the US House of Representatives passed a bill by one vote to extend the length of military service for American draftees. This narrowest of victories could only have strengthened FDR's view that the United States should not enter the war unless and until it was attacked.[48]

Torn between the need to defeat the Axis powers and his desire to ensure overwhelming public support for a US declaration of war, Roosevelt kept waiting for the right circumstances to enter the war. Then, on December 7, 1941, as the linchpin of a broad military offensive in Asia, Japan attacked Pearl Harbor, finding US military authorities in the Pacific shockingly unprepared. Japanese planes sank one battleship, put seven others out of action, and sank or damaged ten other ships. Twenty-four hundred Americans died, and another eleven hundred were wounded. After hearing the news on radio, Churchill cried out, "We shall declare war on Japan." US ambassador John Winant, who was meeting with Churchill, wanted to get confirmation, and they telephoned the White House. Churchill asked, "Mr. President, what's this about Japan?" FDR answered, "It's quite true. They have attacked us at Pearl Harbor. We are all in the same boat now."[49]

Both men benefited from major miscalculations by their enemies. The Japanese decided that a surprise attack by sea and by air would overwhelm the Pacific forces of a country whose economic resources far outweighed their own. They believed that Japan would then be free to expand elsewhere in Asia. Hitler had long wanted to go to war against the United States but feared that he could not do so unless and until Germany developed a much larger surface navy. But the sizable Japanese navy would complement Germany's own. For this reason, Germany repeatedly pledged to assist and join Japan if it chose to go to war against the United States.[50]

The US War Department had already planned to give Europe priority over Asia in case of war with the Axis powers because Germany was the most dangerous power. General George Marshall's planners assumed that Germany would conquer the USSR and that major US forces would eventually need to invade Europe. Although this was only a contingency plan, a large portion of the US fleet had already been transferred from Pearl Harbor to the Atlantic, accidentally sparing these ships from Japan's December 7 attack.[51]

An official in the War Department leaked this "victory program" to Democratic senator Burton Wheeler of Montana, a leading isolationist. Wheeler gave it to Robert McCormick, the isolationist owner and publisher of the *Chicago Tribune*, which unveiled the details on December 4. The three-day uproar among isolationists against FDR's "perfidy" ended abruptly with Japan's attack on Pearl Harbor.[52]

With the American public incensed about Japan, FDR wanted to avoid asking Congress for an American declaration of war on Germany, too. In his now famous "date of infamy speech" on December 8, President Roosevelt asked Congress to declare war only against Japan. There was nary a peep, Secretary of the Interior Ickes wrote, "from an appeaser or an isolationist anywhere except Senator [Gerald] Nye, who was so inept as to permit himself to be quoted . . . saying Japan's assault on our possession was a British plot."[53] Roosevelt resisted entreaties from Secretary of War Henry Stimson and others to act immediately against Germany, partly because he anticipated a German declaration against the United States.[54]

Hitler wanted to convert Germany's diplomatic tie with Japan into a military one. He took heart in the "fact" that the Japanese had not been defeated in 3,000 years, and he assumed that their forces would prevent US military intervention in Europe for some time. A declaration of war against the United

States would enable German U-boats to wreak havoc in the Atlantic with US Lend-Lease shipments to Britain and the Soviets.[55] It would also take the edge off the bad news he had to announce to the German people: heavy German casualties in the East and the unexpected continuation of the war against the USSR into 1942.

In his ninety-minute speech to the Reichstag on December 11, Hitler presented his war in the East as a step he had taken to neutralize a Soviet attack planned by Stalin working secretly in conjunction with Churchill. Hitler depicted Roosevelt as a member of a rich family and the candidate of a capitalist party, whose brain trust was composed of people such as those considered parasites in Germany and removed from public life (i.e., the Jews). The Jews had called Roosevelt to office, Hitler declared, which explained why speculation had flourished and the US economy was in danger of collapse. So, Hitler explained, the president needed a foreign policy diversion, and the Jews around him suggested a "second Purim" for European nations becoming increasingly antisemitic. Roosevelt was determined to destroy Germany, Hitler stated. That the Anglo-Saxon world now made common cause with Bolshevism did not surprise the Nazis, Hitler declared, since they were always linked, meaning, always part of the same Jewish conspiracy. So, Hitler announced that Germany, Italy, and Japan pledged to wage common war against the United States and England.[56] In the process, he resolved Roosevelt's political problem: Congress and the public would not oppose a war effort that concentrated first on Europe. The United States quickly responded in kind to Hitler's declaration of war.

In his announcement, Hitler did not discuss the racial war already in progress and in the process of expansion. But the complications following Pearl Harbor forced Reinhard Heydrich to postpone his secret Berlin meeting to coordinate Nazi

Party and government resources for the Final Solution of the Jewish question. Originally set for December 9, it was rescheduled for January 20, 1942. It later became known as the Wannsee Conference.

THE MYTH OF CHURCHILL'S RESPONSE TO THE HOLOCAUST

Russian-born scientist Chaim Weizmann, later to become Israel's first president, was perhaps the most prominent observer of both Nazi Germany's war against the Jews and Winston Churchill's activities. Weizmann had a friendly relationship with Churchill dating back to their first encounter in 1905, when they had joined a British protest against pogroms against Jews in Russia. Churchill had also opposed a bill designed to block Jews escaping from Russia from immigrating to Britain.[57] Weizmann sensed what the Nazis were about to do before mass executions of Jews started. In a private meeting with Ambassador Maisky in February 1941, Weizmann noted that Soviet Jews were "on firm ground" (because of the nonaggression pact between Germany and the USSR), but that he could not think without horror of the fate of six to seven million Jews in central and southeastern Europe if the Nazis won the war—they would all simply perish.[58]

Amidst a long visit to the United States, Weizmann noticed a key omission in Churchill's August 24 speech. Two days later, Weizmann telegraphed Colonial Secretary Lord Moyne, Churchill's friend, and ally: "Impossible to convey [to] you shocked reaction here to Prime Minister's failure to mention Jews among peoples awaiting restitution and liberation after the destruction of Nazi tyranny."[59] In claiming to convey the reaction of American Zionists to Churchill's failure to mention Jews, Weizmann was suggesting his own sentiments as well. His subtext was that Churchill was not only alienating him but also alienating Jewish

American leaders at a time when the United States was not yet in the war.

In a second, direct appeal to Churchill in September 1941 to create a Jewish fighting force in Palestine for self-defense there or potential use in Egypt, Weizmann clarified his thinking: "Tortured by Hitler as no nation has ever been in modern times, and advertised by him as his foremost enemy, we are refused by those who fight him the chance of seeing our name and flag appear among those arrayed against him." Then he turned to the supposed leverage that "the Jews" had in the current military situation: "I have spent four months in America . . . closely watching the American scene. Forces over there are finely balanced: the position is uncertain. There is only one big ethnic group which is willing to stand, to a man, for Great Britain, and a policy of 'all-out-aid' for her; the five million American Jews." Weizmann stated that Jewish Americans had tipped the scale in favor of intervention during World War I, and they could do so again if Britain sent the necessary positive signal and ceased its rebuffs and humiliation of Jews in Palestine.[60]

A Jewish fighting force in Palestine raised other political problems in the Middle East. The British feared that the Arab world would side with Germany and that a Jewish fighting force would become a political liability later. In October 1941, the cabinet canceled the proposed Jewish division.[61] Still, twice within weeks, Weizmann complained that Churchill and the UK government were ignoring Jewish victims. Weizmann did not recognize Churchill's "crime without a name" as referring to Jewish victims, and he had no sense that Churchill grasped the Nazi focus on killing millions of Jews.

It is difficult to transform Churchill's "crime without a name" into a synonym for the first wave of the Holocaust. At most, one could say that these mass executions, which we recognize today as part of the first wave of the Holocaust, provoked this section of Churchill's speech. But some historians and biographers have given Churchill credit for recognizing the Holocaust, too. In Martin Gilbert's rendition, Churchill could not mention Jews directly when highlighting mass executions, for fear of exposing British codebreaking.[62] The implication is that *we* know what he really meant. Churchill actually risked far more by mentioning German police battalions because it was no secret that Hitler had threatened to kill Jews.

Historian David Stafford writes, "After reading them [decryptions of mass shootings of Jews] for several weeks, Churchill stopped, wearied by their sickening predictability."[63] There is no source for inferring that Churchill instructed MI6 to cease briefing him on the executions, let alone that he was weary of reading about them. He did not keep a diary or otherwise reveal his emotions. He may well have just focused on what MI6 gave him, and he had plenty of other problems to solve.

Biographer Andrew Roberts observes that Churchill spoke of the terrible massacres of civilians—"especially Jews and Communists." But these categories do not appear in his speech, so Roberts injects what he thinks Churchill meant. Roberts mistakenly claims that Bletchley Park managed to decrypt the radio reports of the Einsatzgruppen.[64] One could argue plausibly that Churchill delivered pro-Soviet comments for specific reasons of state but not that he spoke about the Holocaust. All of this is to let hindsight overwhelm the contemporary evidence.

The most detailed defense of both Churchill and MI6 comes from former British intelligence official Michael Smith in a book chapter entitled "Bletchley Park and the Holocaust." Smith claims intimate knowledge of intelligence procedures at that time. His version of the sequence of events is roughly as follows: Early on August 24 the analysts in Hut 6 at Bletchley Park decoded a message that the Tenth Infantry Regiment of the First SS Brigade had shot 65 "Bolshevik Jews," that Friedrich

Jeckeln's Einsatzgruppe shot 70 Jews, and Battalion 314 of Police Regiment South had shot 294 Jews. In addition, Battalion 45 had shot dead 61 Jews and the Police Squadron had shot dead 113 Jews. Smith believes it "possible" that this information was sent by teleprinter to MI6 in time for Menzies's meeting that day with Churchill. If that happened, it would have led to a discussion, since Churchill was much interested in this data. Menzies would "certainly" have reminded Churchill of the danger of disclosing too much information, so "possibly there was a compromise made." For Churchill to have spoken about both German police troops and about Jews, Smith asserts, would have left no doubt that Churchill had access to German radio messages, so he did not mention Jews, perhaps because there were others killed, too (in smaller numbers not given here).[65]

In this account, Smith goes way beyond the surviving documentation. And if Churchill had agreed to such a hypothetical compromise, it worked out badly, because Churchill had no need to speak publicly about German police troops, whereas it would have surprised few knowledgeable people that Hitler was interested in carrying out his repeated threats to kill Jews. Smith concedes that Churchill endangered the secrecy of Bletchley Park's operations. The multivolume official history of British intelligence in World War II does not mention this episode and relegates a selection of Nazi executions to one short appendix in one volume. It also fails to discuss the subject of the Holocaust.

Some of Churchill's latter-day advocates transition swiftly from the "crime without a name" on August 24, 1941, to a message Churchill sent to the *Jewish Chronicle* on November 14, 1941, to commemorate its centenary. The *Chronicle* had already reported that thousands of Jews in Ukraine had been killed in pogroms.[66] Churchill's message to the paper probably did reflect what he had learned following August 24: "None has suffered more cruelly than the Jew the unspeakable evils wrought on the bodies and spirit of men by Hitler and his vile regime. The Jew bore the brunt of the Nazis' first onslaught upon the citadels of freedom and human dignity. He has borne and continues to bear a burden that might have seemed to be beyond endurance . . . Once again, at the appointed time, he will see vindicated those principles of righteousness which it was the glory of his fathers to proclaim to the world."[67] These sympathetic words may have consoled Jewish Britons who had greater knowledge of events in the East, but the passage could not have educated or warned Jews on the continent who lacked such information.

A man of great talent, great failures, great successes, and an astonishing political afterlife as a hero of World War II and the Cold War, Churchill enjoys far more admirers than detractors. However, something is at work here beyond the latitude given to a man regarded as a national hero in two major countries, and with honorary US citizenship. Numerous authors had developed strong views of Churchill the man before seeing intelligence sources released during the past thirty years.[68] The practice of making a person's character dominate over situational influences is frequently misleading, and it is here.

One of Churchill's unusual qualities was a long record of friendly relations with individual Jewish Britons combined with *positive* stereotypes about Jews in general in an age when antisemitism was stronger than it is today. It was natural for later admirers of Churchill to project the conclusion that Churchill was horrified by what we call the Holocaust and that he spoke out to denounce it. That puts heavy weight upon Churchill's "crime without a name" speech—the only viable candidate for an early public statement—despite the fact that it contains no mention of Jews.

In his quite sympathetic study of Churchill and Zionism, Michael Makovsky observes that, despite the horror Churchill felt, he did not focus on the Holocaust or on ways to combat it. His cardinal wartime principles, such as an economic blockade of Nazi-occupied Europe, conflicted with potential efforts to save Jewish lives.[69] Churchill the warrior focused on survival and then on military victory, for which he needed powerful allies.

Churchill sought to strengthen the UK's ties with both the United States and the USSR, a key part of his strategy to win the war. The twenty-first-century moral problem is not with what he said but what he did not say on August 24. Churchill had to avoid the risk of saying too much about mass executions based solely on his access to decoded German radio messages, yet he did not choose his words wisely. If he was trying to preserve the secrecy of Bletchley Park's successes, he said too much. If he was trying to warn about what later was called the Holocaust, he said too little. A clearer moral test would come later, when Churchill could have used media reports about the killing of millions of Jews as a cover for what he gleaned from signals intelligence. Still, the historiographical problem is that others have made or tried to make him an early voice for conscience during the Holocaust.[70]

CHAPTER THREE

STALIN'S ANNIVERSARY

On August 24, 1941, from the stage of an auditorium in Moscow, four Soviet Jewish speakers stressed the Nazi war against the Jews. Solomon Mikhoels, a prominent Yiddish actor and theater director, and the Ukrainian-born writer Ilya Ehrenburg, perhaps the most renowned Soviet journalist of his generation, spoke in Russian. The poet Peretz Markish used Yiddish, and the famous film director Sergei Eisenstein, whose father was Jewish but who did not think of himself as Jewish, displayed his fluent English. Soviet authorities prescreened their remarks, arranged their broadcast, and had them filmed for newsreels.[1]

These four were also among those who addressed an audience of thousands in Moscow's Park of Culture later that day. The crowd approved the resolution they and more than twenty other Soviet Jewish cultural figures had drafted, which asked Jews throughout the world to support the Soviet Union in its desperate struggle against Germany.[2]

Mikhoels declared that the Nazis planned the total annihilation of the Jewish people.[3] He must have learned from friends, relatives, and colleagues that Nazi forces had already executed large numbers of Jews in conquered Soviet territories, including his native Latvia. Unlike many Soviet Jews, he took seriously Hitler's repeated public threats to annihilate the Jews of Europe. And he warned that even American Jews were in danger if Germany won the war.[4]

Ehrenburg, who had lived in France and was well connected in West European political and literary circles, turned personal:

I grew up in a Russian city. My mother tongue is Russian. I am a Russian writer. Like all Russians, I am now defending my homeland. But the Nazis have reminded me of something else: my mother's name was Hanna. I am a Jew. I say this with pride. Hitler hates us above all. And that is our distinction. . . . I appeal now to the Jews of America—as a Russian writer and as a Jew. There is no ocean behind which to take cover. . . . We Jews are the main target of the beast. . . . We will not forgive those who are indifferent.[5]

The fact that these men aired their views in the Soviet media was unusual. That they spoke on August 24, 1941—the same day Churchill gave his "crime without a name speech"—showed their capacity to recognize the direction of Nazi actions early in the Holocaust. They had no need to read decoded German radio messages to do so.

STALIN'S PREVIOUS VIEWS OF ANTISEMITISM AND NAZISM

It had been nearly five years since Stalin's government had directly criticized Nazi racial fanaticism. On November 6, 1936, the eve of the anniversary of the Bolshevik Revolution, Vyacheslav Molotov, the nominal head of the Soviet government, proclaimed the need to stand up to the fascist bullies. A few weeks later, during a speech about the impending proclamation of a new Soviet constitution, Molotov condemned fascism for its hostility toward Jews. He then quoted Stalin as having said that "anti-Semitism, like any form of racial chauvinism, is the most dangerous vestige of cannibalism."[6] The term racial chauvinism fit Nazi Germany, but "vestige of cannibalism" might have seemed an odd political epithet. Perhaps Stalin struggled to find an appropriately primitive and disgusting taboo to contrast Nazism with what he considered the forward march of socialism. According to Molotov, Stalin expressed fraternal feelings for the Jewish people whenever and wherever antisemitic atrocities occurred. Molotov's quotation, the only contemporary public record of Stalin's words, came from Stalin's notes for a speech in December 1930.[7]

Molotov deployed Stalin's phrases in support of Soviet foreign policy. In the summer of 1936, the Soviet Union came to the aid of the beleaguered Spanish Republican government fighting against right-wing military, Catholic, and fascist forces during the Spanish Civil War. Germany and Italy both gave military aid and sent some of their own forces to assist the Spanish rebels led by Francisco Franco. At that time, Moscow also committed itself and the Communist International to a "Popular Front" policy in Europe, in which Communists and Communist organizations under USSR direction made common cause with left-of-center democrats and socialists. Having signed a mutual assistance treaty with France in 1935, the USSR officially favored collective security measures against Germany. Stark Soviet denunciation of antisemitism could help to unite the left against fascist countries and fascist movements.

Molotov was an ideal critic of antisemitism because his wife was Jewish.[8] But his quote from Stalin was an instrument for a purpose, not a moral expression, let alone one of Stalin's core beliefs. If Stalin wanted to denounce fascist antisemitism convincingly, he could easily have done so himself.

On November 25, 1936, Stalin broadcast a long speech to the Eighth Extraordinary Congress of Soviets in defense of the draft of the new Soviet constitution, which he had worked on for years. He dismissed fascist critics who had called the Soviet constitution deceptive, and he discounted bourgeois democracy as "democracy for the strong, democracy for the propertied minority." The USSR's constitution was, according to Stalin, "the only thoroughly democratic constitution in the world." He did not mention antisemitism; he could have criticized, for instance, Germany's Nuremberg Laws, enacted just over a year earlier, which had turned German Jews into pariah subjects. Stalin also spoke against—and thus killed—talk of a proposed amendment to the constitution that would have replaced the phrase "state of workers and peasants" with "state of all the races and nationalities inhabiting the territory of the USSR."[9] Like most committed Marxists of his era, he considered himself an opponent of nationalism, although shortly after the Bolshevik Revolution he had made use of nationalism to strengthen Bolshevik control in non-Russian areas. He served briefly as People's Commissar of Nationalities, largely because he was not a Russian but a Georgian, and his only "major" pre-revolutionary written work was *Marxism and the National Question* (1913).[10]

In private, Stalin used pejorative Jewish stereotypes in the manner common in Russia, and some of his most hated opponents, such as Leon Trotsky or Grigory Zinoviev, had been intellectuals of Jewish origin. He also worked closely with individual Communists of Jewish descent who were from working-class backgrounds, such as Lazar Kaganovich, one of Stalin's longest associates and a senior party and government authority. Still, Stalin probably found it unnatural to criticize antisemitism. One of his biographers found increasing antisemitism in his inner circle during the 1930s.[11]

Soviet-sponsored cultural activities could emphasize Nazi persecution of German Jews when it seemed opportune. The 1938 film "Professor Mamlock" is considered the first dramatic film to attack Nazi antisemitism. Herbert Rappaport, an experienced Austrian filmmaker, was invited to the USSR in 1936 to upgrade Soviet cinema to international standards. He teamed up with native Russian director Adolf Minkin to adapt a 1933 play by Friedrich Wolf, a German. Although the play depicted a surgeon named Professor Mamlock as a Social Democrat and a Jew, the Moscow screenplay made him politically apathetic and Jewish in name only. He was beaten, persecuted, and ultimately killed by Nazi storm troopers despite his having saved the life of a Nazi official. The film also portrayed Mamlock's son as a dedicated Communist who first opposed the rise of the Nazis and then resisted the Nazis in power, which fit the contours of Soviet propaganda. Released in September 1938, the film drew large audiences in the United States as well as the USSR, in part because of fortunate timing. The massive Kristallnacht assault on the German Jewish community followed two months later. The film was the product of the directors, not of government officials, although anything shown on the screen had to pass government censors.[12]

Kristallnacht led to an authorized Soviet demonstration on November 27. The official organization of Soviet writers and architects took part in a meeting at the Great Hall of the Moscow Conservatory, where about two thousand people gathered to protest what were called the "Jewish pogroms" in Fascist Germany. The writer Alexei Tolstoy called the comparison of Nazi Germany with the Middle Ages an insult to the Middle Ages. Recent events in Germany were unprecedented in human history, Tolstoy declared. Mikhoels spoke at this rally as well.[13]

The popular front, collective security activities, and Soviet criticism of Nazi violence did nothing to check or ameliorate

Stalin's own oppression. In fact, they coincided with Stalin's purges of the military and all other branches of government and sectors of society. In 1937, the Soviet ruler purged and executed three of the five Red Army marshals, fifteen out of sixteen army commanders, sixty of sixty-seven corps commanders, and 70 percent of division commanders. Absolute loyalty to Stalin trumped military expertise, but even loyalty counted for little.[14] In 1937–1938, Stalin's broader purge of anti-Soviet elements throughout society, known as the Great Terror, resulted in the execution of an astonishing 634,000 persons. The size of this bloodbath, which continued on a lesser scale in 1939, was kept largely secret, but the fact that Stalin perceived those killed as enemies was not.[15]

None of Stalin's "national operations" (purges of those accused of nationalism, most importantly Poles) during and after the Great Terror was aimed at Jews, per se. Those Jews arrested or executed were targeted because they were members of suspect political elites or other elites. Poles, Ukrainians (especially from West Ukraine after 1939), and Koreans were targeted, though the Koreans were "merely" administratively resettled. Still, Stalin became wary of the People's Commissariat of Internal Affairs (NKVD), which itself had carried out earlier purges, and he made sure to extend the current cleansing into the secret police. He also made some comments that were interpreted as calling for the purge of the disproportionate number of Jewish officials there. In Ukraine, the arrest of many Jewish officials fueled an impression that there was a secret policy of antisemitism—secret because officially, antisemitism was illegal. In any case, the NKVD became far less "Jewish" in the year or so before World War II.[16]

Nevertheless, antisemites in many countries continued to associate Jews with Communism or with the Soviet Union, and this soon had some political and lethal repercussions. Nationalist forces in Eastern Europe, whether or not they collaborated with Germany against the USSR, often attacked Jews as alleged Communists. Recent scholars have re-employed the Nazi and contemporary East European term Judeo-Bolshevism to signify this misleading association, which remains a staple of antisemitic extremists today.[17]

The German destruction of Czechoslovakia in March 1939 ruptured European collective security links. When both Britain and France asked Soviet ambassador to Great Britain Maisky whether the USSR would publicly declare support for any further victims of aggression, Stalin, through Foreign Minister Maxim Litvinov, counter-proposed an anti-Nazi Triple Alliance. Britain and France declined. Perceiving an intra-capitalist war on the horizon, Stalin then shifted signals. In May, he dismissed Foreign Minister Litvinov, who was Jewish, because of his allegedly disloyal attitude, and Molotov took over the post. Other officials of Jewish origin in the Soviet Foreign Ministry were arrested, more an effort to alter the USSR's image than a specific mark of antisemitism. Maisky, surprisingly, was able to hold onto his post. Stalin's new Soviet profile was a precondition for discussions with Germany.[18]

THE HITLER–STALIN PACT

Stalin began asking a subordinate to bring him available literature on Hitler and the social origins of Nazism. He spent an evening reading the limited edition Russian translation of Hitler's 1925 memoir and political tract *Mein Kampf*. A onetime high party official, Grigory Zinoviev, had translated the book for the party bosses in 1933.[19] Zinoviev could have told Stalin a good deal about the early Hitler, but in 1936 the USSR had invented charges that Zinoviev was a terrorist and spy; he was tried, convicted, and executed.

Stalin read and underlined passages in the book about Hitler's goal of acquiring territory in the east. He also studied Konrad Heiden's history of Nazism and *Hitler Rearms* by British author Dorothy Woodman, both published in 1934 and translated into Russian the following year. Woodman showed how Germany prepared for war ideologically even before it could do so materially.[20] Despite or because of this background reading, Stalin gained a positive impression of Germany's dynamism. He apparently concluded that it was better to come to terms with the European power willing to carve up or absorb smaller states, not with those defending the status quo.

The Russian translation of Heiden's book bore the title *History of Fascism*, a revealing shift. Stalin had criticized the fact that Hitler's party called itself the National Socialist German Workers Party or just National Socialist. Stalin found this name deceptive: there was nothing socialist about Hitler's regime. In 1934, the Soviet dictator declared that it contained "not an atom of socialism"; its methods marked the weakness of the bourgeoisie, which could no longer rule by parliamentary methods.[21] Stalin certainly wanted to clarify the political differences for ordinary workers and peasants, but there were probably additional considerations for preferring the term "fascism." It was a general concept that fit into the Marxist formula of the historical process; it qualified as a variant of imperialism, which Lenin had written about long before as the highest stage of capitalism. National Socialism, however, was unique.

Some contemporary Western politicians and diplomats had seen resemblances between Hitlerism and Stalinism.[22] Both were bloody dictatorships with secret police controls and a single authorized mass party. Both dominated culture and education, using them to strengthen the state and party. Both dismissed Western liberal standards and killed large numbers of citizens. Stalin may have wanted as much linguistic distance as

possible between Germany and the Soviet Union because he
was aware of some perceived similarities. A diplomatic rap-
prochement between Germany and the USSR would likely increase the number of critical comparisons, the forerunner of
later theories of totalitarianism.

German Foreign Minister Ribbentrop and Soviet Foreign
Minister Molotov carried out secret preparatory negotiations
for a mutually beneficial treaty. On August 20, 1939, Hitler
wrote Stalin to suggest a nonaggression pact right away. Seeing
that a German attack on Poland was imminent, Stalin welcomed the opportunity to expand Soviet influence to the west.[23]
The Molotov-Ribbentrop pact was really the Hitler-Stalin pact,
with their deal to carve up territories in Eastern Europe contained in a secret protocol.

Reinforcing his choice publicly, on October 9, 1939, Stalin inserted a passage into an editorial in *Izvestiya* that a war to eradicate Hitlerism made no sense: "It is a senseless and stupid brutality to exterminate people for the fact that someone does not
like certain opinions and a certain world view. . . . One can respect or hate Hitlerism, as in the case of any system of political
views."[24] Using very similar language, Molotov told the Supreme
Soviet that war against Hitlerism under the slogan of preserving
democracy was criminal. During the following months, the Soviet press ceased to report on the condition of Jews in Nazi occupied or Nazi dominated European countries.[25] Nazi antisemitism became a taboo topic. One consequence was that some
Soviet Jews, especially those far from the pre-1939 Soviet bor-
derlands with now occupied eastern Poland and the Baltic
countries, remained unaware of the Nazis' persecution of Jews
in German-occupied Poland.[26]

During the fall of 1939 and in 1940, Soviets conquered
eastern Poland and took over Latvia, Lithuania, Bessarabia, and
Northern Bukovina. As a result, the USSR's Jewish population

rose from three to five million. Many of these new "Soviet" Jews became especially vulnerable—unattached to the Soviet economic and political system and regarded as unreliable or hostile. They also resided near or closer to a border with Germany that had expanded to the east.

The Soviet Union accepted about forty thousand able-bodied Jews who fled the German occupation zone of Poland after they agreed to work in the north and east of the Soviet Union, as well as in mines in Ukraine. Most subsequently became Soviet citizens. Perhaps as many as twelve thousand additional Jews were among the politically or socially suspect elements whom the Soviets deported from recently annexed Latvia, Lithuania, and Estonia shortly before the German invasion.[27] A good many deportees died from harsh treatment in the Soviet Gulag, but the deportation eastward of some as "special settlers" and the evacuation of others as Soviet citizens saved them from mass murder by Nazi forces after June 22, 1941.[28]

In November 1940, Stalin signaled willingness to join Germany, Italy, and Japan in an expanded Tripartite Pact if given more territorial incentives.[29] He did not care that closer Soviet association with Germany would severely test the loyalty of many Communists and sympathizers outside the USSR and of Soviet Jews such as Mikhoels and Ehrenburg. Stalin's own Politburo would not check him: Politburo members threatened by recurring purges told him what they thought he wanted to hear.[30]

Stalin reasoned that Hitler, having failed to subdue Britain, would shy away from a two-front war that had proved fatal to Germany in World War I. Plus, the Nazi-Soviet Pact had benefited both sides: Stalin knew that Soviet exports of raw materials alleviated Germany's shortages. He may have assumed that any planned German attack would be to gain specific objectives, and if it materialized, it would come only after Germany tried to extract major concessions.[31] Biographer Stephen Kotkin views Stalin as "mesmerized by the might and daring of Germany's parallel totalitarian regime" and "bafflingly slow to come to grips with the centrality of ideology in the Nazi program."[32] Stalin thus overlooked one of Hitler's most prominent features—that of the ideologue who considered the Soviet Union an adjunct of the international Jewish conspiracy against Germany.

INTELLIGENCE FAILURES

For many years the Soviet dictator had taken extreme measures to defend his vision of socialism against perceived internal enemies—his actual or potential political rivals, suspect nationalities, or anyone who showed an independent streak. His massive purges had ravaged Soviet intelligence to the point where they increased external dangers to the USSR. A Czechoslovakian military intelligence officer, meeting in 1936 with his Soviet counterparts, found them ignorant of Germany.[33] By January 1939, 275 of the 450 Soviet secret police officials stationed in other countries had been brought back and arrested: the foreign branch of the NKVD was essentially destroyed.[34] Its successor, the Commissariat for State Security, lacked an analytical section; only Soviet military intelligence performed some analysis. Stalin insisted on receiving intelligence reports directly, which essentially meant that he was the one interpreting them—picking and choosing the items he believed accurate.[35]

Talented Soviet agents and officials who survived the purges often found their information overlooked or discarded because it did not fit Stalin's preconceptions. Stalin never trusted the now famous spies inside the heart of the British establishment who worked for the USSR at least partly for reasons of conviction. Recruited at Cambridge University, they have become known as the Cambridge Five.[36] The Soviet dictator disregarded one 1940 report that came directly or indirectly from German diplomat Rudolf von Scheliha indicating that Hitler had authorized preparations for an invasion of the USSR. In March 1941, the Soviet military attaché in Berlin, Vasily Tupikov, wrote a one-hundred-page overview of the German military, concluding that an attack on the Soviet Union would take place between May 15 and June 15. These are samples of a larger mass of intelligence warnings.[37] Tupikov's estimate would have been correct if Hitler had held to the original schedule, but the German military needed a slight delay.

On May 4, 1941, Stalin took over Molotov's post as prime minister. Stalin's most powerful position remained general secretary of the party, but he was also head of its Politburo, and, on August 8, 1941, he became supreme commander in chief of the Soviet armed forces. He held far more concentrated power than Lenin had.[38]

On June 17, 1941, the former Soviet ambassador to Germany, now head of the newly established People's Commissariat for State Security, sent Stalin an intelligence report stating that a German invasion would come very soon. With his green pencil Stalin wrote on the document: "To com. [comrade] Merkulov: You can send your 'source' from German aviation HQ to his fucking mother. This is not a 'source' but a disinformation."[39] Multiple warnings of an imminent German attack on the night of June 21–22 reached Stalin and his Politburo, who discussed the situation until three in the morning. Stalin took no action. Shortly afterward, Army Chief of Staff General Georgy Zhukov telephoned with news of the invasion. According to Zhukov's 1956 account, Stalin responded with an order to the troops, "This is a provocation by the German military. Do not open fire to avoid unleashing wider action."[40]

Later that day, Stalin avoided announcing the war to the Soviet people or calling for resistance, leaving that task to Molotov.
Since Molotov was the one who signed the nonaggression treaty
with Germany, Stalin let him reveal its failure. The dictator did,
however, draft much of Molotov's text because he believed he
had a gift for distilling ideas into simple phrases. Loudspeakers
throughout Moscow carried Stalin's and Molotov's words at
noon to the public.[41]

If the Soviet public expected an easy war, Soviet propaganda
was largely to blame. For years, party and government officials
had asked citizens for sacrifices at home in order to build up the
strength of the military. A popular 1938 propaganda film, "If
War Should Come Tomorrow," suggested that the USSR had no
need for allies. After an unidentified imperialist power attacked
the USSR, the Red Army counterattacked and carried the battle
across the border. Workers there revolted to give the Soviets
military victory with minimal bloodshed.[42] The Soviet Ministry
of Defense published a book that same year projecting similar
optimism. *The First Blow: The Story of the Coming War* depicted a surprise German air attack quickly routed by Soviet
fighter planes. The USSR responded by bombing German industrial targets in Nuremberg-Fürth, and then followed up with
a Soviet invasion of Germany in what might be called an idyllic
war.[43]

On June 25, 1941, Pantaleymon Ponomarenko, the top Communist Party official in Belorussia, wrote to Stalin that "an an-
imal fear has taken hold of [the Jews]; in place of fighting, they
are running away." He noted that Nazi propaganda focused on
the struggle against "Yids" and Communists, treating them as
synonyms.[44] But Soviet authorities themselves evacuated professionally or politically valuable citizens from western areas of
the USSR, and many others fled on their own. Those evacuated
or fleeing included perhaps as many as 1.5 million Soviet Jews.[45]

The Soviets thus unintentionally rescued such Jews from the Holocaust.

At the end of June, David Ortenberg, deputy editor of the army newspaper *Red Star*, learned that he would be promoted to editor-in-chief. Ortenberg knew that the new post was risky for anyone, let alone for a Jew; three previous editors had disappeared during the purges. But General Lev Mekhlis, also of Jewish descent, told him that Stalin had approved the appointment with the proviso that Ortenberg use the byline Vadimov, constructed out of his son's name Vadim, because it did not look Jewish. Ortenberg believed that, even after a week of fighting, Stalin was still trying to avoid steps that would antagonize Hitler. Ortenberg then brought in journalists and writers of renown such as Ehrenburg and Aleksei Tolstoy, a distant relative of the great novelist. Stalin regarded both men as talented.[46]

STALIN AS SUPREME DEFENDER

Field Marshal Fedor von Bock's German Army Group Center aimed to follow Napoleon's route toward Minsk, capital of Belorussia, then Smolensk, and then Moscow, in total, some six hundred miles. On June 29, after the Germans encircled some 400,000 Soviet troops and took Minsk, Stalin finally recognized the catastrophic scale of the losses and the near desperate state of the military command. Leaving the Commissariat of Defense, Stalin remarked to Molotov and supplies chief Anastas Mikoyan, "Lenin left us a great legacy. We, his heirs, have pissed it all away." Then, seemingly shaken by his misreading of Hitler and his mistakes as commander in chief, he secluded himself in his dacha for two days.[47]

In his first post-invasion speech on July 3, from radio facilities newly set up in the Kremlin, Stalin uncharacteristically addressed the population personally: "Comrades, citizens, brothers and sisters, and warriors of the army and navy. I turn to you my friends." British journalist Alexander Werth, who was in the USSR then, thought that his words suited the atmosphere. Novelist and poet Konstantin Simonov later described Stalin's voice as soft and toneless with a heavy Georgian accent: "Once or twice, during his speech, you could hear a glass click as he drank water. His voice . . . might have seemed perfectly calm, but for his heavy, tired breathing, and that water that he kept drinking during the speech. . . . There was a discrepancy between that even voice and the tragic situation of which he spoke; and in that discrepancy there was strength."[48]

Stalin explained away Germany's ultra-rapid advance as the result of its full mobilization and advance preparations. He greatly exaggerated German casualties in the early battles. He termed the war a matter of life and death for the Soviet state and the peoples of the USSR, the national culture and statehood of the Russians, Ukrainians, Belorussians, Lithuanians, Latvians, Estonians, Uzbeks, Tatars, Moldavians, Georgians, Armenians, Azerbaijanis, and the other free peoples of the Soviet Union. He did not mention the Jews. He said that this war was not between two armies but between the entire Soviet people and the fascist German invaders. He called on Soviet civilians to recognize the depth of this danger, to organize a partisan struggle in German-held territory, and to remove or destroy resources from areas the enemy controlled or threatened. In calling the conflict a patriotic one, Stalin drew upon the precedent of the Patriotic War of 1812 against Napoleon. World War II soon became "the Great Patriotic War." Stalin must have hoped that invoking the fatherland would resonate more than appeals to Communism. He also reassured his audience that the USSR had powerful friends in this struggle. And despite his recounting of difficulties and dangers, the public gained confidence that he would lead effective resistance.[49]

Stalin relied on the party for tighter methods of control even within the military. He appointed political commissars—loyal party officials—who were attached to commanders at every level. The Bolsheviks had used political commissars during the Civil War; they had been abolished, brought back in 1937, and abolished again, only to be reintroduced after the German invasion.[50] They enforced the strictest political control, with the result that between June 22 and October 10, more than ten thousand Red Army officers and soldiers were executed. On August 16, Stalin made it illegal for soldiers to surrender and be taken prisoner. They were to be killed if they could be bombed or otherwise targeted, and their families deprived of benefits. Deserters could simply be shot. Stalin's reaction to one defeat after another was to look for scapegoats and for traitors. But some of these threatened measures were not carried out.[51]

From July 22 to August 17, German bombers repeatedly attacked Moscow, a city with many wooden buildings easy to set afire. The first raid came without any warning, but as Moscow's air defenses were built up, German pilots found anti-aircraft fire heavier than what they had faced a year or so earlier over Britain. Still, by the end of the six-months-long air assault, they had hit the Kremlin sixteen times and killed ninety-six men in its garrison. More than two thousand Muscovites were killed, with three times as many wounded. The Luftwaffe failed to bomb the population into submission, but they did raise the level of anxiety. Many other German air missions over the USSR hit targets to support the German army's advance toward Moscow.[52]

SOVIET MEDIA AND THE HOLOCAUST

On August 16, a small group of culturally accomplished Soviet Jews proposed a Jewish rally in Moscow aimed at public opinion in the United States, Britain, and other countries. Their gathering would feature Jewish academics, writers, artists, and Red Army soldiers. Unable to keep track of Stalin's frequent purges, the organizers had listed among potential speakers at least one air force officer (and Spanish Civil War veteran) already arrested, Smushkevich, a Jew from a religious family in Vilna.[53] That problem was resolved by adjusting the lineup of speakers. Then Solomon Lozovsky, deputy minister for foreign affairs and deputy chairman of the Soviet Information Bureau (Sovinformburo), pushed the proposal through.[54] It paralleled Stalin's goal of improving ties with the West in order to press for American and British help against the Germans.

Three of the Soviet Jewish cultural leaders featured in the broadcast on August 24, 1941—Ehrenburg, Mikhoels, and Eisenstein—had struggled during the period of the Nonaggression Pact. Ehrenburg, living in France (until June 1940), declined to return to the USSR. He then had his dacha seized and fell into depression for months. When he returned after the German conquest of France, no one met him at the station. He was clearly suspect. He was not allowed to publish much; *Izvestiya* would not accept his articles at all. The regime did nothing to mark his fiftieth birthday.[55]

Former NKVD chief Nikolai Yezhov, under brutal interrogation, had named the great writer Isaac Babel as a spy. Babel, himself tortured, falsely implicated Ehrenburg, Mikhoels, and Eisenstein, while also "confessing" that he was part of a Trotskyite organization.[56] Yezhov was executed, and Babel too, by firing squad in 1940. But Stalin spared the three men accused by Babel. He liked one of Ehrenburg's novels and told him so in a phone call. And he had watched Mikhoels perform "King Lear." Stalin fancied himself a patron of Soviet culture.[57]

Public Soviet Jewish activities could attract material aid and impress foreign Jews who might be able to influence their

governments. In the summer of 1941, Stalin released two Polish
Jews, Henryk Erlich and Viktor Alter, as part of an effort to appeal to Western labor movements. These two leaders of the
Bund (Jewish Labor Party) in interwar Poland had been impris-
oned after they fled to the USSR in the fall of 1939. They sought
to bring Soviet Jews and Jewish refugees from German territory
into an international committee and to form a Jewish Legion
within the Red Army, with American volunteers. But soon ex-
ceeding the very limited tolerance of Soviet officials, they were
placed in solitary confinement (where they both died later,
Erlich by suicide). The Jewish Anti-Fascist Committee, established in the spring of 1942, carried out an "anti-fascist" campaign among Jews abroad to garner material and political
support.[58]

On August 11, 1941, *Pravda* described how Nazi authorities
in Minsk liquidated Jews in one section of the city. A few days
later, an *Izvestiya* correspondent wrote that Jews across the occupied Soviet territories were being tortured and then killed. In
mid-August, Ponomarenko wrote Stalin about the merciless annihilation of the Jewish population in occupied Belorussia. On
August 16, the Sovinform, in a long report on German crimes,
included a mention of bloody Jewish pogroms in the Ukrainian
province of Zhytomyr. By the end of the month, an NKVD report reached similar conclusions about Nazi mass executions of
Jews in several regions of occupied Ukraine, though it is unclear
whether this last report reached Stalin.[59] Preoccupied with the
fighting and with his efforts to secure large-scale assistance
from the West, for months the Soviet dictator did not raise the
subject of the Jews himself.

From a room next to his Kremlin office, Stalin sent strategic
and tactical instructions to the fronts by telegraph. Lacking military expertise, he frequently overreached, especially during the
first two years of the war. He insisted on trying to hold every

piece of territory with the result that the Germans were able to encircle and destroy entire armies. Army Chief of Staff General Zhukov, the son of a shoemaker, wanted to evacuate Kiev in early September to avoid encirclement, but Stalin refused. Zhukov requested to be removed from his post and sent to the front. Stalin agreed, so Zhukov went off to manage the defense of Leningrad. When German troops took Kiev, they seemed to have blown the southern front open. They captured well over 600,000 Soviet troops—four Soviet armies. Only 15,000 ever returned. Although this victory vindicated Hitler's decision to emphasize the southern front, the result was mostly attributable to Stalin's blunders.[60]

A week and a half after German forces took Kiev, Sonderkommando 4a, assisted by more than two German police formations, Wehrmacht units, and Ukrainian auxiliaries, carried out the massacre of 33,771 Jews at the nearby Babi Yar ravine, the largest single mass killing of the first wave of the Holocaust. Another six thousand plus were killed over the next few days.[61]

The Soviet media reported some additional killings of Jews in September. When the Red Army retook a town in the Smolensk province *Izvestiya* and *Trud* (the daily newspaper of the trade unions) both wrote about Nazi shootings of locals just because they were Jews. On September 27, *Izvestiya* carried an unusually broad article under the byline of N. Petrov, a pseudonym. Much later, it became known that Petrov stood for Soviet head of state (chairman of the presidium of the Supreme Soviet) Mikhail Kalinin. Alexei Tolstoy may have ghostwritten the article for Kalinin entitled "The People's Hatred." In 1926, Kalinin had given a speech at a national meeting to spur Jewish agricultural settlement in which he urged the Jews to retain their culture and ethnicity. One of the largest Jewish collective farms, established in the Kherson region of southern Ukraine, was named Kalinindorf.[62] Now "Petrov" warned that all Soviet Jews faced severe danger because fascist ideology blamed the Jews for bringing disasters to Germany, and accordingly, the Jews had to be destroyed.[63] It was not Stalin's kind of article because it stressed the ideology that Stalin had ignored for many years. Kalinin stood in for Stalin as Molotov had done in November 1936. On the other hand, the article at least associated the Soviet media with criticism of Nazi murders of Jews. Such coverage could appeal to foreign Jewish organizations, and it might go over well in London and Washington.

LEND-LEASE ASSISTANCE

British and Americans officials understood that shipping weapons and ammunition to the Soviets would help their own cause. Seeing Stalin's personal courage during an air raid in late July and his general steadfastness, FDR's special envoy Harry Hopkins cabled home his favorable assessment of Soviet military prospects. Leaving Moscow, Hopkins made it across the Atlantic in time to join FDR and Churchill at their shipboard meeting at Argentia Bay, Canada. There Hopkins reiterated that Stalin and the USSR could manage to stave off defeat if the United States and UK gave them sufficient support.[64]

Stalin deemed the ensuing Western aid negotiations in Moscow so critical that he and Molotov led the Soviet side. In late September, Lord Beaverbrook and Roosevelt's personal representative Averell Harriman offered Stalin an ongoing flow of military equipment in lieu of the new second front on the continent he had demanded. The only way to satisfy the USSR's extensive military needs was to divert some of the American arms promised earlier to Britain under the Lend-Lease Program.[65] On October 1, 1941, the United States, UK, and USSR reached an agreement providing the USSR with generous quantities of arms and supplies, a billion dollars from the United States, and medical supplies. The final communiqué indicated that the agreement reflected practically everything the USSR had asked for.[66] But Stalin wanted Britain to open a second front on the continent at least as much.

THE DEFENSE OF MOSCOW

In an October 3 radio address to the German people, Hitler announced a new military operation of gigantic proportions that would smash the enemy in the East, though he did not name the target. A renewed German offensive to take Moscow, codenamed Operation Typhoon, had begun a day earlier. German troops swept into Orel, only about two hundred miles from Moscow, with many Soviet troops fleeing. Still, close to seven hundred thousand soldiers were encircled and captured. German general Heinz Guderian believed that the bulk of the Soviet army had now been destroyed.[67]

Demanding a counterattack, Stalin was told it was impossible. The Soviet media did not at first report Hitler's speech or the initial Soviet defeats, but by October 8, *Red Star* conceded that the USSR was in grave danger. By October 12, even *Pravda* wrote in the same spirit and warned of enemy agents, spies, and provocateurs trying to create panic—a thinly veiled warning against anyone expressing defeatist sentiments.[68]

On October 8, Stalin reminded Zhukov, whom he had recalled from Leningrad to take command of Moscow's defense, of Lenin's desperate decision in early 1918 to sue for peace with Germany at great territorial cost in the Treaty of Brest-Litovsk. Would he have to do the same? A prominent fighter pilot summoned to Stalin's office listened as he wailed: "A great misfortune, a great sorrow has befallen us. . . . What are we going to do? What are we going to do?" On that very day, Stalin ordered preparations to destroy plants and factories in and around the capital.[69]

Some twelve thousand volunteers with virtually no military training were organized to fill in gaps in the approaches to Moscow left uncovered by the army. Other volunteers, including at least six hundred women, were absorbed into decimated army sub-units along with new conscripts. Fortunately for the Soviets, the first snow on October 7 thawed, turning Soviet roads into mud, and the German advance toward Moscow slowed. Overstretched German formations were also weakened when some units were diverted to other objectives to the north and the south.[70]

When top Communist officials met on October 15, Stalin announced that the Germans might break through to Moscow at any time. He ordered the evacuation of government offices and foreign diplomatic missions to Kuibyshev, 770 miles southeast on the Volga River, but he refused to surrender the capital. He declared that he would stay as long as possible, although he did prepare a plane for a last-minute departure if necessary. Suddenly on October 16, the city's basic services collapsed: no newspapers, no buses, no trams or trolleys, no police. Many workers who went to work that morning found factories closed, or they were sent home. Looting and burglary spread. In his diary a Soviet historian compared the city to an ant heap, with the ants acting like strangers to each other. Large numbers of civilians, including some high Communist officials, fled toward Kuibyshev, the fortunate ones by train. By the time the planned and spontaneous evacuation ceased in late November, two million people out of a peacetime population of four million had left.[71]

During these critical days, Stalin read biographies of Ivan the Terrible, the sixteenth-century ruler of Moscow who declared himself tsar of all Russia, and Marshal Kutuzov, the imperial Russian commander who defeated Napoleon in 1812 with a

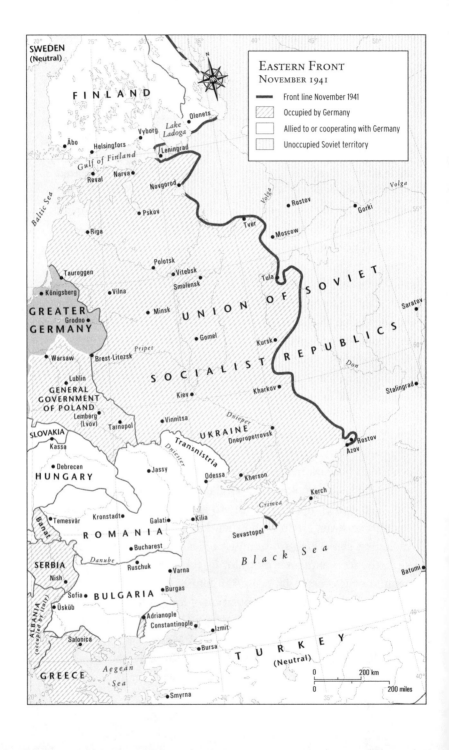

EASTERN FRONT
NOVEMBER 1941

— Front line November 1941
Occupied by Germany
Allied to or cooperating with Germany
Unoccupied Soviet territory

SWEDEN
(Neutral)

FINLAND

Olonets
Lake
Ladoga
Vyborg

Åbo
Helsingfors
Gulf of Finland
Leningrad
Reval
Narva
Novgorod
Pskov
Rostov
Gorki
Volga
Volga

Baltic Sea
Riga
Tver
Moscow

Tauroggen
Polotsk
Vitebsk
Smolensk
Königsberg
Vilna
Tula
Saratov
GREATER
Grodno
Minsk
UNION OF SOVIET
GERMANY

Warsaw
Brest-Litozsk
Pripet
Gomel
Kursk
REPUBLICS
Don
SOCIALIST
Lublin
GENERAL
GOVERNMENT
Kiev
Kharkov
Stalingrad
OF POLAND
Lemberg
(Lvov)
Tarnopol
Dnieper
SLOVAKIA
Vinnitsa
UKRAINE
Kassa
Transnistria
Dnepropetrovsk
Rostov
Dniester
Azov
Debrecen
Jassy
HUNGARY
Odessa
Kherson
Kerch
Temesvàr
Kronstadt
Galati
Kilia
Crimea
Banat
ROMANIA
Sevastopol
Bucharest
Black Sea
SERBIA
Danube
Ruschuk
Varna
Nish
Batumi
Sofia
BULGARIA
Burgas

Üsküb
Adrianople
Constantinople
Izmit
Salonica
Bursa
TURKEY
GREECE
Aegean
(Neutral)
Sea
Smyrna

0   200 km
0   200 miles

strategy of attrition. Two momentous decisions, perhaps reflecting or reinforced by his reading, helped stabilize the situation. As early as October 12, he summoned about 400,000 troops, 1,000 tanks, and 1,000 planes from the Far Eastern Army to rush to Moscow. (This time Stalin credited intelligence that Japan was not going to attack the USSR in the east.) He also declared a state of siege to restore control in Moscow, authorizing summary execution of spies and agents provocateurs. The NKVD shot about two hundred people on October 16 alone. Stalin was reassured when on October 16 or 17, General Zhukov expressed confidence that Moscow could be held. Even so, it was not until October 19 that the dictator firmly decided to remain. German troops were then fifty miles away from the capital, in some spots nearer. By late October, the city, converted into an improvised fortress, began to revive with a reduced population.[72]

STALIN'S SPEECHES

November 7, the anniversary of the Bolshevik Revolution of 1917, was normally a day of major ceremonial events.[73] For this twenty-fourth anniversary, Stalin decided that the propaganda value of holding traditional speeches on the evening of November 6 and the following day, capped off by a parade, outweighed the risk of casualties from a German air attack. But he would give his first speech at a protected location, the ornate hall of the Mayakovsky Metro Station, largest in the system. Zhukov approved anniversary plans, stipulating that additional fighter planes be brought in from other fronts. He also wanted to supply roughly two divisions of manpower to provide security and to march in the parade. Stalin hedged his bets by keeping all anniversary preparations secret until the very last minute, knowing that he could cancel in case of a military emergency—

and that he could coerce people into attending without advance notice.[74]

Stalin was not a brilliant speaker. He had needed inspiring oratory neither to rise to dictatorial power nor to maintain it. His Georgian accent was a handicap, and his vocabulary was filled with commonly used phrases. He generally spoke to the public only on important or necessary occasions, and he had not done so since July 3. But after the near collapse of the Soviet system he wanted to project strength.

The Moscow Soviet, the communist version of a city council, hosted the November 6 evening event. The hall filled with delegates of Soviet, party, and trade union organizations, representatives of the armed forces, and ordinary citizens. Immediately after Soviet chair Vasili Pronin introduced Stalin, enemy aircraft approached Moscow, and Soviet fighters and anti-aircraft batteries scrambled. Because the air raid sirens would have interfered with the broadcast, the officer in charge wisely decided not to sound them. German bombs fell elsewhere. The sound of bombing did not register inside the hall, but the next day *New York Times* correspondent Daniel Brigham described a constant drone, attributed to the large aerial attack. Brigham portrayed the atmosphere as electric with suspense. He was probably right, but he could draw upon only long-distance perception because he had been listening by radio from Bern, Switzerland.

Stalin spoke simply and deliberately, in a soft voice that was difficult to hear given the poor acoustics and frequent interruptions by applause. Brigham timed Stalin's speech at fifty-two minutes.[75] British journalist Werth called Stalin's presentation a strange mixture of black gloom and complete confidence.

This year, Stalin stated, he would not discuss Soviet successes in the construction of socialism. Instead, he would give an account of the war since June 22, which he said represented a turning point for the USSR. Stalin accurately observed that the

Nazis had prepared a surprise invasion, but they had miscalculated, expecting the Soviet system to collapse within six weeks to two months. This comment suggested that Stalin had begun to credit good Soviet intelligence about Hitler's expectations. The huge German casualties (Stalin claimed a very inflated 4.5 million killed, wounded, or taken prisoner) and the continued resistance of Leningrad and Moscow showed how German planners had underestimated the Soviet armed forces and people. Stalin seemed to recognize that bourgeois democracies had some virtues and that not all imperialists were alike: "the Hitlerite party" was one of the most rapacious imperialists among all the imperialists of the world. The USSR's allies, Britain and the United States, were democracies different in nature than Germany. Although they were not presently fighting German armies directly, they were helping with supplies, and Stalin hoped that Britain would soon open a second front in the German rear. This coalition was a growing reality, he said. This alliance enjoyed the moral advantage of defending itself and seeking to liberate much of Europe from Nazi oppression. Stalin concluded, "Our cause is just. The enemy will be beaten. Victory will be ours." The applause lasted for ten minutes.[76]

Aware of Nazi mass murders of Soviet Jews, Stalin mentioned the subject directly once, saying that the Nazis were carrying out medieval "pogroms" just as eagerly as the tsarist regime had done.[77] Here he apparently wanted to reach his Soviet audience with a comparison to known events, and he preferred familiar terms, even if they underplayed what he knew to have occurred. Elsewhere, he claimed to have found on the body of a fallen German lieutenant the text of an address of the German high command calling upon soldiers "to kill every Russian, every Soviet. Do not halt even if before you there is an aged man or woman, boy or girl. Kill in this way and you will save yourself from destruction. You will secure the future of your family and you will become famous forever." No such document survived the war; it was likely Stalin's invention. But perhaps the Nazi killing of Jewish men, women, and children inspired it.

Stalin quoted Hitler as saying that to conquer the world, to create a great German empire, Germany had to drive out and destroy the Slavic peoples. In their "moral degradation," the German invaders sank to the level of wild beasts and thereby doomed themselves to perdition, Stalin predicted. In response, the task of the Soviet military would consist of exterminating to the last man all Germans who invaded Soviet territory. Werth's translation is the most pointed: "The German invaders want a war of extermination against the peoples of the Soviet Union. Very well then! If they want a war of extermination, they shall have it. (Prolonged stormy applause)." The provocative *Times* sub-headline read, "He [Stalin] Says Nazis Will Be Annihilated with U.S. and British Help."[78] The Associated Press and United Press correspondents, based in London, both carried major articles but without the full text and with a softer tone and fewer quotes. Both emphasized Stalin's call for a second front, and both lacked the phrase war of extermination.[79] It was a term that Hitler and other high Nazi officials used most frequently for the Jews. Stalin borrowed it, at least as a rhetorical flourish.

Stalin's audience in the Mayakovsky Metro Station and his radio audience throughout the USSR (as newspaper readers abroad) would not have grasped even a fragment of the first wave of the Holocaust from his November 6 speech. Tsarist-type pogroms barely registered next to a massive war characterized as a war of extermination. Stalin generalized the threat of extermination, perhaps so that all the Soviet people would feel the threat facing the country, but likely because he really believed in the danger. On the other hand, by including the Jews as victims, Stalin signaled that the subject of Nazi killing of Jews was at least open for discussion. And on the same day it reported this speech, the *New York Times* also carried a front-page article announcing that Maxim Litvinov, former People's Commissar of Foreign Affairs, advocate of collective security, and implicit opponent of the Nazi-Soviet Nonaggression Pact, had been named Soviet ambassador to the United States. Litvinov was Jewish.[80]

Stalin's November 6 speech had repercussions for Soviet media reportage on Holocaust events. On November 19, *Pravda* and *Izvestiya* both reported that the Germans had executed fifty-two thousand Jews in Kiev—men, women, and children.[81] Although the two Soviet papers cited the Soviet TASS News Service in New York, it looks like the information came from Moscow, because the story had not yet surfaced in New York. Six days later, the Jewish Telegraphic Agency published a similar story that originated "on the German frontier" but had been delayed. Some fifty-two thousand Jews in Kiev had been killed not in a pogrom but by "merciless, systematic extermination," in "one of the most shocking massacres in Jewish history." Historian Walter Laqueur thought that this information did not come from Soviet sources, but possibly from Polish circles. In any case, the *New York Journal American* soon ran a similar story on page two.[82]

The *New York Times* did not carry any version of the news about the Kiev massacre, nor did other major US newspapers during November. AP reporter Ernest G. Fischer managed to get to Kiev while embedded with German troops in late October. His October 23 article on the German occupation of Kiev, drawing mostly on German sources, mentioned Jewish forced laborers in Rowno, but he wrote nothing whatsoever about the complete disappearance of more than forty thousand Kievan Jews. It may be relevant that Fischer, a native of Texas who was raised in a German-American community, made other antisemitic comments in public and in his diary.[83]

In relative terms, Soviet media coverage of the Babi Yar massacre was a little exaggerated but not far from the actual scale. Stalin left a clue that shows he approved of one media story on mass killings of Jews, although it involved Romanian troops. On November 16, *Pravda* published an article about Romanian atrocities in Odessa on October 23. The draft of the article specified that the killing of two hundred Romanians by an exploding Soviet mine had led the Romanian army to organize the murder of twenty-five thousand Jews, described as "one of the biggest mass murders of Jews in history." Stalin removed the section about the Soviet mine being the catalyst but let the rest stand.[84]

The optics of Stalin's November 7 speech were more dramatic than his address in the Mayakovsky Metro Station the prior evening. Stalin stood on a platform in Red Square in front of the Kremlin, as German and Russian artillery boomed in the distance and Soviet fighters patrolled overhead. The audience consisted mainly of soldiers and sailors returned from the fronts or soon to head back. Stalin led with a favorable but exaggerated comparison of the current dire situation with that of November 1918, when "three-quarters of the country was in the hands of foreign invaders." He reprised some key points from his speech the previous evening: there was no doubt that Germany could not maintain the strain of its current casualties; the USSR had greater reserves; a second front in Germany's rear would be opened soon; the Soviet war of defense was also a war of liberation for Europe; and the Soviet people could draw inspiration from their heroic ancestors. He repeated his successful line: "If they want a war of annihilation, they will get it." Stalin made no mention of Jewish deaths this time. He concluded with the slogan "death to the German occupiers." A military parade followed in mostly precise fashion, as if these forces had been practicing it. The audience on Red Square felt that they were participating in "a drama of patriotism and defiance."[85]

Nowhere is the link between Nazi war and genocide more evident than in the Soviet Union during the second half of 1941, where the killing fields for Soviet Jews were not all that distant from the battlefields, and where some German military units facilitated mass killing. In theory, it would make sense that Soviet reactions to Nazi genocide came quickly. But for personal and political reasons, Stalin and other high Soviet officials folded the story of Nazi genocide against Soviet Jews into the larger crisis of the war and huge Soviet military and civilian casualties. How much did the plight of Soviet Jews matter compared to the survival of the rest of the Soviet people and of the Communist regime? No one in Moscow would have been surprised if Stalin had failed to mention the Jews at all.

In his November 6 anniversary speech, Stalin did the minimum, likely for foreign policy reasons, to show that he recognized systematic Nazi killings of Soviet Jews. But something else apparently bothered him, and it was certainly not the killing itself. The Nazis reverted to an older, discredited style of brutal antisemitism, a backward lurch of the historical process. Hence his one-time comparison with cannibalism and his November 6 mention of tsarist pogroms: he believed that the Soviet experiment represented the forward progress of the human race and the Nazis the opposite.

In a totalitarian system even a minimal response by the dictator is important. Stalin's anniversary speech showed other Soviet officials that the subject of Jewish casualties was not taboo. It freed Soviet Jews like Mikhoels or citizens of Jewish origin like Ehrenburg to continue their efforts, which had preceded Stalin's own. That large numbers of Soviet Jews fled the Nazi dragnet had multiple causes. Some heard about mass killings from Polish Jewish refugees. But others may have read what the Soviet media reported, and there were a number of journalists of Jewish origin in key positions in the Soviet media.

The mass shootings of Jews in the occupied Soviet territories came early in the Holocaust. Most extermination camps were still under construction; deportations of German Jews had barely begun. Ghettos existed in occupied Poland and in Latvia, Lithuania, and Belorussia, but they were not yet comprehensive or completely sealed off. Only a portion of the Jews across Europe had a firm sense of what Nazi Germany and its allies might do in areas they conquered or otherwise controlled. For this reason, early news of the first stage of the Holocaust could have been generally important, even where the escape of Jews seemed improbable or initially impossible, assuming that such news would have been widely disseminated. But the Western media did not pay much attention to unsourced stories in the Soviet media. Given better knowledge and more time, many more Jews might have evaded or hindered the Nazi roundups of Jews across the continent.

The Jewish press in Palestine was somewhat attentive to Soviet Jewish events and Soviet media stories. The trade union federation's newspaper, *Davar*, wrote approvingly about the appeal by Soviet Jewish intellectuals (on August 24, 1941) to Jews throughout the world to aid the Red Army against the Nazis. But the paper recognized that the Jews themselves and the democratic world had virtually no leverage to prevent the Nazis from carrying out their crimes. Only the threat of international justice after the war might deter Nazi criminals, *Davar* maintained. The Yiddish newspaper *Forverts* in the United States began to publish major stories about Nazi mass murder of Jews in Ukraine in March 1942, but it was cautious about the numbers, and it took some time before it abandoned the view that these actions resulted from eruptions of rage by the killers in the field. The only response, *Forverts* stated, was for Jews to help the Allies in every way. The paper displayed a tenuous sense of Nazi extermination policy only in the second half of 1942.[86]

The Soviet government used some of its accumulated information about Nazi atrocities to try to solicit more outside support. On January 5, 1942, Vyacheslav Molotov sent a long diplomatic note about Nazi crimes against the peoples of the USSR to the ambassadors and ministers of all the countries with which the Soviets maintained diplomatic relations. He also published it in the Soviet press in an effort to stir the public's emotions.[87]

Molotov argued that all Nazi crimes emerged from an organized campaign by the German government and army high command to unleash the bestial instincts of German troops and to destroy as many people and as much Soviet property and culture as possible. Molotov included an exhaustive number of incidents, ranging from the execution of a seventy-seven-year-old peasant who asked soldiers not to burn his house, to the widespread rape of women, to the use of forced labor and concentration camps. Late within this document of more than five thousand words came a few crimes against Jews, such as the June 30, 1941, massacre of hundreds under the slogan "kill the Jews and the Poles" in Lvov. Molotov also mentioned the killings of fifty-two thousand in Kiev (at Babi Yar) but described the victims as Russians, Ukrainians, and Jews. (When he described the execution procedure, admittedly, he did refer to the victims as Jews.) He wrote of Nazi executions of primarily Jewish working people in some other Ukrainian places.

On the same day this document went out, the now optimistic Soviet commander in chief met with the high command to insist on a broad general counterattack from Leningrad to Kharkov. Stalin convinced himself that underequipped German troops were near collapse. A limited Soviet counteroffensive might have done considerable damage, but this one, launched on January 7 with the goal of winning the war in 1942, exceeded Soviet capabilities. It weakened the Soviets more than the Germans and helped facilitate Germany's own offensive in the spring.[88]

Perhaps any summation of Nazi atrocities was too close to home for Stalin to put his name on it. Still, other examples show him playing down Nazi killings of Jews. On January 14, NKVD chief Lavrenti Beria sent Stalin copies and translations of a captured order issued on October 10, 1941, by General Walter von Reichenau, commander of the German Sixth Army. Apparently having received complaints and expressions of concern from below about the mass shootings of Jewish civilians, Reichenau explained that "the main goal of the campaign against the Jewish-Bolshevik system is the total smashing of the state power and the extermination of the Asiatic influence on European culture." The German forces had "a mission to liberate the German people once and for all from the Asiatic-Jewish danger." The troops needed to have a "full understanding of the necessity of the harsh but justified revenge on Jewish subhumanity." Experience also showed, Reichenau wrote, that Jews were responsible for inciting uprisings in the army's rear. Stalin had *Pravda* publish this German document, a translation, and a related editorial the next day. The translation omitted all the references to Jews, except one: "Asiatic-Jewish danger." The editorial, probably written by Stalin, claimed that Hitler had approved Reichenau's order, which allegedly aimed at the extermination of the male population of the occupied territories. Beyond that, according to the editorial, the Nazis threatened the physical extermination of the Russians, Ukrainians, Belarusians, and all the other peoples of the USSR.[89]

Stalin clearly wanted to focus on the Nazi threat to the state and people of the USSR, and he must have believed that references to the Nazi war against the Jews could only distract from that. He made no further public comments about Nazi killings of Jews for the rest of the war. But in 1942, Soviet ideologues portrayed racial ideology as a natural stage of imperialist society.[90]

CHAPTER FOUR

SECRETS PRESERVED

For six months after Germany declared war on the United States, Nazi killings of Jews in the East remained largely out of Western view. Nazi officials had developed sophisticated methods to disguise their murder operations. Churchill protected his intelligence sources and methods. Pursuit of the war against the Axis powers overrode Allied concerns about even urgent humanitarian issues. On occasion, Hitler spoke publicly about the Nazi policy of genocide, but his rhetoric was vague enough to be discounted, and it was mixed into reports on the war that attracted greater attention. Hitler's inflammatory insults of Churchill and Roosevelt drew more attention than his verbal attacks on Jews.

On January 30, 1942, Hitler spoke to a large crowd of Berlin workers, military nurses, and wounded soldiers gathered at the Berlin Sportspalast, plus a radio audience throughout much of the world. He again prophesied that the war would result not in the extermination of the European Aryan peoples but in the annihilation of the Jews. He said that he had not been hasty (or premature) in making that statement in 1939. *New York Times* reporter Daniel Brigham botched the translation of Hitler's line by calling it an "inconsiderate prophecy," making the comment harder to decipher. As usual, Hitler misdated his prophecy: instead of January 30, 1939, he gave the date as September 1, 1939, an intentional or subconscious conflating of World War II with the war against the Jews. The dictator charged that international Jewry operated in league with Germany's enemies.[1]

On January 30, Hitler attacked Churchill as a drunkard and one of the most dangerous warmongers of all times. He described Roosevelt, who turned sixty that day, as a paralytic and a lunatic.[2] Implying that the war in the East had not gone as he had planned, Hitler explained that Soviet resistance and the winter had forced the German army into defensive positions. Because of that shift, he said, he himself took over as commander in chief of the army. Hitler had feared that a full-scale retreat would lead to a Napoleonic-style disaster. He sacked the heads of the three German army groups in the East, as well as commander in chief Field Marshal Walther von Brauchitsch.[3]

Hitler offered German listeners several reasons for optimism. Within a couple of months, he said, Germany would launch new offensives in the East. The Wehrmacht represented the most powerful army in the world, German U-boats were savaging Allied ships in the Atlantic, and Japan's entrance into the war would greatly improve the strategic situation for the Axis powers. Although Hitler did not make it public, Germany and Japan had in fact considered meeting up in South Asia and the Indian Ocean, with Germany penetrating into the Middle East from North Africa and through the Caucasus Mountain region of the Soviet Union, and Japan moving west from Southeast Asia. Hitler privately recognized that the war might continue for years, but hoped that cutting off Britain from its empire and from oil would strangle it and perhaps break the unnatural ties among the Allies.[4]

British and American journalists emphasized what seemed to them to be new in Hitler's January 30 speech—namely, his caution about Germany's war situation.[5] Hitler was not cautious in his remarks about the Jews, except in that he chose not to reveal the messy details of carrying out his threats. Nazi mass killing had begun in secret with Germany's disabled population. Sometime in the summer of 1939, Hitler decided to enact a program of murdering many German adults with disabilities and perceived genetic defects. As far back as 1935, he had talked about compulsory "euthanasia" to take effect when war broke out: those who were unworthy of life would be killed. He and his subordinates made no effort to balance economic benefits against the costs and political risks. Hitler simply wanted to do this to improve the German "race." In September 1939, officials in Hitler's Führer Chancellery began this program, codenamed T4, sending patients in asylums and other institutions to six gassing centers in Germany. A smaller effort to kill children with disabilities used toxic medication instead. Officials in Hitler's private chancellery developed techniques to mislead patients and their families, and they eventually learned that information leaks could bring political damage. Heinrich Himmler's SS and police empire did not run or oversee this euthanasia operation, but they absorbed some of its lessons and soon inherited some of its key personnel.[6]

At the end of 1941, Nazi Germany began assembly-line mass murder of Jews. Himmler had plans for a constellation of extermination camps in annexed Polish territory and in the occupied General Government of Poland to resolve what the Nazis called the Jewish question.[7] The first stationary gassing center, located in the middle of a small village called Chełmno near Lodz (in the German-annexed Warthegau), began to operate on December 8, 1941, although SS units had previously used mobile gas vans

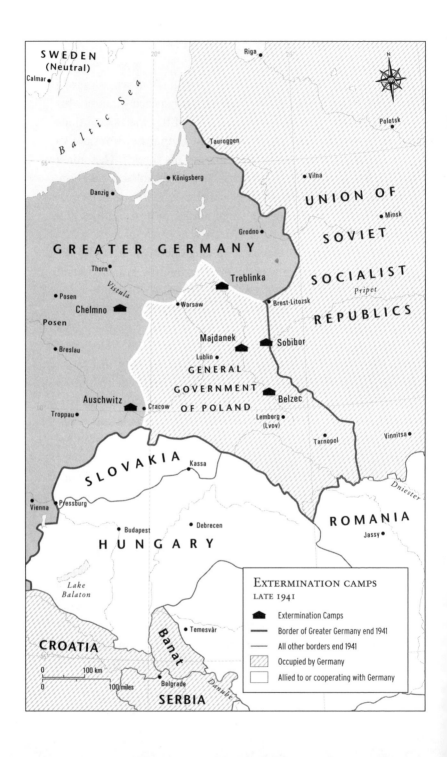

SWEDEN
(Neutral)

Calmar •

Baltic Sea

Riga •

N

Polotsk •

Tauroggen •

• Königsberg

• Vilna

Danzig •

UNION OF

• Minsk

Grodno •

SOVIET

GREATER GERMANY

Thorn •

Vistula

Treblinka

SOCIALIST

Pripet

• Posen

Chelmno

• Warsaw

Brest-Litozsk

REPUBLICS

Posen

Majdanek

Sobibor

• Breslau

Lublin •

GENERAL

GOVERNMENT

Belzec

Auschwitz

• Cracow

OF POLAND

Troppau •

Lemberg •
(Lvov)

Vinnitsa •

Tarnopol •

SLOVAKIA

Kassa

Dniester

Vienna •

• Pressburg

ROMANIA

• Budapest

• Debrecen

HUNGARY

Jassy •

Lake
Balaton

EXTERMINATION CAMPS
LATE 1941

Extermination Camps

• Temesvàr

CROATIA

Banat

Border of Greater Germany end 1941

All other borders end 1941

Occupied by Germany

0   100 km

Allied to or cooperating with Germany

0   100 miles

Belgrade •

Danube

SERBIA

on a small, experimental basis in Soviet territory and in occupied Poland.[8]

A special unit headed by Herbert Lange, a euthanasia veteran, supplemented by other SS men, rounded up Jews from communities near Chełmno. After telling the victims they were to be sent to Germany for work, the Nazi officers explained that they had to be disinfected first. The Jews were led into the basement of a manor house, then through a corridor into a sealed van, which was flooded with bottled carbon monoxide. Between December 8 and January 15, about 6,400 Jews were murdered in this fashion. Two other vans, equipped to recycle their own exhaust gas, arrived from Berlin to expand the daily quota. Reich Security Main Office official Adolf Eichmann carried out an early inspection of the process.[9] On January 7, 1942, Otto Dietrich's Reich press office ordered the German press not to report anything about anti-Jewish measures in the occupied eastern territories.[10]

JOINT ALLIED MILITARY PLANNING

At the end of 1941 and for the first two weeks of January 1942, the president, the prime minister, and their top military advisers met in Washington, DC, to work out a coordinated military strategy in discussions called the Arcadia Conference. During most of that time, Churchill resided in the White House and set up his map room in the James Monroe Room, the proximity indicating his increasingly close relationship with FDR.[11] The two Western leaders confirmed earlier contingency plans to give priority to the war in Europe, given that Nazi Germany represented their most dangerous enemy. That choice was not automatic for Roosevelt after the Japanese attack on Pearl Harbor, but it suited Stalin's needs and demands. It made good sense then and looks wise today.

Churchill and Roosevelt preferred to build up British and American forces in the UK and to launch an invasion of France only when they were well prepared. If the Western Allies prematurely rushed into a difficult campaign in France, they might well suffer defeat against battle-hardened German troops. But if the Western Allies delayed any offensive, they would have to deal with Stalin's fury and, at worst, with a German victory in the East. As a result, the two governments agreed on a near-term move into French Northwest Africa. Churchill pushed this idea as the "true" second front of 1942. A successful amphibious invasion would prevent Germany from taking control of this region and put German General Erwin Rommel's North African forces (and Italian troops) in a vise. British troops based in Egypt were already fighting Rommel in Libya. The proposed offensive in Northwest Africa would also reopen the Mediterranean route to the Suez Canal and give the Allies another base to move against Italy and Germany later. Moreover, American soldiers could get battlefield experience under easier circumstances than they would encounter in France.[12]

Obstacles and disagreements surfaced within weeks. Japanese advances in Asia threatened to cut off Australia and New Zealand, which forced Roosevelt (strongly encouraged by Churchill) to divert American forces to the Pacific. German U-boats took a heavy toll of Allied ships in the Atlantic, making the direct route to the UK risky and delaying shipments of arms to the USSR. The vision of a spring 1942 offensive in Northwest Africa turned into a mirage, which led to disagreements about when and where the Western Allies could attack in the Eastern Hemisphere. Churchill was inclined to wait until Allied bombing, the naval blockade, and resistance uprisings had softened German defenses in Western Europe. Eventually, Roosevelt insisted on offensive action during the calendar year 1942, which brought Northwest Africa back as a target.[13]

Any strategic decision would influence the duration of the war in Europe and North Africa, which in turn, would affect the Nazi war against the Jews. The longer the war in Europe lasted, the more Jews would be killed or would die. In that sense, the selection and outcome of Western military offensives affected the Holocaust even though Roosevelt and Churchill were not motivated by the Holocaust. As it turned out, the North African campaigns directly affected the geographical reach of the Holocaust.

During his stay in Washington, Churchill gave the president what historian David Stafford called a big-picture view of Britain's Bletchley Park decoding effort. How far their discussion went is unclear. The only written evidence is a letter Churchill wrote after returning to London, for the British ambassador to deliver personally to FDR, reminding him of their conversation. Churchill asked Roosevelt to handle the matter by himself: he wanted the fewest possible number of people to know about it. He also asked FDR to burn the letter afterwards, which the president did not do.[14]

SECRET HOLOCAUST INFORMATION

If Churchill had been told that he violated—or was about to violate—security during his speech on August 24, 1941, he would have been all the more careful not to say much to Roosevelt about what he had learned from decoded German radio messages.[15] There is no evidence that he raised the subject of Nazi killings of Jews with FDR.

Secret information about Nazi persecution and mass murder of Jews continued to accumulate in London. Shortly after Churchill returned from Washington, the Postal and Telegraph Censorship Department within the Ministry of Information issued its third in a series entitled "Reports on Jewry." Officials stationed in Liverpool drew upon materials submitted by various imperial posts for the period between May and October 1941. They read and excerpted private telegrams and letters to offer snapshots of what was happening to Jews in different parts of Europe and the Middle East, as well as of Jewish attitudes toward Britain. When this practice of intercepting private communications later came up for discussion in Parliament, Minister of Information Brendan Bracken, one of Churchill's closest advisers, defended it as necessary for the prosecution of the war.[16]

The first part of the third Report on Jewry, dated January 22, 1942, had a mixed bag of short excerpts about Jewish attitudes toward Britain, conditions of Jews in different countries on the continent, and Nazi practices. One excerpt sometimes contradicted the next. The censors received and reviewed letters from Jews in Palestine, Berlin, Cologne, Hanover, Vienna, and elsewhere.

The censors often cited specific individuals or institutions, but there was one egregious exception. Under the general heading "Situation on the Continent," the editors began with a subheading "Policy of Extermination." An unattributed comment followed: "The Germans clearly pursue a policy of extermination against the Jews. From an official German document the statement is quoted: 'The only things Jewish that will remain in Poland will be Jewish cemeteries.' Of the ten hostages shot in Paris (about September 20), four were Jews."[17]

Such a German document could have arrived in British hands later than October 1941, because the report was issued three months afterward. But, whether in October, November, December, or January, historians today do not know of any German document of this kind dated this early. This purported document revealed more information than was available to top officials in major branches of the Nazi government and party.

The flat British editorial statement of Nazi policy and application to the area of Poland, which still had more than two million
Jews, is stunning. If there was such a document, who could have
written it, and how could the British government have obtained
it? These will likely remain unsolved mysteries.

Still, by January 1942, a branch of the British Ministry of Information put out a limited distribution report with one small
but clear statement of Nazi policy toward the Jews. And it extended what British intelligence had concluded earlier about
Nazi executions of Jews in conquered Soviet territory. It reinforced what Hitler had said repeatedly about his prophecy.

In his memoirs, MI6 agent H. Montgomery Hyde discussed
isolated successes in opening diplomatic pouches at the
British station on Gibraltar and other ways of separating foreign diplomatic couriers from their pouches at the British
censorship station in Bermuda and the Caribbean. Britain
began to copy and share the fruits of this (illegal) intelligence
with the United States even before it entered the war—in contrast with the Bletchley Park decodes. The Chilean consul in
Prague, Gonzalo Montt Rivas, was a particularly good source
because of his sympathetic attitude toward Nazi policies and
because Reinhard Heydrich, Himmler's right-hand man, held
the post of Reich Protector of Bohemia-Moravia and spent
time in Prague.

On November 24, 1941, Montt Rivas wrote to his government:

The Jewish problem is being partially solved in the Protec-
torate, as it has been decided to eradicate all the Jews and
send some to Poland and others to the town of Terezin, whilst
looking for a more remote place. . . .

The German triumph [in the war] will leave Europe freed
of Semites. Those [Jews] who escape with their lives from
this trial will certainly be deported to Siberia, where they will

not have much opportunity to make use of their financial capabilities.

In proportion to the U.S.A. increasing its attacks on the Reich, Germany will expedite the destruction of Semitism, as she accuses international Judaism of all the calamities which have befallen the world.[18]

This translated Chilean diplomatic despatch (found in the US National Archives but originating with the UK) reveals that some well-placed observers could fathom Nazi extermination policy in late 1941, and that the United States had access, with months delay, to some good British intelligence sources.

Of course, the United States also had intelligence facilities and sources of its own. The American embassy in Berlin operated until December 11, 1941, and American journalists remained in and reported from Germany until then. Leland Morris, first secretary of the embassy, wrote at the end of September 1941 that the Nazis had intensified anti-Jewish propaganda, such as charging that the Jews sought to exterminate the German people. In mid-October, Morris wrote of rumors of mass deportations of Jews to ghettos in occupied Poland, part of an effort to move all Jews out of Germany to Poland and other eastern areas.[19] The American military attaché in Berlin, William D. Hohenthal, wrote one despatch in early November 1941 that reached Roosevelt's closest adviser Harry Hopkins. According to an informant, Hohenthal wrote, SS units operating in many cities, towns, and villages of conquered Soviet territory segregated Jews and then shot them.[20]

In October, Nazi officials took nine foreign correspondents, including several American journalists, on a guided 660-mile tour of German conquered territories in the East in apparent anticipation of German victory over the USSR. Lochner and some other correspondents turned the invitation down because they feared being out of touch with major announcements in Berlin. But some Americans, such as Fred Oechsner of United Press and Ernest Fischer of Associated Press, accepted and went to the East. While traveling, they were able to send stories back to their offices in Berlin via the Propaganda Ministry. After they had returned to Berlin, they found, however, that their writing had been heavily censored.[21] When Howard K. Smith tried to include discussion of Nazi censorship in his regular radio CBS broadcast from Berlin, Nazi censors told him that that information was censored, too.[22]

The inability to reach and investigate killing sites hampered Western media coverage of the first stage of the Holocaust. Nazi propaganda about alleged ties between the Allies and the Jews made even experienced reporters leery of writing about Nazi atrocities without strong evidence.

THE INTERNMENT AT BAD NAUHEIM

Hitler's declaration of war against the United States turned the American observation post in Berlin into a liability. American diplomats frantically destroyed documents and sensitive materials. Meanwhile, authorities in Washington took German diplomats and some German correspondents into custody as likely spies. The German prisoners were sent to the luxury Greenbrier Hotel in White Sulphur Springs, West Virginia, where they were treated like guests and allowed to go into town.

Germany retaliated against 115 American men, women, and children—diplomats, journalists, and families. The Americans, led by embassy first secretaries Leland Morris and George F. Kennan, were transported to the Jeschke Grand Hotel in Bad Nauheim, a spa town north of Frankfurt am Main. This nineteenth-century hotel had once been magnificent, and, as a small boy, Franklin Roosevelt had stayed there with his father, who tried out the mineral springs. Built for the summer season, Jeschke was not well insulated, had shut down in September 1939, and was no longer in operating condition. The US correspondents, calling it the Grand Refrigerator, initially spent a good deal of time huddled under covers. Limited food rations were heavy on potatoes and turnips.[23]

A UP stringer named Robert Best, a South Carolinian veteran of World War I, hated Jews and Roosevelt. After receiving noticeably better rations and treatment than the other journalists, he was released on March 2 and turned his efforts to making propaganda broadcasts on German shortwave radio. He took the radio name "Mr. Guess Who," becoming the American counterpart to the British pro-Nazi broadcaster nicknamed "Lord Haw-Haw."[24]

The other Americans had virtually no personal contacts outside the hotel grounds; at times, they were locked in the hotel. They could not send or receive mail during what became a five-month internment. They were, however, given access to propaganda-laden German newspapers. Their one good link to the outside world was a portable, battery-powered radio that had been smuggled in, and they were able to listen secretly to German, British, and some other foreign broadcasts. Louis Lochner was able to receive some reports from AP's German staff.[25] After a while, twenty-one Americans from other occupied countries joined them, bringing a little more news. This internment effectively limited recent German information reaching the State Department in Washington, and it cut down the number of well-informed articles about Nazi Germany that appeared in US newspapers. The journalists at Bad Nauheim spent part of their time preparing or thinking about stories they could use after they were released; they could not send them out before then. Some began to work on books.[26]

Some experienced American journalists luckily managed to avoid internment. Sigrid Schultz of the *Chicago Tribune* was back in the United States when Germany declared war. Schultz had been injured during a British bombing raid on Berlin in 1940, and she had gone back to the United States to recuperate. William L. Shirer, well known for his CBS radio broadcasts from Berlin, returned to the United States at the end of 1940. CBS's Howard K. Smith took a train to Switzerland on December 7, 1941. He wrote up his experiences and reflections in a 1942 book. But the sequence of Nazi killing programs—first euthanasia, then the war against the Jews—meant that these journalists in the United States knew more about the earlier euthanasia gassings than about the first wave of the Holocaust in the East.[27]

Schultz, who was hoping to go back to Germany, talked privately about what she knew about euthanasia. Drawing partly on leaked information from American diplomats, Shirer, however, wrote about what he knew in three articles and in his 1941 book, *Berlin Diary*, which became a main selection of the Book of the Month Club and was reviewed by Eleanor Roosevelt. Moreover, he was able to publish one article in the conservative *Reader's Digest*, offering some protection against the charge that he served up left-wing or Jewish propaganda. Shirer wrote of rumors of poison gas experiments and a total of 100,000 euthanasia victims but cautioned that he thought the real total might be around several thousand. Still, American and British readers remained skeptical. Today it is estimated that between January 1940 and August 1941, the six T-4 gassing centers disposed of more than seventy thousand people considered genetically deficient by the Nazis.[28]

The Bad Nauheim internees pursued a range of educational and recreational activities to keep busy. George F. Kennan lectured on Russian history; that was the most popular course at "Badheim University," whose motto was "education of the ignorant by the ignorant." For the would-be athletes, a whittled stick served as a baseball bat, and the ball was composed of a champagne cork, pajamas cut into strips, sticky tape, a sock, and stitching from medical supplies.[29]

Fifteen journalists and two military officers devoted a good deal of time to a study of war propaganda. Military attaché William Hohenthal wrote up a detailed questionnaire, and the participants discussed their responses. By March, when the group's release seemed close at hand, each individual wrote up his thoughts, most in considerable detail, and Hohenthal included his own views. The group was all male, and none (to my knowledge) was of a minority, except for at least one Catholic. One wrote that he had lived with a German family, and one (Lochner) had a German wife. With those demographic limitations and influences, their product reads like a sincere effort to boil down American experiences in Nazi Germany into practical lessons for the Western Allies during the war. It is possible that some of these journalists hoped to play a subsequent role in an American government information campaign against Germany.[30]

The Bad Nauheim group believed that Nazi propaganda had proved effective with the German public. Part of the reason was simple repetition. Lochner wrote of once sensible Germans who, after years of propaganda, came to parrot the Nazi line regarding despoliation and elimination of the Jews. He reported saying to one of them, "have you lost all power of thinking?"[31] Hitler's direct or indirect appeal also helped to make propaganda effective. Plenty of Germans would complain about specific features of the Nazi regime, but they did not blame the Führer, and they closely followed his speeches. This led a number of US journalists to recommend against Allied propaganda attacks on Hitler.

The participants believed that radio was the most important conduit of Nazi propaganda, and that the Nazis themselves were aware of that. Clifton Conger noted that the Propaganda Ministry avidly followed foreign news broadcasts even though it distributed little of the information. Hitler's headquarters had its own listening post for foreign broadcasts, and he was believed to get the text or summaries of Churchill's and Roosevelt's speeches to study in advance of any formal German response.[32]

Many of those surveyed felt that Hitler, Goebbels, and other Nazi officials occasionally overshot the mark with extravagant claims, such as the announcement by Propaganda Ministry official Otto Dietrich of impending victory over the USSR, or scurrilous attacks on foreign leaders. A couple of journalists specifically mentioned the Nazi insults of FDR as a lunatic and a cripple, showing that the group had listened to Hitler's speech of January 30, 1942. On the other hand, Conger thought that the long-term pattern of radio (and press) attacks on American leaders and media as 100 percent Jewish-owned and operating in British interests was at least partially effective. US leaders were accused of being biased against Germany (*deutschfeindlich*) and of faulty logic. They were "depicted as political opportunists or war profiteers, and maligned in both moral and political character on the basis of true, distorted, or invented reports." Roosevelt, for example, was said to be the real author of a plan to sterilize all Germans, something proposed in a 1941 self-published book by an unaffiliated New Jersey Jewish writer named Theodore Kaufman. The Propaganda Ministry ordered all German newspapers to publish long reviews of this book, entitled *Germany Must Perish*, and Goebbels wrote that it was an open secret that FDR inspired and personally dictated the most important parts. The Propaganda Ministry also held a press conference to introduce a genealogist who traced Roosevelt's family tree, showing that he had a Jewish ancestor. And after all, his mother's name was Sara.[33]

Conger wrote that Kaufman's sterilization plan perfectly illustrated what the Allies should not do. That sort of rhetoric
would only make the German people desperate. In general, the
journalists thought it possible to drive a wedge between the
German people and the Nazi regime, but believed that success
might require the prior achievement and announcement of real
Allied military victories. Aware that some combination of fac-
tual reporting and counter-propaganda by the Allies would not
win the war by itself, the journalists believed they could help.

Some study participants commented specifically about using
accounts of Nazi atrocities against Jews, without describing
atrocities themselves. Paul C. Fisher of NBC wanted American
broadcasts to stress the corrupt judicial system, Gestapo abuses,
barbaric pogroms against the Jews (presumably Kristallnacht),
and outrages by the SS in Poland and other occupied areas. But
he warned against making the Jewish situation prominent in
US propaganda or allowing Jews to disseminate it. He added, "I
say this not in bigotry or in any dislike for the race, but merely
because I know that anything that smacks of the Jewish angle or
has a Jewish ring will be suspected and will not be well received
in Germany." J. M. Fleisher of UP warned that any use of atrocity
stories had to be supported by evidence so strong that there
could be no doubt about their authenticity. Frederick Oechsner
of UP advised against impassioned defense of the Jews. Alvin
Steinkopf of AP recommended against using Jews to disseminate Allied propaganda and against relying on threadbare stories from Jewish immigrants who "had their own reasons for
hating Germany." Only Glen Stadler of UP favored detailed de-
scriptions of the concentration camps and death rates, with information about the Jews within them. Hohenthal joined the
prevailing sentiment when he recommended against champi-
oning the Jewish cause vigorously.[34] These recommendations by
no means precluded the journalists from writing stories about

Nazi atrocities once they were free to do so. Some of them indeed wanted to pursue a good and important story. But they did
suggest that US and UK government officials might be leery of
releasing or endorsing such information.

The Allies sought to win the war as expeditiously as possible.
Accounts of Nazi mass killings of Jews would not separate the
German people from the regime or depress German morale.
And some journalists' comments suggested that milder forms
of antisemitism in the West might complicate the situation
there, too.

By contrast, more than a few of the journalists thought it
would be beneficial to broadcast leaked information about the
Nazi euthanasia program. On August 3, 1941, Bishop Clemens
von Galen had criticized the regime in a sermon, copies of which
had circulated among some Germans. A larger pattern of leaks
of information before then had generated more than occasional
signs of public discontent. On August 24, Hitler decided to shut
the gassing centers for this reason, but the killings continued in
a decentralized and even more secretive manner.[35] Wider circu-
lation of information that the Nazi regime was still killing Germans with disabilities might have alienated the German public.

One revealing incident illustrates how far and how high the
reports of Nazi euthanasia spread. The German military attaché
in Washington, Friedrich von Boetticher, had a son who, as a
teenager, had been diagnosed as schizophrenic; in his early
twenties he had made critical comments about the Nazi regime.
In the mid-1930s, he was indicted for plotting treason. His father was able to quash these proceedings, but a German government decree ordered the son to report for compulsory sterilization. Instead, the younger Boetticher joined his father in the
United States. When war broke out, he resided in an institution
in Towson, Maryland, diagnosed as manic-depressive. Boetticher asked the State Department for permission for his son to

remain there after the United States entered the war. Apparently, on December 19, 1941, the cabinet discussed the likely consequences if he returned to Germany.[36]

Attorney General Francis Biddle mentioned that Boetticher had requested "that his insane son be allowed to stay in a hospital in this country to prevent his being chloroformed if he were sent back to Germany." FDR told the cabinet that the Nazi regime was doing away with wounded German soldiers on the battlefields and with the elderly generally.[37] Such misinformation showed his tendency to absorb what others passed on to him if they reinforced his view that the Nazis threatened all of humanity. Roosevelt also read a copy of Bishop von Galen's sermon, given to him by William J. Donovan, soon to become head of the Office of Strategic Services (OSS), the forerunner of the CIA. But if FDR said anything about Nazi killings of Jews, Attorney General Biddle did not record it.[38] (Boetticher's son remained in the United States and joined the American Air Force upon his release from treatment in 1944.) Today it is known that toward the end of the war, the Nazi euthanasia program expanded to dispose of geriatric patients, bombing victims, and foreign forced laborers.[39]

The Americans finally left the Jeschke Grand Hotel on May 12, 1942, arriving in Lisbon two days later. Stadler and Grigg were able to craft their news stories to get them past Portuguese censors while waiting for the exchange ship *Drottningholm*, which reached New York on May 30. Grigg ended up going to London instead. Stadler wrote of Hitler's firing squads having executed nearly 400,000 people while engaging in vast looting of conquered areas of Europe. He relegated Jews to the one paragraph about mass murder in the Baltic States. In Lisbon Grigg wrote a general account of the war situation, but once he reached London, he revealed that the Nazis had already massacred 200,000 Jews in Eastern Europe—Russia, Poland, and the

Baltic States—and that millions had been driven into ghettos. The victims of mass shootings had been forced to dig their own graves, he related. Grigg reminded readers that on January 30, 1939, Hitler had threatened that war would result in the destruction of the Jews: "Those of us who lived in Germany know that he and his agents have done everything possible to make this prophecy come true."[40]

OPERATIONS ANTHROPOID AND REINHARD

In late May 1942, a spectacular assassination carried out by a British-Czech team and Nazi retaliation to it thrust Nazi atrocities into the consciousness of much of the world. Czech resistance in Bohemia-Moravia had given the German occupation problems, but the situation changed dramatically in September 1941, when Reinhard Heydrich became Reich Protector. Although Heydrich remained Himmler's subordinate in the SS and police, in his Prague post Heydrich reported directly to Hitler. The Czech underground, fearing Heydrich's brutal reaction to any more acts of sabotage, decided to lay low. But Edvard Beneš, head of the Czech government-in-exile in London, believed that passive acceptance of Nazi rule would compromise the country's future in a peace settlement. So, he was eager to carry out a high visibility attack, whether or not the Czech underground approved of it.

After establishing a new Special Operations Executive (SOE) under the Ministry of Economic Warfare, Churchill had encouraged Minister Hugh Dalton to "set Europe ablaze," by encouraging resistance sabotage and uprisings in conquered countries. An SOE dossier on Heydrich described him as the second most dangerous man in Europe, perhaps because he was more charismatic and more outwardly aggressive than his superior Himmler. A mission to assassinate Heydrich seemed to meet the needs of both SOE and the Czech government-in-exile. It was codenamed Operation Anthropoid.[41] Its approval had little to do with the fact, unknown to the Allies, that Heydrich was a key figure in implementing the Final Solution of the Jewish question. He had chaired the Wannsee Conference, the January 20, 1942, meeting where high Nazi government and party officials administratively coordinated the Final Solution.

Neither sponsor of Operation Anthropoid wanted the limelight. SOE wanted to hide the fact that a British government agency involved itself in an assassination, and Beneš hoped to make it seem like an action by the Czech underground, not the government-in-exile. On December 28, 1941, British pilots flew two former members of the Czech Brigade trained by SOE to a site not far from Prague, where, after parachuting in, they linked up with the underground. They spent months studying Heydrich's movements and selecting the right spot for an attack, settling on a hairpin turn on the road leading out of Prague. When they learned that Heydrich was heading off for a meeting with Hitler on May 27, 1942, and following that, would be away from Prague for some time, they decided to act. The first agent, Josef Gabčik, tried to shoot Heydrich with his machine gun, but it jammed. Heydrich stopped his open Mercedes and emerged to fire at them, which allowed the second agent, Jan Kubič, to throw a bomb, seriously wounding the Reich Protector.[42]

Within the hour, Hitler ordered the execution of ten thousand Czech civilians as punishment, and Himmler wanted at least one hundred executed that same night. But Heydrich's deputy Karl Hermann Frank, deducing that authorities in London were behind the mission, argued that a massive retaliation against the Czech population would backfire, so they held retaliation in abeyance. Heydrich died of a septic infection on June 3, the assassins temporarily vanishing into the Czech underground. Later tracked down and trapped, they committed suicide to avoid capture.

On June 9, Himmler delivered the eulogy for Heydrich, and Hitler also spoke at Heydrich's lavish funeral in the New Reich Chancellery in Berlin. Both portrayed Heydrich as a Nazi role model and a fierce opponent of all the enemies of the Reich. After the funeral, vengeance began. The small Czech town of Lidice was chosen on the basis of unfounded rumors that someone there had assisted the assassins. Hitler ordered the execution of all men and the imprisonment of all women in a concentration camp. The Nazis examined the children to see which ones were or seemed racially suitable to be Germanized, but only nine were given to German parents. In the end, 199 males between the ages of fourteen and eighty-four were killed, as were most of the children. Every building in the town was destroyed and the rubble cleared away. Lidice no longer existed, Nazi propagandists proudly proclaimed to the outside world. But they did not advertise the fact that, in Heydrich's honor, the program to eliminate the Jews in Poland was given the codename Operation Reinhard.[43]

On June 10, Churchill's War Cabinet discussed a potential response to Lidice. The prime minister had told Beneš that RAF bombers would wipe out three German villages, and Churchill suggested that the force "fit it in when they can." But other ministers opposed the idea, warning that it risked the lives of British pilots and might provoke German bombing of British villages. Churchill reluctantly conceded to the majority, so there was no direct British reprisal. But the heavy bombing campaign of German cities initiated by Commander Arthur "Bomber" Harris continued.[44]

The destruction of Lidice and the killing of thousands of suspected members of the Czech underground did not suffice for Propaganda Minister Goebbels. Because he always regarded the

Jews as the force behind Germany's enemies, he wanted to return fire in that direction somehow. In an editorial in the June
14, 1942, issue of his periodical *Das Reich*, he proclaimed that
stepped-up British bombing raids on German cities would not
go unanswered: yes, Churchill was responsible, but so were the
Jews. They had turned this war into a sacrilegious game, and
they would pay for it with the extermination of their race in Europe and perhaps beyond. Goebbels read this essay on German
radio even before it appeared in print. American newspapers
took notice, with significant articles in the *New York Times* and
the *Washington Post*.[45]

Front-page newspaper stories across the world brought the
fate of Lidice to millions of readers. Some American towns
changed their name to Lidice, as did towns in Mexico, Peru, and
Brazil. In her regular column, Eleanor Roosevelt described
Lidice as unforgettable, and withering editorials against Nazi
atrocities were widespread. In the United States, Nobel Prize–
winning German novelist Thomas Mann denounced Heydrich
as Hitler's hangman, as well as deploring Nazi retaliation for his
death; Mann's recorded broadcast went out on the BBC broadcast to Germany. After some time, his brother Heinrich Mann,
also in US exile, wrote a novel about Lidice, and Hollywood entered the fray, too.[46]

The story of the vanished town and its murdered and impris-
oned inhabitants might easily have overshadowed Goebbels's
threat against the Jews, which had no explicit tie to the assassination of Heydrich. But, contrary to what one might have
guessed, Lidice and other Nazi retaliatory executions in Bo-
hemia did not blot out the threats against the Jews. An editorial
in the *Minneapolis Star Tribune*, probably written by executive
editor Gideon Seymour, a former AP executive in Europe, as-
tutely observed that, coming only days after the "inconceivable
bestialities" at Lidice, the editorialist(s) wrote, "we are amply

justified in accepting the sincerity of the [Goebbels] threat and
to give recognition to the probability of being carried into execution." Lidice "may only be the beginning, the prelude to
greater blood-lettings and vaster exterminations that are being
painstakingly plotted in the hate-rotted Nazi minds. . . ." The
editorial continued:

> We have every right to assume that the Nazis, when they
> begin to feel the full pressure of the United Nations, will liter-
> ally take refuge behind the conquered women and children of
> Europe and that the Jews will be their first barricade as Goe-
> bbels has formally announced. Their ultimate resistance will
> be the weakness of our humanity, our horror of holocausts of
> the innocent and helpless, which they will be prepared to
> carry out with methodical callousness.[47]

This editorial used the term holocaust for something close to
what it has come to mean today. It also showed that even some
of those who were very much interested in Nazi atrocities did
not have much information about what the Nazis had already
done to destroy the Jews.

The same editorial also reinforces a point that may vanish in
the hindsight of the twenty-first century. Access to information
about the genocide taking place in Eastern Europe was only the
first obstacle. The second problem was accepting that an advanced Western country in the twentieth century could do such
things. All too many Westerners remembered or read about
anti-German atrocity propaganda during World War I that
turned out, after the war, to have been invented or exaggerated.
People did not want to be gullible or manipulated, especially
those who feared that Jews might be doctoring these stories for
their own purposes. And the notion of assembly-line mass
murder was psychologically difficult to accept. This was one

basic argument of Walter Laqueur's classic 1980 work, *The Terrible Secret*. But Lidice convinced some people that the Nazis were capable of anything.

IMPLICATIONS FOR PALESTINE

In May 1942, David Ben-Gurion estimated that a quarter of the Jews of eastern and southeastern Europe would be killed or would die during the war. Chaim Weizmann foresaw that two to four million stateless and homeless European Jews would need resettlement in Palestine.[48] But the future prime minister of Israel and its future president did not recognize how far Hitler's bloody crusade against the Jews had already advanced.

Ben-Gurion and Weizmann each spent long stretches of 1942 in America, trying to generate government sympathy and Jewish-American support for the future Jewish state. Both men spoke at a large Zionist conference arranged by the American Emergency Committee for Zionist Affairs, which met during May 9 to 11, 1942, at the Hotel Biltmore in New York. Ben-Gurion advocated the postwar establishment of a binational state in which Jews and Arabs would have equal rights. The Biltmore Conference revealed a marked shift toward Zionism among a heterogeneous Jewish American community and a reasonable attempt to begin planning and action for a later day. But the only *emergency* visible at the gathering was an effort to press Allied governments to establish a Jewish military force to help defend Palestine, which, Ben-Gurion and Weizmann both felt, would protect against German encroachment into the region and further long-term Zionist goals.[49]

Despite previous expressions of sympathy for Zionism, President Roosevelt well knew that by no means all Jewish Americans were Zionists.[50] Years of battles against isolationists and against even more virulent Nazi propaganda had made Roosevelt skittish about endorsing specific Zionist goals. He was cautious when asked to supply a statement to the American Palestine Committee's May 25 dinner at the Mayflower Hotel in Washington. This bipartisan, Christian organization, founded in 1941 and chaired by Senator Robert F. Wagner of New York, built political support for a Jewish homeland in Palestine. It offered FDR some political cover.[51]

In a presidential statement that Wagner read to more than 500 congressmen, diplomats, and other prominent figures at the Mayflower, Roosevelt noted that he had backed previous efforts to implement the Balfour Declaration of 1917 that had put Britain on record as favoring the establishment in Palestine of a national home for the Jewish people. He praised the development of Palestine over the past two decades and linked its progress to humanity's march toward freedom from fear, freedom from want, freedom of speech, and freedom of worship—a reference to his four freedoms speech of January 6, 1941. FDR also declared: "The immediate military danger to Palestine, which existed some time ago, has been very definitely removed." The *Philadelphia Inquirer* put his military assessment into its headline, and the *New York Times* also emphasized it.[52] Events over the next months, however, showed that the Holocaust could easily have spread to Palestine.

CHAPTER FIVE

THE ALLIED DECLARATION

I n the fall of 1942, Britain and the United States intensified the war on both sides of North Africa, while the Soviets had to face a new German offensive in Ukraine, the Caucasus, and the Volga region. By the end of the year, the Allies had gained the upper hand on these key battlefronts. Meanwhile, evidence of the killing of Jews in Europe expanded exponentially during the second half of 1942. Enough credible information had reached the corridors of government and the media that both the United States and the UK agreed to formulate an Allied government statement about the Nazi policy of murdering all the Jews.

A moral critic may ask why Roosevelt and Churchill themselves did not speak out. Historians and philosophers may complain that it is impossible to show why someone did *not* do something. But historians can assess likely military, diplomatic, and domestic repercussions if Churchill or Roosevelt had used their rhetorical skills to denounce what we call the Holocaust. Did the two Western leaders consider the effects of a speech denouncing the Holocaust? And how do we assess their actions or inaction now?

To answer those questions, we need to reconstruct the atmosphere and linkages of this crucial period through a chronological narrative. Only then can we judge the moral argument that more active and more motivated leaders could and should have done more to counter Nazi genocide.

A harrowing glimpse of Nazi mass murder in Eastern Europe emerged in the West in June 1942. The Bund, the Polish Jewish labor party, prepared a very detailed report on mass killings in occupied Poland, dated May 11. It was dispatched from Warsaw on May 21 with the assistance of Swedish businessmen; it reached London at the end of the month. Revealing that 700,000 Jews had already been killed in Poland, the document listed specific Nazi killing actions, including the operation of gas vans at Chełmno. According to the Bund, all this was part of Hitler's effort to kill off all the Jews, and the number of Polish Jews threatened was in the millions. The BBC, the closest thing to an international news service during World War II, broadcast a condensed account of this story on June 2. The Polish government-in-exile sent a note to Allied governments on June 6 drawing on the Bund report and claiming that "extermination of the Jewish population is reaching an unbelievable scale." The Bund's representative on the Polish National Council in London, Shmuel Zygielbojm, met with British journalists to place the story in a general newspaper, and the *Daily Telegraph* carried the story on June 25. The BBC then redoubled its efforts in broadcasts to Germany and Poland, in which Zygielbojm himself took part. One historian has discerned the hand of British Minister of Information Brendan Bracken in the temporary willingness of the BBC, and to a lesser extent, the British media generally, to report atrocities against Jews at this time. Bracken later destroyed his own papers, but if he was involved with this story, it means that Churchill was at least aware of it and did not disapprove of this publicity.[1]

Churchill had broader Anglo-American issues on his agenda when he headed off to America once more, this time by airplane from Scotland on June 17. On June 19, the prime minister flew from Washington to Hackensack Airport in New Jersey. Roosevelt picked him up in his Ford equipped with hand-controls, and drove him to his Hyde Park, New York, estate on the Hudson. After Churchill praised the scenery and the pleasant company in Roosevelt's home, they got down to business. Churchill warned that British military planners saw no prospect of success for any offensive on the European continent against the Germans by September 1942. This was to lead to postponement of a US/UK front in Europe. Even though he had promised Moscow that the United States expected to open a second front before the end of the year, Roosevelt would nevertheless agree with Churchill on Northwest Africa as a substitute for a cross-channel invasion. The two leaders discussed atomic research with Harry Hopkins and may have agreed to share information and work on equal terms (they put nothing in writing).[2]

They took a train to Washington the next evening, and it was in the White House, on June 21, that FDR received a telegram with the news that the British force of about thirty thousand men at the port city of Tobruk, near Libya's border with Egypt, had surrendered to General Erwin Rommel's considerably smaller Afrika Korps. All the more humiliating for Churchill to hear about this devastating defeat from the president! By contrast, the United States had just checked the Japanese advance in the Pacific at the decisive naval battle near Midway Island. Roosevelt asked Churchill what the United States could do to help. The prime minister quickly asked for as many of the new medium Sherman tanks as the United States could manage to send. Roosevelt agreed on the spot, because both men appreciated that there was little to stop Rommel from entering Egypt, taking the Suez Canal, moving into Palestine and beyond, and taking the oil wells of the Middle East. That advance would be a big step toward the Germans meeting up with Japanese forces in Asia. It also meant that more than 550,000 Jews in Cairo and Palestine were in their path. But if Churchill and Roosevelt discussed the situation of the Jews in Palestine and in Europe, there is no record of it. The two leaders decided to plan simultaneously for invasions of Northwest Africa and France, with the invasion of Northwest Africa to have top priority, later in 1942.[3]

Intensifying his lobbying for a Jewish fighting force to defend Palestine, in late June, David Ben-Gurion met FDR's intelligence adviser William J. Donovan (about to become director of the new Office of Strategic Services), Assistant Secretary of War John J. McCloy, and Undersecretary of War Robert Patterson. McCloy promised to pass Ben-Gurion's memo about a Jewish division to the Combined Chiefs of Staff, and Patterson recommended sending a copy to the president as well. Ben-Gurion warned that time was of the essence because a German conquest of Palestine would mean "the end of our nation." Seeing a parallel with the Ottoman Empire's murder of more than one million Armenians during World War I, Ben-Gurion said, "Now the German generals will do the same with the Jews." At the beginning of July, Ben-Gurion wrote up his views about the danger to the Jews in Palestine and sent them to Supreme Court Justice Felix Frankfurter. He asked the justice to pass them on to President Roosevelt, but there is no confirmation that this happened.[4]

At a White House meeting on July 7, Weizmann pressed the case for a Jewish division, and he wanted the British to transfer Major Orde Wingate from India to Palestine to take command of it. The Scottish Wingate had learned Hebrew, was known to be pro-Zionist, and had commanded joint British-Jewish units during the 1936–1939 Arab uprisings in Palestine. Roosevelt responded that he wanted to delay any statement about a Jewish force for ten days, mentioning that the British feared that the Egyptian army would turn against them if they established an all-Jewish force. Afterwards, FDR told Henry Morgenthau that the immediate issue was to prevent Alexandria and Cairo from falling to the Nazis.[5]

Roosevelt knew that German control of the region would be disastrous. But creation of a large Jewish fighting force would complicate the political and military prospects of an Allied invasion of largely Muslim Northwest Africa, the idea of which was still in dispute in Washington. Army Chief of Staff General George Marshall and other key generals thought North Africa a diversion from the main show in Europe, and they were privately scornful of Roosevelt's motives: "The leader in a democracy has to keep the people entertained," Marshall said. At that time, General Dwight D. Eisenhower called Roosevelt's July 25 decision in favor of invading Northwest Africa the blackest day in history. If FDR was naïve about the tradeoffs involved in a peripheral offensive strategy, he was correct in sensing that it was time to attack the Germans somewhere and that an invasion of France was far too risky for untested American troops.[6]

The overall Allied military effort was still sputtering. Stalin believed that the severe winter of 1941–1942 left weakened German forces vulnerable to counterattack. In May, he ordered an assault to encircle and destroy German forces at Kharkov (today Kharkiv) in Ukraine. Although Soviet troops punched some holes in German lines, the Germans had concentrated tanks in the region, and they were able to encircle the would-be encirclers. The Red Army took 267,000 casualties, and the Germans captured another 240,000 men at the end of May. A month later, German troops complemented by Romanian and Hungarian forces began their major Case Blue offensive designed to cross the Don River and take both the Caucasus region and the city of Stalingrad. If the Soviet forces collapsed, it might have succeeded, but if they carried out timely retreats, the Axis forces would be stretched too thin and their supply lines would be vulnerable. The Axis situation was all the riskier because Hitler had ordered the withdrawal of some units to strengthen defenses in France against an Allied invasion.[7]

Stalin was understandably suspicious about the slipping Western timetable for a second front in Western Europe. Allied reverses, however, proved daunting. Losses of shipping in the Atlantic, the Caribbean, and the Gulf of Mexico reached a peak level of 173 ships in June. General Rommel forced the British Eighth Army to retreat further to El Alamein in Egypt, only 160 miles from Cairo. Churchill went to Egypt to see whether the Eighth Army's commander, General Claude Auchinleck, should be replaced. He was ousted after he declined to launch an offensive.[8]

Ultimately, Roosevelt had to force through the amphibious invasion of Northwest Africa—renamed Operation Torch—over the vehement opposition of Marshall and other top US military planners, who suspected the British were seeking to prop up their fading empire. Roosevelt and Churchill also had to settle disputes over where to land. Churchill also had the unenviable task of meeting with Stalin to convey the unwelcome news that there would be no Anglo-American cross-channel invasion of France in 1942, and that Torch would have to substitute. This was the most important US/UK initiative of the year. In October, Churchill confided to Foreign Secretary Anthony Eden, "If Torch fails, I'm done for and must go and hand matters over to you."[9]

The media and the public in the United States and the UK followed the course of the fighting in the East and in the Middle East, the debate over a Palestinian Jewish fighting force, and the publicity about killings of Jews in Poland. On July 8, the Polish National Council passed a resolution denouncing the systematic destruction of the "vital strength of the Polish Nation and the planned slaughter of practically the whole Jewish population." The next day, at a press conference at the Ministry of Information, Bracken, introducing other speakers, expressed horror at Nazi crimes in Poland, especially atrocities against Jews.[10]

Nazi forces and non-German collaborators began carrying out comparable but disguised measures against Jews in occupied countries of Western Europe. While most of the killing would occur only after deportation to the East by train, observers who closely followed the news from Eastern Europe could see the pattern forming. On July 17, German radio announced that the mass arrest of all alien Jews living in (German-occupied) Paris had begun. An estimated twenty thousand Jewish refugees (this number was exaggerated) from Germany, Austria, Poland, and Czechoslovakia would be deported to the East. An article in the *Manchester Guardian* cited evidence that Jews in Vichy France were likely to suffer harsher treatment, too, for they had recently been forced to wear the Star of David. Another World News Service article reported that after weeks of preparation, Nazi officials had begun the deportation of all Dutch Jews to what was said to be Polish ghettos and occupied Soviet territory. Trains carrying at least six hundred Jews from Western Europe left daily. The Dutch were informed that they would not see one Jew left in the country.[11]

In North Africa, General Rommel appreciated the military potential of stirring up Muslim antagonism to the British and the Jews. In late June, after German troops crossed the Libyan border into Egypt, Rommel requested that Berlin supply suitable propaganda, and millions of pamphlets, leaflets, and flyers were flown in for distribution in Egypt and North Africa. By the end of August, German forces had distributed more than eight million pieces of Arabic-language propaganda, and there were

plans to make Cairo a center of German propaganda for the
Islamic world. One leaflet showed Stars of David planted on
Jerusalem, Beirut, Amman, Damascus and Aleppo, Mosul and
Baghdad, and Alexandria and Cairo. The caption under the
map read, "Roosevelt, Churchill, and Chaim Weizmann divide
the Arab countries for the Jews."[12] A German shortwave broadcast to the Middle East on July 7 called upon Egyptians to kill
the Jews before the Jews killed them. On July 29, another
German broadcast in Arabic proclaimed, "It is the duty of Mos-
lems, whenever the British exaggerate in their evil doings and
oppressions, to invoke the name of Allah to fight them."[13]

Hitler and Himmler planned to use obedient and secretive
killing forces in North Africa and Palestine once those areas were
conquered. On July 1, SD Foreign Intelligence chief Walter
Schellenberg discussed a "deployment in Egypt" with Himmler.
That afternoon, Himmler spoke with Hitler, which led Himmler's key subordinate Karl Wolff to contact the Army High
Command. On July 13, the SS and the army agreed that an SS
Einsatzkommando, a mobile killing squad commanded by Ober-
sturmbannführer Walter Rauff, would be attached to Rommel's
Afrika Korps but would receive its instructions directly from the
Security Police and SD, carrying out its actions under its own
authority against the civilian population. On July 20, Rauff, one
of the inventors of the gas van, flew to Tobruk.[14] Allied leaders
knew none of this at the time, because British intelligence could
decipher little of the German radio traffic and because they did
not yet know what an Einsatzkommando was.[15] But they knew
that the Jews of Palestine were in danger.

The American Jewish Committee, B'nai B'rith, and the
Jewish Labor Committee organized a large rally at Madison
Square Garden on July 21, 1942, persuading both Roosevelt and
Churchill to send messages to the gathering. Roosevelt's general
statement seemingly addressed to the Jewish crisis in Europe,

made it clear that he knew the situation was dire: "Citizens regardless of religious allegiance will share in the sorrow of our Jewish fellow-citizens over the savagery of the Nazis against their helpless victims. The Nazis will not succeed in exterminating their victims any more than they will succeed in enslaving mankind." The text also pledged postwar trial of the perpetrators of Nazi crimes and the ultimate triumph of the four freedoms largely inspired by Christian and Jewish teachings.[16]

Churchill repeated his own October 25, 1941, statement that Jews were Hitler's first victims and had since then been in the forefront of resistance to the Nazis. He then danced around the issue of a Jewish army in Palestine, arguing that Palestinians (Palestinian Jews) were already playing a role in British armies, and that Britain's primary emphasis must be on ensuring the success of those armies. The prime minister might have been able to inject enough emphasis and emotion into his final sentence if he delivered it himself in the House of Commons, but the reader in Madison Square Garden must have been relieved to reach the end of Churchill's convoluted last sentence: "His Majesty's Government in the United Kingdom took risks in the dark days in 1940 to discharge their obligations in the Middle East and they have throughout been animated by the determination that the Jewish population in Palestine should in all practicable ways play its part in resistance of the United Nations to oppression and brutalities of Nazi Germany which it is the purpose of your meeting this evening to condemn." The meeting was not a rally in favor of a Jewish armed force, but the organizers did not control all the speakers. Republican Senator Henry Cabot Lodge, recently returned from Libya, spoke in favor of a Jewish military component "side-by-side with their British and American friends." Rabbi Stephen S. Wise, head of the American Jewish Congress and the most prominent American Jewish leader, then supported it, too.[17]

Roosevelt's language about Nazi extermination came from a recommendation by Rabbi Wise, although it is doubtful that FDR knew the full extent of Nazi plans for mass murder.[18] On the same day as the Madison Square Garden rally, the AP sent out a story suggesting that Jews in many parts of occupied or satellite Europe were being used as forced laborers.[19] It would take more evidence and much more repetition by credible sources to convince large numbers of Western readers that the Nazis were killing most Jews.

In late July, President Roosevelt decided in principle to condemn German, Japanese, and Italian military and civilian atrocities as crimes against humanity and to appoint a renowned jurist to gather evidence and prepare for eventual prosecution. Assistant Secretary of State Adolf Berle discussed this policy with Arthur Sweetser, a high official of the Office of War Information (OWI). This was a newly established executive agency that dealt with information policies and warfare but also engaged in some collection of intelligence abroad. Sweetser worried that some Americans, "especially those hostile to the president, might charge him with conducting a single-handed crusade for American punishment of people in Germany, Italy, and Japan." Sweetser thought an international pronouncement would be much better, but there was no appropriate international organization ready to act.[20] He expressed more politely what some American journalists had written at Bad Nauheim: Nazi propaganda and isolationists in the United States would exploit any real or imaginary tie between FDR and the Jews. Denouncing atrocities in general terms was better psychological warfare than focusing only on the killings of Jews, but, still, Sweetser wanted to avoid a unilateral American initiative.

The OWI also consulted its advisory committee, which consisted of representatives of the State Department, the War Department, the navy, the Joint Psychological Warfare Committee, the Coordinator of Inter-American Affairs, and the Office of Censorship—a broad swath of US government agencies. On September 2, 1942, this group examined questions related to publicity regarding characterization of the enemy and enemy atrocities. The committee drew on statements by the president and many others to define the enemy as the militaristic and fascist rulers of enemy countries. It determined that information about these rulers should be freely released to the American people and the world whenever it would clarify the enemy's character and purposes, according to the draft statement. On the other hand, information that would merely foment hatred of the German, Italian, or Japanese people should not be made public. This distinction led into a guideline on atrocities: "barbarous actions and cruelties not serving directly to illuminate the nature of the enemy, but merely to excite horror and hatred of all members of the races [sic] guilty of such actions, would not be released."[21]

The committee avoided specific terms that might have drawn both foreign and domestic criticism. It nonetheless implied that Germans would react badly to such publicity about atrocities against Jews because they would think that Americans and Britons would hate all Germans. And German antisemites would see it as confirmation that the Allies were fighting on behalf of the Jews. But Americans would not be motivated to fight harder, because antisemitism was a factor in the United States, too.

RIEGNER'S TELEGRAMS

The most influential evidence about Hitler's plan to eliminate the Jews of Europe to reach Washington during 1942 came in telegrams from Geneva written by the young lawyer Gerhart M. Riegner, representative of the World Jewish Congress in

Switzerland. Riegner managed to get an alarming message into the right hands in the West. The German source of the information needed anonymity, so the document has become known as the Riegner telegram. Actually, Riegner sent two slightly different messages, one to London and the other to Washington, about Hitler's plans.

On July 29, 1942, the German chief executive of a huge Silesian mining corporation with headquarters in Breslau made a hurried trip to Switzerland. Despite his prominent position in the German economy, Eduard Schulte had never joined the Nazi Party and secretly hated the Nazi leaders, whom he considered gangsters. He previously visited Switzerland regularly on business and for pleasure, and also to pass useful information to Allied intelligence agencies. On this visit, however, he hoped to contact Jewish representatives based in Switzerland. They presumably would care the most about the terrible secret he carried.[22]

When Himmler inspected the Auschwitz camps in mid-July 1942, he witnessed the gassing of Jews at Birkenau and authorized a major expansion of the gas chambers and crematoria. During his visit he had met with local and regional officials, and word of his priorities spread. Otto Fitzner, the number two man at Schulte's firm Georg von Giesches Erben, was very friendly with the Nazi Party Gauleiter of Lower Silesia, Karl Hanke. Fitzner thus learned about the Hitler's plan to annihilate the Jews of Europe through the use of poison gas, and Schulte likely plied this information out of his subordinate. Then he arranged a trip to Zürich.

Schulte's financial adviser in Switzerland recommended contacting Benjamin Sagalowitz, press officer for the Association of Swiss Jewish Communities. Sagalowitz turned to Riegner, who was gathering information about Nazi Germany. Sagalowitz told Riegner that the source of the report was reliable and anti-Nazi: he had given accurate information in the past. But the source insisted on strict anonymity, for he had returned to Germany. Riegner learned the industrialist's name in October 1942, but he maintained his pledge of secrecy and felt bound to confidentiality even after Schulte's death. Schulte was identified as Riegner's source only in 1983.

Riegner wanted Western governments, as well as the World Jewish Congress, to receive and respond to this message. Knowing that diplomatic channels were quicker and more secure than the regular mail, he decided to share the information with local American and British officials in the hope that they would send it to their governments. So, he drafted a short telegram and also consulted Swiss professor Paul Guggenheim. Guggenheim advised him, in order to make the message credible with the diplomats, to delete a phrase about a huge crematorium under construction and to add some note of caution about the source. Guggenheim also gave him a letter of introduction to American Consul Paul Squire in Geneva. In the end, Riegner's message read:

> Received alarming report stating that in Fuehrers headquarters a plan has been discussed and being under consideration according which total of Jews in countries occupied controlled by Germany numbering three and half to four millions should after deportation and concentrated be at one blow exterminated in order resolve once and for all Jewish question in Europe STOP Action is reported to be planned for autumn ways of execution still discussed STOP It has been spoken of prussic acid STOP In transmitting information with all necessary reservation as exactitude cannot be controlled by us beg to state that informer is reported to have close connections with highest German authorities and his reports to be generally reliable.

On August 8, Riegner took two nearly identical telegrams to the British and American consulates. British Vice-Consul Armstrong in Geneva agreed to send one cable to Sidney Silverman, chairman of the British section of the World Jewish Congress and a member of Parliament. The telegram to Silverman contained an important addition at the end: "Inform and consult New York."

Riegner was a cautious man. He thought that the Foreign Office would likely deliver a telegram to a prominent MP. He was less optimistic about the State Department giving it to Rabbi Stephen Wise, head of the American Jewish Congress and the most prominent Jewish-American spokesman, but a private citizen. To ensure that Wise received the information, he wanted Silverman to contact Wise.

Squire was on vacation, so Riegner met at the US consulate with Vice-Consul Howard Elting, Jr., who found Riegner greatly agitated. Elting said he would send the telegram to the US Legation in Bern for transmittal to Washington, but he warned Riegner that higher-ups might discount a report from an unknown source. In a cover letter to US Minister Leland Harrison in Bern, Elting tried to convey that Riegner was a serious person convinced of the accuracy of the report.

Harrison was skeptical. In his commentary to the department on Riegner's message, he noted that the report "has the earmarks of war rumor inspired by fear and what is commonly understood to be the actually miserable condition of these refugees."[23] Nevertheless, he sent the text to Washington. A State Department summary described Riegner's message as a "wild rumor inspired by Jewish fears." One official in the Division of European Affairs pointed out that Rabbi Wise might well "kick up a fuss" if he found out later that the State Department had withheld a telegram to him. Another argued that they should hold it back "in view of the Legation's comments, the fantastic nature of the allegation, and the impossibility of our being of any assistance if such [Nazi] action were taken. . . ." The department then directed the legation not to accept such unsubstantiated messages for private citizens in the future. Weeks later, Squire informed Riegner that his text had failed to reach Wise. In London, Foreign Office officials also expressed doubt and worried about potentially embarrassing publicity. But in the end, they decided to pass it on to a member of Parliament. On August 29, Silverman telegraphed it to Wise, as Riegner had requested.[24]

On September 2, Wise showed the telegram to Under Secretary of State Sumner Welles. The under secretary was a close and trusted friend and associate of the president. As a youngster, Welles had been a page at FDR's wedding. Welles had handled Roosevelt's refugee initiatives in 1938, and he and Wise had become well acquainted. Wise knew that Welles was a liberal in a generally conservative department, and that he was close to the president.

Unaware that several of the State Department's experts on Europe had sat on this information for more than three weeks, Welles consulted them. They told him that the Nazis were putting Jews deported to the East to work, as they had done with Russian prisoners of war. Welles accepted this plausible opinion: Why should Germany waste valuable labor? He called Wise to question the information in Riegner's cable. Wise asked, "May we feel reassured?" Welles responded cautiously, "Who can tell, seeing that you are dealing with that madman [Hitler]?" He asked Wise not to publicize Riegner's cable until the State Department thoroughly investigated the evidence of Nazi atrocities against Jews.

On September 4, a new cable from (Orthodox) Agudath Israel sources in Bern renewed Wise's horror. The new information was that in Warsaw 100,000 Jews had recently been killed, with their corpses used to make soap. While the first part of the report was true, the latter part turned out to be inaccurate. Wise spread the news of both cables to his friends and allies. He hoped that someone would tell Roosevelt, even if the president would be unable to do much.

The Union of Orthodox Rabbis in the United States had called an urgent meeting of American Jewish organizations to devise a strategy for responding to reports of systematic killing of Jews on a huge scale. After an inconclusive first meeting on September 4, the American Jewish Congress arranged a second meeting on September 6. Wise told the representatives about his meeting with Welles and Welles's request to avoid publicity until the State Department completed its investigation. Participants considered three options: (1) Roosevelt should appeal directly to the German government to stop the killing, (2) neutral governments should be asked to intervene on behalf of Jews in Poland, or (3) the US government should threaten to take reprisals against German aliens in the United States unless the massacres ceased. The Jewish organizations agreed that Wise should set up a committee to study the matter. Another meeting on September 9 added several ideas, such as placing the evidence of mass murder before Democratic senators Wagner of New York and Tom Connally of Texas, getting other members of Congress in both houses to denounce Nazi crimes against Jews, and marshaling important church and lay opinion to influence a broad public audience. But the first and most important item was to appeal to the president to make a strong statement expressing "the revulsion of the civilized world to mass murders and mass deportations of civilian populations."[25]

As for the State Department investigation, Welles asked Harrison to meet with Riegner and his colleague Richard Lichtheim, representing the Jewish Agency for Palestine. Harrison should find out what additional evidence they had and explore other sources. By October, Harrison found other accounts consistent with Riegner's message. On October 22, Riegner and Lichtheim presented Harrison with a set of documents they had written and collected about the Nazi policy of extermination. They called for the collection of specific evidence against those responsible. More importantly, they urged the strongest possible pressure on the governments of Italy, Hungary, Romania, Bulgaria, and Vichy France not to cooperate with deportations of Jews. This represented a potentially feasible strategy to make use of information without the application of Allied military force.

A day earlier, Roosevelt met off-the-record in the White House with Rear Admiral Henry Kent Hewitt and General George S. Patton. As commander of the *Indianapolis*, Hewitt had taken FDR on a month-long trip in 1936. Now the admiral commanded the fleet for Operation Torch. He summarized the plan: it would consist of a fleet 300 warships and 400 transport and cargo vessels crossing the Atlantic to land more than 100,000 troops on the shores of Morocco, while another fleet steamed from the UK into the Mediterranean to land troops at sites in Algeria. Three-quarters of the soldiers were American and under Patton's command. The hope was that the eight French divisions in both territories would not resist an American-led operation, given a history of good ties between the two countries and the fact that the United States and Vichy France still maintained diplomatic relations. If the French authorities in North Africa did not oppose them, American and British troops could head quickly for Tunisia, pinning Rommel's Afrika Korps between Torch and the British Eighth Army advancing west, and setting up a base for a later landing in Italy. Patton declared that he would either leave the beaches as a conqueror or as a corpse. Smiling, the president asked whether he would charge with his saber drawn. Patton said the fate of the war depended on their success, so that he had to go ashore with the troops. The overall commander of Torch, General Eisenhower, would wait nearby in Gibraltar until it was secure for him to take charge in Northwest Africa. Years later, he would remember the hours in Gibraltar before the November 8 landings as his most excruciating ones of the entire war.[26]

Good news arrived before the landings. Churchill's selection of General Bernard Montgomery as the new commander of the British Eighth Army created a new dynamic in Egypt. Timely decoding of German Enigma messages gave Montgomery a priceless asset, which he exploited. And Roosevelt had sent convoys loaded with advanced military equipment, including shipments of three hundred Sherman tanks of the first armored division, directly from the United States to Montgomery, giving him tank superiority over the Germans outside El Alamein.[27] As it happened, Rommel was in Germany reporting to high authorities and recuperating when Montgomery launched an offensive at El Alamein just before midnight on October 23-24. Rommel rushed back by plane on October 25, but to reinforce and supply his force was another matter. The British sank numerous German resupply ships.[28]

Notifying the Army High Command that he could no longer hold the El Alamein front, Rommel requested approval for his retreat. However, in a typical refusal to recognize uncomfortable reality, Hitler insisted on victory or death. Rommel's superior Albert Kesselring advised him to disregard the Führer order, and the Afrika Korps' November 4 retreat was partly successful. Montgomery captured about 30,000 German and Italian troops, while Rommel led about 7,500 west toward Libya. Hitler, who had valued Rommel highly, now thought he had lost his nerve. Churchill found a suitable rhetorical frame for the event in a November 10 speech: "Now, this is not the end. It is not even the beginning of the end. But it is, perhaps, the end of the beginning."[29]

The British victory at El Alamein sharply reduced the chance of an Axis victory barring the collapse of the Soviet Union. The battle also removed the immediate German threat to Palestine and its 550,000 Jews, limiting Nazi mass murder of Jews largely to Europe. But the success or failure of Operation Torch would determine whether the war would turn into a bloody stalemate, or be a gradual progression toward Allied victory, with an Italian collapse in relatively short order, and the dire consequences that would have for Germany's position. To a great extent, the fate of Europe's remaining Jews would depend on the duration of the war in North Africa and then in Europe.

On October 7, the White House issued a presidential statement that Nazi war crimes were continuing. Along with other Allied countries, the United States was establishing a United Nations War Crimes Commission to gather evidence so that Nazi perpetrators could be tried and punished.[30] Meanwhile, the Foreign Office had discounted Riegner's telegram at least as much as the State Department bureaucrats had, and there was no one comparable to Welles in London to push the issue. In fact, the private secretary to Foreign Secretary Anthony Eden wrote in his diary that Eden hated Jews, and Eden himself admitted that he preferred Arabs to Jews.[31] A leading member of the British section of the World Jewish Congress complained to his American colleagues that it had been "absolutely impossible" to get anything from the Foreign Office: "We are received with cold courtesy and skepticism; there is never any action."[32]

In Bern, Harrison continued to gather corroborating evidence about the Final Solution. Carl Burckhardt, a high official of the International Committee of the Red Cross and former League of Nations High Commissioner for Danzig, offered highly detailed testimony about Hitler's policy to make German territory free of all Jews by the end of 1942.[33]

Myron Taylor, FDR's representative to the Vatican, had already met in Rome with Pope Pius XII and with Vatican Secretary of State Cardinal Luigi Maglione.[34] Maglione said that the pope had made statements in the past "without descending to particulars," and that another statement might come forth in October, but that the pope could not speak out daily.[35]

Taylor and Welles met with FDR on October 16, and Taylor left other documents with the president at that meeting. FDR or Welles suggested that Taylor might also brief Rabbi Wise.[36] In an October 20 meeting with Wise, his son James Waterman Wise, and World Jewish Congress leader Nahum Goldmann, Taylor reported confirmation of reports of atrocities against Jews in France, Poland, and Yugoslavia, and noted he had left supporting documents with the president. Taylor added that welfare agencies were prohibited from operating in Poland, and such a ban would probably continue until the war situation changed radically enough to affect the Nazi plan of extermination; that he would urge the president and the secretary of state to issue another condemnation of Nazi inhumanity; and he would urge the Vatican that the Pope do likewise. Taylor thought a new presidential statement might prompt the Vatican to act.

On November 8, Operation Torch, the first large amphibious operation by the United States in forty-five years, ran into serious difficulties. French political authorities and military officers in Algeria and Morocco chose to follow orders from Vichy France's head of state, Marshal Henri-Philippe Pétain, and to resist the British and American invasion. In the ensuing fighting French forces inflicted substantial casualties on Allied ships and troops at the nine different landing sites. Except in Algiers, it took several days for American and British troops to establish and expand secure beachheads. When further resistance became too costly, the French forces surrendered. But French officials in neighboring Tunisia, a critical future objective for any Allied move into Italy, remained loyal to Vichy. In a November 20 speech, Vichy France's premier Pierre Laval declared that he hoped for a German victory in the war. Otherwise, he warned, the Jews and communists would seize control of France and would extinguish French civilization. Notably, this statement came *after* Germany had responded to the Allied invasion of Northwest Africa by seizing control of what had been the unoccupied zone of France without any French resistance.[37]

American collaboration with high French officials who surrendered in Morocco and Algeria turned sour. For example, the tarnished Vichy admiral (and former Vichy premier) Jean-François Darlan, who happened to be visiting Algiers, was given the post of high commissioner in Algeria, which led to a major political controversy in the United States and some tension with the UK. But the biggest short-term military problem was the delay in advancing Allied troops and equipment eastward. Worried about German and Italian reinforcements being sent to Tunisia, on November 18, Eisenhower wrote: "If we don't get Tunisia quickly, we surrender initiative, give the Axis time to do as it pleases in that region, encourage all our enemies in the area . . . This battle is not, repeat *not* won."[38]

After Eisenhower landed in Algiers on November 23, a rumor circulated in Arab neighborhoods that "he was a Jew sent by the Jew Roosevelt to establish a Jewish state in North Africa." American officials took this problem seriously enough that they began a leaflet campaign to stress Eisenhower's Protestant faith. Darlan, meanwhile, kept Vichy's antisemitic laws in force, supposedly to avoid provoking the Arabs. Vichy had taken away citizenship from Algerian Jews in 1940, and the Jews wanted citizenship rights back. Tensions rose between Jews and Muslims, who lacked citizenship, and Nazi propaganda exploited Muslim resentment.[39]

Generals Patton and Mark Clark had no interest in mediating ethnic and religious conflicts in this region. Patton was antisemitic, greatly respectful of Germans, and sympathetic to French officials' complaints about Moroccan Jews "of the lowest order" who hoped to take over the country and who were stirring up trouble against the French. Although Clark's mother was Jewish, he blamed unassimilated immigrants for communism and anti-Americanism in the United States and was also a racial segregationist; he rejected the notion of the melting pot. But Patton and Clark's military credentials were fine, and they enjoyed Eisenhower's trust.[40]

The day after the Torch landings, Taylor stopped in to see the president again, perhaps to congratulate him but more likely to check on his interest in a statement denouncing Nazi extermination.[41] FDR, however, was not about to make any moves that might interfere with the battle in French Northwest Africa. Vichy France had just severed relations with the United States. Roosevelt issued a press release that day declaring that American ties with the French people would endure despite Vichy's action.[42]

Convinced of the truth of reports from Switzerland about the Nazi plan to annihilate the Jews, Welles asked Rabbi Wise to come to Washington. On Tuesday, November 24, the under secretary informed Wise that the investigation "confirmed his deepest fears." In an account to Jewish leaders that evening, Wise quoted Welles as saying: "For reasons you will understand, I cannot give these to the press, but there is no reason why you should not. It might even help if you did."[43]

Officials of the European Division were skeptical and unsympathetic, Welles knew, which meant that there would be a fight if he tried to go public. A larger problem was that the State Department, officials in other US agencies, and the military viewed pursuit of the war and simultaneous criticism of the Nazi campaign against the Jews as contradictory. Whether or not they accepted the report of mass extermination of Jews, they believed that the United States could not effectively fight the war and try to defend the Jews. But the most immediate problem was the politically delicate situation in Northwest Africa. American and British officials feared that Muslim pro-Axis sentiment would affect the battlefields. If Welles thought he could not disclose this information himself, then he would have realized that it was highly unlikely that the president would give a speech or issue a statement about the Nazi policy of exterminating Jews.

Wise had hoped for government action of some kind even if the only feasible military action (in North Africa) was already in progress. Now, he was on his own, but at least he was freed from a promise of confidentiality that had left him in agonizing limbo—he feared that tens of thousands of Jews were murdered each day. Publicity could spread public awareness, and he could seek additional political allies for some action that might take clearer shape in the future. Getting presidential endorsement of the facts was critical. And getting stories in the news at least showed that he and other Jewish representatives were doing something, even it if was minimal.

Wise spoke to an AP reporter in Washington, who broke the first story: Hitler had issued an order to extinguish the Jewish "race."[44] Then Wise called a small press conference attended by half a dozen reporters. In an expanded AP article (without byline), Wise was quoted as saying that the State Department confirmed the information that two million out of four million Jews in Nazi-occupied territories had already been killed in a campaign of extermination. He also stated that the president's personal representative (i.e., Myron Taylor) had confirmed the evidence. The article carried evidence of mixed reliability about different means of execution. The second AP story spread widely, with at least 213 US newspapers carrying the story, even

if newspaper editors treated it cautiously by attributing everything, including State Department confirmation, to Wise.[45]
After Wise held another press conference in New York, a story
about the documents assembled during the investigation made
the front page of the *New York Herald Tribune* and several other
papers; the *Times*, however, played it down.[46]

Just after Thanksgiving, Welles told Wise that FDR had agreed
to receive a delegation of Jewish leaders who could present the
evidence of the Nazi plan to him. General Edwin "Pa" Watson,
FDR's gatekeeper, nevertheless tried to divert them to the State
Department. Wise wrote the president directly to protest, and he
also alerted FDR's adviser on Jewish affairs, David Niles, to warn
that if the president avoided this meeting there would be political
trouble. In the end, Roosevelt consented to a meeting but only if
it included representatives of the various branches of the Jewish
community.[47]

The potential killing of millions of Jews was only one of the
president's problems: North Africa was very much on his mind.
Patton had told Eisenhower that the Arabs wanted the Allies to
retain a Vichy French official in Morocco. Patton noted that his
removal and the revocation of Vichy's anti-Jewish laws would
provoke so much unrest that it would take sixty thousand
troops to control the situation. Patton was certainly biased
against Jews, but he was also indispensable, and he convinced
Eisenhower of the necessity of working with French officials in
North Africa to avoid wasting Allied troops on occupation duties. And Assistant Secretary of State Adolf Berle wrote in his
diary, "I gather only God could tell whether the Arab tribes
would rise."[48]

The military situation in Eastern Europe, however, improved
dramatically when Soviet armies completed their encirclement
of German, Romanian, and Hungarian troops at Stalingrad. On
the same day as newspapers published Wise's account of the

Nazi extermination plan, some US papers also carried a heartening diagram of the Soviet counteroffensive at Stalingrad.[49]

JAN KARSKI IN LONDON

The Polish government-in-exile reinforced Riegner's evidence of the Nazi Final Solution. On December 4, Polish Prime Minister Sikorski met with Welles and gave him documentary evidence from Polish underground sources. Some of it, perhaps all of it, came through the now famous diplomat-courier Jan Karski (real name Jan Kozielewski), who had sent microfilmed documents to London on November 17, probably from Gibraltar, and who arrived in London on November 25. Polish officials in London condensed his report and released a version to the press even before Karski arrived there. Sikorski afterwards described the document he gave to Welles as a report concerning the atrocities suffered by the Polish and Jewish populations at the hands of the German occupants. But it has not been found in the Welles Papers.[50]

In London, Karski was taken into custody and held incommunicado until he agreed to answer questions from British intelligence officials. After he refused given his official Polish government status, they compromised on allowing Polish government representatives to attend the debriefing. MI19, a branch of British Military Intelligence, rated him C (a low ranking) as an informant.[51]

Karski's first report, most likely a variant of the condensed one already prepared by Polish officials, focused on killings and deaths in the Warsaw Ghetto, mentioning deportations to several death camps near the end. He estimated that only 100,000 out of an original population of 450,000 Jews in the Warsaw Ghetto were still alive.[52] Subsequently, an unidentified member of the Polish government gave a longer report to Silverman and

Alex Easterman of the British Section of the World Jewish Congress. This second Karski report repeated the first but contained additional comments about Jews who were left alive for slave labor; about Janusz Korzcak, writer and director of the Jewish orphanage, who went to his death with his children; about Nazi mass murder disguised through the myth of resettlement; and about methods of executions, including (but not limited to) gas chambers.[53]

Hoping to induce action from the British government, on November 26, Silverman and Easterman brought the second Karski report to Richard Law, parliamentary under-secretary in the Foreign Office, who was skeptical. Silverman argued that this report was consistent with Riegner's telegram. He urged Law to bring about a four-power declaration that the United Nations (all the allied countries) had been informed and would punish the perpetrators. Law conceded that Karski's account was consistent with Riegner's telegram, but that did not mean that he believed either one. He cautioned his Foreign Office colleagues, however, that the government might find silence awkward if both reports turned out to be true.[54]

On December 2, Karski met with the two Jewish members of the Polish National Council: Ignacy Schwarzbart, who had ties with the World Jewish Congress, and Zygielbojm, who represented the Bund. In a building near Piccadilly where the Polish interior ministry was based, Karski explained that he had been in the Warsaw Ghetto in August 1942 and in Belzec at the end of September. (It turned out, as he explained later, that he was in a sorting camp near Belzec, not in the actual extermination camp.) On his arduous trip from Poland to London, he had talked with British diplomats who listened to his horrific stories. The diplomats showed sympathy for the stress he had experienced but said that it must have made him overwrought, and that his account could only be partially true. After the three men talked for some time on December 2, Karski said that he had been asked to deliver some information from a Bund member identified as B (thought to be Leon Feiner) only to Zygielbojm. Schwarzbart excused himself from the room, and then Karski told Zygielbojm:[55]

> "B" requested me to inform you, Mr. Zygelboim [sic] and all other Jews of the following: 'Tell them 'there' (outside the Nazi-invaded countries), that there are moments when we hate them all. We hate them because they are safe 'there' and do not rescue us . . . because they don't do enough. We are only too well aware that in the free and civilized world outside it is not possible to believe all that is happening to us. Let the Jewish people, then, do something that will force the other world to believe us . . .
> We are all dying here. Let them not retreat until the civilized world will believe us—until it will undertake some action to rescue those of our people who will remain alive. Merely protests and threats are not sufficient. . . .'
> Of the three and one half million Jews in Poland and the five to seven hundred thousand who were brought there from other Nazi-occupied countries only a small number remains alive. It is not any longer a question of oppressing Jews, but of their complete extermination by all kinds of especially devised and perfected methods of pain and torture.[56]

The Jewish representatives in Poland (Karski later wrote) recommended that the Allies publicly and officially threaten the German government and the German people with reprisals and systematic destruction of the German nation if the persecution of Jews continued. This was the only step that might prove effective.

On December 2, the intelligence branch of the British Political Warfare Executive (PWE), more impressed with Karski than other British agencies, incorporated a long section based on a Polish summary of Karski's testimony into its secret weekly intelligence report on Europe. It also drew on other Polish or British intelligence, briefly traced the chronology of the Final Solution, then concentrated on the details of the liquidation of the Warsaw Ghetto, some of which Karski had seen firsthand. The Polish report, "written in a very sober style . . . confirms the view expressed more than once in previous [PWE] *Summaries*, that it is the deliberate policy of the German Government to wipe out the Jewish race in Poland." It named Belzec, Sobibor, and Treblinka as sites of execution for deported Jews, but it refrained from any statement about the use of poison gas. Although the narrator (Karski) could only testify about events up until September, he said that it was very unlikely that the liquidation in Warsaw ceased afterward. The report explicitly discounted the view that most Jews were being used for slave labor. And yet, in its conclusion, the summary discussed the German policy of exterminating the Polish nation and others, "the most hideous manifestation of which was the recent mass murder of the Jews. . . ."[57] It was politically inexpedient to single out Nazi extermination of the Jews.

THE UNITED NATIONS DECLARATION

On December 1, Polish ambassador Count Edward Raczyński met with Foreign Secretary Eden to recommend a gathering of the governments in exile of Nazi-occupied nations to express their view about "the wholesale destruction of Jews in Poland which was causing great agitation among Jews all over the world." Eden thought such a meeting would be "cold comfort" for the Jews, but Raczyński persisted. He also thought such a gathering might issue a warning to French Premier Laval.[58]

A delegation of Jewish Britons asked US ambassador John Winant to petition the US government to intervene to bring about public condemnation of Nazi killings of Jews. Winant had previously failed to get constructive responses from the Foreign Office to Riegner's telegram, but he tried again. On December 2, Soviet ambassador Maisky told Eden that a Jewish delegation had asked him to see if the USSR would associate itself with a declaration denouncing the extermination of the Jews. Maisky said he favored the idea. Count Raczyński also presented evidence of Nazi policy (presumably from Karski) to Eden. On December 4, the Polish government-in-exile contacted all the United Nations to suggest a joint declaration denouncing Nazi killings of Jews and threatening punishment of the perpetrators. Winant and Eden gave their tentative approval to such a joint effort, as did Maisky.[59] A draft declaration for the big three powers emerged, and Winant forwarded it to Washington on December 8.[60]

On December 7, Eden notified the British ambassador in Washington that he now had little doubt that the German authorities were carrying out a gradual policy of exterminating the Jews. The Polish government had supplied evidence, and it was convincing, Eden wrote.[61] After Wise had publicized the investigation of Riegner's telegram, Eden apparently thought the United States wanted some response for Jewish American audiences and authorized Lord Halifax to cooperate and coordinate. Eden also recognized that important British opinion leaders such as William Temple, the Archbishop of Canterbury, favored at least some kind of statement.[62] Like Arthur Sweetser earlier, Eden must have recognized that an international approach had advantages over a unilateral statement: it was less binding and politically less risky.[63]

December 8 was the day of the meeting between Jewish American representatives and Roosevelt, as well as the first anniversary of FDR's date of infamy speech about Pearl Harbor. Properly interpreting Roosevelt's remarks at this unusual meeting requires understanding the immediate military and diplomatic context and avoiding twenty-first-century hindsight. FDR believed that the fortunes of war had shifted in favor of the Allies. The encirclement of German, Romanian, and Hungarian troops at Stalingrad looked highly promising for the Soviets and for the Allies generally. Roosevelt hoped that the combination of German defeats on their eastern front and in North Africa would break the morale of the German people—if the Anglo-American offensive in Northwest Africa succeeded. On December 5, he told visiting Canadian Prime Minister Mackenzie King that he thought the German situation resembled that of 1917–1918: Germany "might crumple up at any moment."[64] This view of a collapsing Germany was wildly optimistic at the end of 1942, and he could not talk about it in public for fear of creating unrealistic expectations. Importantly, he wanted to avoid pushing all Germans to fight to the finish. Any emphasis on Nazi atrocities against Jews would not go over well in Germany and in German-dominated Europe, first, because it would seem to support Nazi propaganda about the Roosevelt administration, and second, because of antisemitism among Germans and others in Europe. The notion of threatening the destruction of the German nation ran directly counter to this strategy.

At noon on December 8, four Jewish American representatives entered the Oval Office. The president sat behind his cluttered desk, smoking a cigarette. He greeted Wise—the only one whom he knew personally, and Wise introduced the others: Adolph Held of the Jewish Labor Committee, Rabbi Israel Rosenberg of Agudath Israel, and Henry Monsky, representing B'nai B'rith. A representative of the American Jewish Committee, Maurice Wertheim, was scheduled, but could not make it in time.[65] Held prepared a report about the meeting. He noted the president's introductory comments and then turned to the substance of the gathering:

> Rabbi Wise said: "Mr. President, we have an orthodox Rabbi in our midst. It is customary for an orthodox rabbi to deliver a benediction upon the head of his country, when he comes in his presence. Will you, therefore, permit Rabbi Rosenberg to say the prayer of benediction?"
>
> "Certainly" the President answered.
>
> Rabbi Rosenberg rose and put on his scull-cap. We all rose. The President remained seated, and, as Rabbi Rosenberg commenced to recite the prayer in Hebrew, the President bowed his head.
>
> "O, God Lord of Kings, blessed be Thy name that Thou bestowest a share of Thy glory upon the son of men."
>
> "Thank you very much"—the President said.
>
> The President seemed to be moved, and so were we all.

Wise read a small portion of a long memorandum entitled Blue Print for Extermination, appealing to FDR to bring this to the world's attention and "to make an effort to stop it." Held recorded Roosevelt as responding:

> The government of the United States is very well acquainted with most of the facts you are now bringing to our attention. Unfortunately we have received confirmation from many sources. Representatives of the United States government in Switzerland and other neutral countries have given up proof that confirm the horrors discussed by you. We cannot treat these matters in normal ways. We are dealing with an insane man—Hitler, and the group that surrounds him represent an example of a national psychopathic case.[66] We cannot act

toward them by normal means. That is why the problem is very difficult. At the same time it is not in the best interest of the Allied cause to make it appear that the entire German people are murderers or are in agreement with what Hitler is doing. There must be in Germany elements, now thoroughly subdued, but who at the proper time will, I am sure, rise, and protest against the atrocities, against the whole Hitler system. It is too early to make pronouncements such as President Wilson made, may they even be very useful. As to your proposal, I shall certainly be glad to issue another statement, such as you request.

When Roosevelt asked the delegation for other suggestions, Held suggested asking neutral countries to intercede with Germany on behalf of Jews. There were few other proposals.

FDR then shifted the discussion to North Africa. He mentioned that he had given orders to free Jews from concentration camps there and to abolish Vichy's special laws against Jews. He then balanced this statement with another complaining that Muslims had also suffered discrimination by the French— they had had fewer rights than Frenchmen and Jews, and there were seventeen million Muslims. The United States would fight for equal rights for all—it was not in favor of greater rights for one group over another. Without saying so directly, FDR had signaled to the assembled leaders that the concerns of Jews would not necessarily take precedence over those of other peoples. At the close of the twenty-nine-minute meeting (they had been scheduled for fifteen minutes), as the group stood up, FDR said that they could issue a statement about the meeting, and they could use the statement he had given Wise in July again—if they quoted him exactly. He added, "we shall do all in our power to be of service to your people in this tragic moment."

Wise, who had a stake in the success of the meeting, was pleased afterward. In a thank you note to David Niles, who had arranged the meeting, Wise praised FDR, noting he "could not have been more friendly or helpful: The word he gave us will carry through the country and perhaps serve in some degree as warning to the beasts. . . . Thank God for Roosevelt. We ought to distribute cards throughout the country bearing just four letters, TGFR, and as the Psalmist would have said, thank Him every day and every hour."[67]

On the one hand, Wise had shown other Jewish leaders that he had access to the president, and Roosevelt had empathized with their pain. On the other hand, FDR could have played a more direct and more active role in highlighting Nazi genocide and in convincing Americans to believe it. His comments about the need to avoid alienating the German people and his concerns about conditions in Northwest Africa explain why he did not do so. He sought a pragmatic course to win the war as quickly as possible, not an opportunity to educate the public about genocide. And he preferred international sponsorship to presidential endorsement of any declaration denouncing the Nazi policy to murder all the Jews. Clearly, he had not yet received word of the draft declaration of the big three powers sent that very day by Ambassador Winant.

The twenty-first-century critic may regard these presidential choices as inadequate—as rationalizations for inaction in Europe. But the historical evidence indicates that the Nazi war against the Jews extended into Nazi-occupied Tunisia and would have spread to Palestine but for the Allied military campaign. Roosevelt's role in that campaign (and Churchill's) must be taken into consideration. And what action would have had a substantial effect in Europe? If Roosevelt or Churchill had known enough about the assembly-line procedure of mass murder and the location of extermination camps to try to interfere with them, they had no feasible military options. All the extermination camps, located in what had been prewar Poland, challenged the range of British and American bombers in 1942 (and 1943). Precision bombing was still a misnomer. Later, British and US bombers increasingly punished German civilians as well as German military-industrial targets, but for better or worse, this was general military strategy, not punishment for atrocities or attempts to prevent further ones.

Even Allied psychological warfare emphasizing Nazi mass murder of Jews carried risk of backfiring if the German people believed that the bombs raining down on them were punishment for the mass murder of Jews. In December, Goebbels launched a new and reinvigorated antisemitic propaganda campaign, partly to reinforce the goal of mass extermination, partly to remind the German people that they were implicated in Nazi Jewish policies. If the Germans failed to achieve victory in the war, Nazi propaganda suggested, the Jews would exact vengeance. In this context, some ordinary Germans came to believe, without evidence, that Allied bombing *was* a form of Jewish retaliation. Although many blamed and feared the Jews, some quietly criticized the Nazi leaders.[68]

On December 9, Polish Foreign Minister Raczynski sent Eden and American ambassador A. J. Drexel Biddle, Jr. (the ambassador to the governments-in-exile in London) a nine-page summary of Polish evidence of Nazi extermination policy. The lead paragraph contained charges that the Nazi occupation intended to reduce Poles to slavery and ultimately to exterminate the Polish nation. But most of the document traced Nazi Jewish policy in occupied Poland. It summarized the significance of Himmler's visits to Poland and his orders to clear the territory of Jews. It mentioned sites of execution, with poison gas used at Chełmno and electrocution allegedly being used at Belzec. Auschwitz was not listed. The account focused on the step-by-step liquidation of the Warsaw Ghetto and several other ghettos. It concluded that at least one-third of Poland's 3.1 million Jews had already been killed. Receiving a copy of this document the next day, Churchill asked the Foreign Office for further information.[69]

On December 14, at a meeting of the War Cabinet, Eden stated ambiguously that the Polish accumulation of evidence might be true, but that there was no confirmation of an overall extermination policy: "It might well be that these transfers [deportations] were being made with a view toward wholesale extermination of Jews." The War Cabinet then approved the principle of a joint Allied statement condemning Nazi policy.[70] While Eden thought the situation ambiguous, those British officials with access to the British decodes of German police radio messages knew they could trust reports of extermination as they had seen many examples of confirmation.

In response to War Cabinet discussions, Foreign Office official F. K. Roberts prepared a formal reply for Eden in case he wished to send it to Churchill. Roberts wrote: "The Polish Government's note summarized and confirmed information which had already reached me from reliable Polish and Jewish sources indicating the intensification of German anti-Jewish measures in Poland. As I informed the War Cabinet on December 7th, I proposed early last week to the United States and Soviet Governments that we should issue a joint Declaration condemning these German measures, expressing sympathy with the victims and reminding those responsible of the retribution awaiting them. . . . In view of parliamentary interest I think our statement should be made in Parliament. I have throughout been in touch with representative Jewish spokesmen." But Roberts received a handwritten reply the next day that Eden did not think he needed to send this note to Churchill.[71] He apparently thought that Churchill concurred with the proposed Allied declaration and did not intend to press the matter further.

When James de Rothschild asked Churchill on December 16 to meet with some leading Jewish representatives to discuss the plight of European Jews, the prime minister's secretary referred the request to Eden without acknowledging it. In any Foreign Office response to Rothschild, the secretary wrote, Churchill wanted them to make it clear that Eden was handling these matters at Churchill's request.[72]

State Department officials, unaware of or unconvinced by Welles's investigation, consistently maintained that the department had not confirmed the Nazi policy of exterminating Jews. On December 15, one department official, Robert Borden Reams, complained to another that if Wise had described Riegner's telegram as a private communication obtained through the good offices of the State Department, little harm would have occurred. But instead, he went to the press and cited State Department sources: "All of these reports are unconfirmed. It is obviously impossible to secure confirmation of German activities in the various occupied countries. . . . It cannot be doubted that the Jewish people of Europe are oppressed . . . Whether the number of dead amount to tens of thousands or, as these reports state, millions is not material to the main problem . . . Our main purpose is the winning of the war, and other considerations must be subordinate thereto." State Department officials continued to distance themselves from Wise's statements after the declaration.[73]

Nonetheless, an Anglo-American draft declaration was sent to Washington and Moscow. Secretary of State Hull approved it on December 16, and, after approval by eleven other governments and governments-in-exile at war with the Axis, plus the French National Committee, it was released the next day.[74] The declaration drew on Riegner's evidence and some of what Karski revealed in London about deportations and liquidation of ghettos. It endorsed reports that the German authorities were carrying out Hitler's oft-repeated intention to exterminate the Jews of Europe. It described transports from occupied countries to Eastern Europe as a means to make most Jews disappear, save a small minority of skilled workers. The able-bodied were worked to death in labor camps, while the aged and infirm were allowed to die or were massacred. The number of deaths was reckoned as "many hundreds of thousands." The declaration lacked any references to specific locations of mass extermination. But these governments of the United Nations condemned this bestial policy of cold-blooded extermination and reaffirmed their commitment to punish those responsible. This declaration was the first official recognition of what we now call the Holocaust by the multiple Allied governments at war with Germany. It was the first step toward any kind of specific response to genocide.

The UK government highlighted the Allied declaration, with Eden reading it in the House of Commons in response to a question posed by Sidney Silverman. Afterward, James de Rothschild spoke for five minutes with tears in his eyes. Then the MPs stood and observed a moment of silence for those victims. In his diary Joseph Goebbels took note of this ceremony, commenting that the House of Commons was a sort of Jewish exchange, that the English were the Jews among the Aryans, and that Eden "cuts a good figure among these characters from the synagogue."[75]

Out of the limelight, Eden showed a different profile. In February 1943, he met twice with Karski, who again described the tragedy of Polish Jews. When Karski brought up the idea of mass air-raids on German cities as retaliation, Eden interrupted him: "The Polish reports on the atrocities had already reached us: the matter will take its proper course." The foreign secretary declined to arrange a meeting for Karski with Churchill because

Eden said that it was his duty to protect the elderly and over-worked prime minister from too many petitioners.[76]

In some ways, Allied recognition of Nazi genocidal policy re-duced the immediate pressure for government remedies, espe-cially since the concept of reprisals against Germans had little support and there were no obvious means of rescuing large numbers of Jews on the continent.[77] On the other hand, given the difficulty of comprehending genocide in the heart of Eu-rope, the declaration helped many people believe that the Nazis were killing some Jews and marking others for very harsh treat-ment, whether or not Western readers and listeners believed the numbers. And it empowered the government agencies involved in printing and broadcasting information to conduct future campaigns emphasizing Nazi antisemitism, which must have reached considerable numbers of Jews on the continent. The general terms in this paragraph apply to both the United States and the UK; in December 1942, their policies were quite sim-ilar, if not perfectly aligned.

The actions of their leaders differed. Roosevelt met with Jewish leaders and used Welles as a sympathetic stand-in to give them a hearing, while Churchill had no personal interac-tion and directed Jewish Britons to the obstructionist Eden.

Roosevelt and Churchill both favored a win-the-war strategy to end genocide. Today we know that FDR's December 1942 ex-pectation that a series of military defeats would soon crack the Nazi regime was wildly optimistic. On the basis of detailed re-search, historian Alexandra Lohse has described the trend of opinion among ordinary German soldiers and civilians: "Shocked when the tide turned in 1943, they reluctantly em-barked on total mobilization. . . . By 1944, when the nation suf-fered a catastrophic bloodletting, many Germans considered the continuation of the war a matter of national self-preservation. Still waiting for the vaunted 'miracle' . . . they were stunned when in 1945 defeat came instead."[78] They were caught in a fantasy world created by Nazi propaganda, their own faith in Hitler, and their own hopes and fears. In retrospect, both Western leaders could have done more to articulate genocide without major damage to the Allied war effort. They might have followed up the Allied declaration of December 17 by speaking out once the troops in North Africa had gained the upper hand. That would have had at least some benefit in alerting potential victims and rescuers in Europe.

CHAPTER SIX

TWO INFLUENCERS IN WASHINGTON

O n Wednesday morning, July 28, 1943, Polish ambassador Jan Ciechanowski and Jan Karski, Polish diplomat and underground courier, entered the Oval Study on the second floor of the White House for a meeting with the president. Scheduled for one hour but lasting longer, their conversation has resonated for many decades.[1] Karski has achieved fame as an eyewitness to the Holocaust who conveyed some of his knowledge to high Allied officials. He simultaneously warned the West against trusting the Soviet Union.

Assistant Solicitor General Oscar Cox helped to arrange Karski's audience with Roosevelt. Cox subsequently worked to convince FDR that fighting the war effectively was by itself insufficient to act against genocide. Though Karski and Cox did not induce Roosevelt to give a speech about Nazi killings of Jews, they did lead him to warn again in general terms against Axis atrocities and to encourage other actions behind the scenes during the second half of 1943. The unheralded Cox also advised high Treasury Department officials in their campaign against obstructionists in the State Department, and it was this Treasury effort that persuaded the president to create the War

Refugee Board in January 1944. Both Karski and Cox tried to determine how the Allies could resist the Holocaust while fighting and winning the war.

KARSKI, THE POLISH UNDERGROUND, AND THE SOVIETS

The Polish government-in-exile in London sought to warn the West against the behavior of Communist agents and activists in Poland and against the aggressive intentions of the Soviet Union. Karski tried in vain to convince British officials of the Soviet danger. But Foreign Secretary Anthony Eden implied that Poland might have to sacrifice territory to the USSR in the peace settlement. Despite Karski's request, Eden refused to let him see Prime Minister Churchill.[2]

The USSR had considerable diplomatic leverage because of its success on the battlefield. In early 1943, Soviet armies encircled and largely annihilated the German Sixth Army, as well as Hungarian and Romanian troops, at Stalingrad. When Roosevelt and Churchill held a summit conference in Casablanca from January 14 to 24, Churchill successfully argued for a continued Mediterranean strategy, with an invasion of the island of Sicily, and then the Italian mainland. Impatient American generals saw this as a diversion and a delay of the knock-out blow—the cross-channel invasion of France.[3] Stalin was not the only one impatient for a second front in Europe.

At the Casablanca summit, Roosevelt announced the Allied policy of unconditional surrender, ruling out a negotiated settlement. Churchill and Roosevelt had long regarded any deal with Hitler as politically and morally abhorrent.[4] The Anglo-American leaders also sought to reassure Stalin that the Western Allies would not arrange a separate peace with Germany. The Soviet dictator feared that the Americans and British might even join with Germany against the Soviets, or just let the two

totalitarian powers bleed each other to death.[5] Without the re-
assurance of the policy of unconditional surrender, Stalin might
have tried to reach his own separate peace with Hitler.

Stalin, who never endorsed unconditional surrender, occasionally referred to the war as (merely) a German-Soviet one.
He permitted "unofficial" secret discussions between Soviet and
German intelligence agents to take place in Stockholm in the
spring of 1943. Whether he was seriously exploring a separate
peace or merely trying to put more pressure on the West for a
second front remains unclear.[6]

In April 1943, Polish-Soviet hostility erupted into crisis. In
the Katyn Forest near Smolensk, German troops found the mass
graves of an estimated ten thousand Polish POWs and civilians
killed years earlier. It was later established that the Soviets'
"Katyn massacre" targeted nearly twenty-two thousand Polish
officers, civil servants, and intellectuals killed by the NKVD at
several different locations. Stalin had personally arranged for
their execution in March 1940. He hated the Poles and had
viewed the Polish prisoners as security threats.[7]

On April 13, 1943, Joseph Goebbels used Radio Berlin to ac-
cuse Moscow of the mass murders at Katyn. He hoped to further divide the Soviets and the Polish government-in-exile, and
he assumed that the news would also poison relations between
the Poles and the Jews—because the Nazis believed that Jews
controlled the Soviet government. Two days later, Radio
Moscow falsely responded that "German-Fascist hangmen" had
carried out these killings in the summer of 1941. But officials of
the Polish government-in-exile knew that nothing had been
heard from these prisoners in several years, meaning that they
disappeared during the period of Soviet control of the region.
So, Germany and the Polish government both asked the International Red Cross to investigate the evidence at the murder
site. On April 21, in "retaliation," Stalin accused the Polish

government-in-exile of collaboration with the Nazis. He blamed
the Poles for a "slanderous campaign" against the Soviets. Four
days later, he severed diplomatic relations with the London
Poles.[8]

In a remarkable act of realpolitik bereft of all moral considerations, both Churchill and Roosevelt, accepting Stalin's anger as
justified, overlooked the evidence against the Soviets. Churchill
called Stalin a warrior, and the Allies obviously needed warriors.[9] The Western Allies could not manage without the Soviet
military if they hoped to end the war within the next few years.

While he stayed in London, Karski spoke with the Jewish
representatives on the Polish National Council, who in turn
communicated his testimony to Jewish organizations in the
United States in ways that would not compromise his identity
or his support network. On March 1, a pamphlet entitled "The
Ghetto Speaks" carried extensive coverage of Karski's observations, lightly camouflaged by altering some details but dis-
cussing his visit to the Warsaw Ghetto and his trip near the extermination camp at Belzec. On March 17, Ignacy Schwarzbart,
a member of the Polish National Council, notified the head of
the Representation of Polish Jews in the United States via telegraph that he had spoken with a special envoy [Karski], who
told him that the complete annihilation of Polish Jewry was certain unless the Allies intervened to save the remnants. In his
diary Schwarzbart quoted the envoy as telling him that the suffering of the Jews was qualitatively different from that of the
Poles under Nazi occupation: "One can fittingly speak about a
biological liquidation of the Polish intelligentsia, whereas you
have to speak in relation to the Jews about the liquidation of a
whole people."[10]

In London, Karski learned of one of the Polish underground's
important secrets. A Polish underground radio operator named
Stefan Korbonski regularly sent current news to London, where it

was edited and broadcast by the secret Polish radio station called Świt (Dawn). Świt claimed to be operating from a secret underground location in occupied Poland, but the broadcast site was actually Woburn Abbey, in Bedfordshire. No wonder the German forces in occupied Poland could never track it down. Karski served at times as an adviser to the Polish broadcast team.[11]

On April 23, a dramatic Świt story revealed that Jewish fighting forces in the Warsaw Ghetto had begun a last-ditch uprising. German forces had already deported much of the ghetto population and were engaged in liquidating the rest. Only thirty-five thousand Jews remained, according to the article (actually, there were about sixty thousand). Although the Germans deployed armored cars and tanks against the desperate fighters, the defenders still inflicted heavy casualties. The story claimed (inaccurately) that the Polish underground had supplied arms and trained commanders to the ghetto fighters. The next step for the Nazis would be to liquidate the Cracow Ghetto, the article stated. Polish sources cited in the story believed that at least 1.3 million Jews had perished so far during the Nazi occupation of Poland.[12] This sketchy account helped to raise consciousness in the West about Jewish resistance because the story reached the mainstream media. Jewish accounts, the first one smuggled out to Stockholm simultaneously with Świt's story, gradually followed, as escaping fighters supplied many details. This doomed Warsaw Ghetto uprising, the first urban revolt against Nazi rule, became a source of pride for Jewish organizations.[13]

KARSKI'S ARRIVAL IN WASHINGTON

Karski quietly arrived in the United States on June 16. On July 3, Ambassador Ciechanowski planned to introduce Karski to key US officials through a series of "small, informal, men's [!]

dinners" at the Polish Embassy. The first one came two days later, with the guests being presidential adviser Ben Cohen, Supreme Court Justice Felix Frankfurter, and Assistant Solicitor General in the Justice Department Oscar Cox—three of the most influential Jewish Americans in government. Their discussion lasted until 1:00 a.m.[14] It had to be a strain for the two Polish officials: a day earlier, Polish Prime Minister Sikorski, who was also commander in chief of the Polish army, died along with his daughter and his chief of staff when their plane crashed in the sea after taking off from Gibraltar.

Over the course of the evening, Karski sketched out the organization of the Polish underground and described life in Poland under Nazi rule. He handled Nazi persecution of Jews "objectively," while occasionally referring to what he had personally seen. Cox was apparently the only guest who recorded his reaction promptly.[15]

On July 6, Cox wrote Harry Hopkins, who had been his superior at the Works Progress Administration in 1935 and again on Lend-Lease matters in 1941–1942:[16]

> If you can find time, you may possibly want to arrange to talk to a man named Karski who has just arrived in town. He is a member of the Polish Underground and left Poland in February of this year. He went through Germany, France and Spain on his way here. His story will make your hair stand on end but it is well worth hearing. The details about the Polish Underground have, I think, both military and political significance and you may want to get the flavor of it. He can be reached through the Polish Ambassador, or, if you wish, I can arrange the date for you.[17]

Hopkins never met with Karski himself, but as the president's closest adviser, Hopkins very likely passed on word of Karski's presence and importance to Roosevelt. In a shorter, similar letter to columnist Walter Lippmann, Cox described Karski's story as "bloodcurdling."[18]

During the evening of July 5, Karski had a side encounter with Justice Frankfurter and Ciechanowski, in which the justice asked for more details about the fate of Polish Jews. Karski recounted what he had witnessed in the Warsaw Ghetto and near the Belzec death camp. After some hesitation and pacing back and forth, Frankfurter said that he had to be frank: "I am unable to believe you." Ciechanowski immediately protested that Frankfurter could not call Karski a liar. Frankfurter clarified that he was not saying that Karski was lying, only that Frankfurter was unable to believe such monstrosities even though he was generally aware of Nazi policies.[19] Frankfurter's comment may have had consequences: Karski's biographers suggest that he never again related his own experiences to American officials.[20]

On July 22, in a White House meeting, Rabbi Wise urged the president to warn Nazi satellites such as Romania and Hungary, which had the largest surviving Jewish populations in Eastern Europe, against further cooperation with Germany in persecuting and killing Jews. He also sought the president's approval of a World Jewish Congress proposal to assist Jews in Romania and France. The WJC suggested that wealthy Jews living in both countries lend money for food, medicine, or escape. Jewish organizations in the West would then reimburse the lenders by depositing equivalent funds in American or Swiss bank accounts that would be blocked until the end of the war. In this way, no new funds would enter Axis territories during the war. The complicated currency maneuvers were necessary to avoid running afoul of the Allied blockade and currency regulations. Wise wondered whether the US government would support the proposal. It had originated with Riegner in Switzerland but had been languishing in various bureaucracies for nearly a month. Roosevelt supported the idea, asking Wise to discuss it with Treasury officials.[21]

Three days before Karski met with Roosevelt, an Italian coup ousted Mussolini and installed Marshal Pietro Badoglio as his replacement. Churchill, with Roosevelt's backing, warned the Italians that they would either have to "stew in their own juices" with their German ally or surrender unconditionally. Roosevelt announced that he would address the nation on radio on the evening of July 28 to summarize progress in the war. Meanwhile, the Soviets had blunted the German offensive against the Soviets near the city of Kursk in western Russia, and with well-prepared armies counterattacked north and south of the Kursk salient.[22] (The battle raged for six weeks, turning into the largest tank battle in history.) Good news for the Soviets was a mixed blessing for the Poles if it meant that Soviets, not Western troops, would eventually liberate Poland.

Shortly after his July 28 appointment with Roosevelt, Karski wrote a long, strictly confidential report to the new prime minister of the Polish government-in-exile, recapitulating the arrangements for the meeting with the president and their conversation itself. The information on how the Karski-Roosevelt meeting came about reflected what Karski had been told and what he believed, not necessarily the reality. Still, Karski's contemporary account is the best primary source available for this meeting, even if some items must be corrected.[23] His writings later during the war were influenced by the need to pursue Polish interests in the peace settlement.

Karski gave most credit to the former US ambassador to France, William Bullitt, for persuading FDR to see him. By this time, however, Roosevelt was furious with Bullitt over his underhanded role in exposing Undersecretary of State Sumner Welles's homosexual encounter with an African American porter on a train. Bullitt gave evidence to Secretary of State Hull, who bitterly resented Welles's close tie with FDR, and Hull forced Welles out. To make matters worse for Bullitt, the president probably heard through Felix Frankfurter that Bullitt was spreading the false story that Roosevelt gave priority to the European theater over Asia in the war effort because of the influence of Jews in the administration.[24]

Karski also credited Ben Cohen, listing him (correctly) as a presidential adviser and (incorrectly) as the author of Lend-Lease; he cited Oscar Cox as assistant attorney general (he was assistant solicitor general) and a confidant of FDR (this applied better to Cohen). Cox was one of the authors of the Lend-Lease bill. After the White House contacted Ciechanowski and asked to see Karski on July 28, the ambassador gave Karski precise advance instructions to stress the activities of the Polish underground and the general conditions of life in Poland; Ciechanowski told him to avoid any exaggerations.

At the White House meeting Ciechanowski introduced Karski as a nonpolitical courier very familiar with the Polish underground. Karski opened with a compliment, saying the Poles respected FDR as a champion of truth and humanity. Roosevelt cut the flattery short, asking whether the situation in Poland was as bad as rumored. Karski responded that it was very bad, describing in detail food shortages and the Germans' seizure of crops. FDR, who sometimes called himself a farmer, asked questions about livestock and property seizures, and asked Karski to compare the food situation in Poland and France (which Karski had passed through on his way to the UK). In response to other questions Karski described German troops and the occupation administration as demoralized and susceptible to bribes.

When Roosevelt asked about German methods of terror, Karski worked in a comparison with the Soviet deportation of hundreds of thousands of Poles to the USSR. The Soviets had incarcerated all persons with an actual or suspected political past, but the Nazis lacked the time and the manpower for this kind of operation. Instead, they applied massive terror and collective responsibility for any subversive behavior or attacks on Germans.

Karski spoke of Auschwitz as the most horrible concentration camp, where close to a hundred thousand Polish members of the intelligentsia had already died. He listed other extermination and concentration camps, too, without distinguishing among them. If one follows the documentary evidence, Karski did not speak of the gassing of Jews at Birkenau, either when he met with officials in London in November and December 1942 or when he saw Roosevelt some eight months later. He had no direct personal knowledge of Auschwitz-Birkenau.[25]

Karski did discuss the general Jewish situation with the president, declaring that many people were unaware of just how horrible the fate of Polish Jewry was: the Nazis had already killed more than 1.8 million Jews in the country. The Nazis wanted to destroy the Polish nation as a nation, he said, leaving peasants and workers but eliminating the political, intellectual, religious, and economic elite. But they sought to destroy the biological substance of the Jewish people. If the Germans did not alter their policy and the Allies did not intervene, there would be no Jews left, he said, within eighteen months after his departure from Poland. The president asked whether Karski's organization and the Jewish underground worked together. The courier replied that the Jewish labor movement took part in underground work cooperating with the Polish Socialist Party. In addition, there was a special organization for the aid and protection of Jews that contained Polish representatives. Karski stressed the limits of what the Poles could do for Jews when many Jews could be recognized by their looks and when the

Nazis applied the death penalty to entire families of any Poles who assisted Jews. He urged the Allies to threaten retaliation against Germans within their reach, attributing this recommendation to the underground Jewish leadership in Poland and international Jewish organizations.[26]

Several years later, Ciechanowski claimed that Karski had presented to Roosevelt some incidents from his own experiences in the Warsaw Ghetto and near Belzec.[27] It is possible, but not likely, that Karski chose to omit them in his report to the Polish prime minister. It is more likely that Ciechanowski misremembered or embellished. In any case, Karski wrote that FDR showed so much interest in his answers that the meeting ran overtime; the president commented that he was half an hour late for his next appointment.

Karski and Ciechanowski received no verbal signal from the president that he would defend Polish interests against the Soviets in the peace settlement. In this sense, their effort was a failure, and Ciechanowski entitled his postwar memoir *Defeat in Victory*. For decades afterward, Karski believed that he had also failed to persuade the president to take greater notice of the Holocaust. His biographers (correctly) conclude that he was mistaken.[28] His impact on Roosevelt must be inferred from the president's behavior and scattered statements afterward, since FDR kept his own counsel and, as usual, did not record his thinking.

Roosevelt quickly stepped up efforts to deter Axis crimes against civilians. At his July 31 press conference, the president read statements he had made on August 21, 1942, denouncing barbaric crimes against innocent civilians in Europe and Asia and threatening those responsible with trials after the war. He then noted his October 7, 1942, statement that a successful close of the war would include provisions for the surrender of war criminals to the Allies, adding "the wheels of justice have been turning since those statements were issued, and are still turning."[29] But he was again unwilling to denounce the Nazi war against the Jews.

In 1978, French documentary filmmaker Claude Lanzmann interviewed Karski extensively but used only a portion of the interview for his nine-hour film, "Shoah." Greater use of the same interview came only in another Lanzmann film, "The Karski Report" (2010). Karski told Lanzmann that at the end of his meeting with Roosevelt, he told the president about his visits to the Warsaw Ghetto and to Belzec. The president, he said, did not ask any questions about the Jews of Poland, but assured him that the Allies would win the war, punish war criminals, and bring about justice.[30] Karski's own contemporary account of their meeting lacks these claims.

Karski's encounter with FDR has spawned other misleading beliefs that have spread among later generations. Karski was *not* the first person to tell FDR about the Holocaust. The president *did* ask questions about Polish Jews, but he did not ask him if published accounts of Jewish casualties were true. Nor was the president stunned by Karski's general statements about the Holocaust.[31] Karski's statements gave added credibility to information FDR had received previously from Jewish sources, including Wise in December 1942 and again on July 22. But Karski *did* make a significant impression on the president with his comments about Nazi mass murder of Jews, as John Pehle, the head of the War Refugee Board, later recalled.[32]

COX

Oscar Sidney Cox, who served in multiple government agencies at a high level, played an unsung but critical role in the war effort. He was born in 1905 into a religious Jewish family in Portland, Maine. His father's name originally was Karakofski.[33]

After briefly attending MIT, Cox transferred to Yale, where he received degrees in philosophy and law. Following some years as an attorney in private practice, he went to Washington to join the New Deal. Working at the WPA, the Treasury Department, the Lend-Lease Administration, the Justice Department, and the Foreign Economic Administration, he demonstrated his talents and made valuable connections. He had close personal relationships with Hopkins, Secretary of the Treasury Henry Morgenthau Jr., and Edward R. Stettinius, the head of the Lend-Lease Administration and later FDR's secretary of state.

The basic idea of simply giving war materiel to US allies before America entered the war came from the president. Cox found an 1892 statute that allowed the secretary of war to lease army property for the public good for a period of five years. Hopkins and Cox drew on this precedent to write up a bill of a mere fifteen hundred words that became the legal and financial vehicle for the United States to assist the enemies of Germany with massive quantities of material goods. Cox was entrusted with the job of maneuvering this Lend-Lease bill through the Senate Foreign Relations Committee and the full Senate, which he did well.[34] Cox stood directly behind FDR during the bill's signing on March 11, 1941. The United States became, in Roosevelt's phrase, the arsenal of democracy—and later the supplier of materiel to the totalitarian Soviet Union, too.[35]

Cox's religious upbringing did not stick or carry over to the upbringing of his own children, but it seems to have affected his perception of the US response to the Holocaust.[36] The December 1942 Allied declaration on Nazi genocide had not generated much in the way of action. Cox grew impatient, along with others inside and outside government.

American Jewish organizations sponsored mass meetings and other forms of persuasion and pressure, which had negligible effect on the Nazi regime but some influence in Washington.

Congress, in a March 1943 resolution, condemned Nazi atrocities
against civilians in occupied countries, including the phrase "especially the murder of Jewish men, women, and children." Senator Alben Barkley, the Democratic Majority Leader, urged neutral countries to request Germany to release all Jews and to
shelter them temporarily.[37] The first notion was unrealistic, but
the second had merit if the Allies gave support and other assurances to the neutrals.

In response to public criticism of inadequate government
policies, the State Department and the British Foreign Office
agreed to hold a private conference on refugee problems in seclusion on the island of Bermuda. On April 1, 1943, seven Jewish
congressmen led by New York Democrat Emanuel Celler
warned the president that the lineup of the delegations and
other early indicators looked bleak. Roosevelt agreed to have
the State Department reconsider the use of emergency visitors'
visas for Jews and said he favored renewed efforts to rescue
Jewish children.[38]

Richard Law, the senior British representative in the Bermuda delegation, said in a private session at the conference that
it was folly for the Allies to assume responsibility for any sizable
portion of twenty to thirty million "useless people" who were a
liability to Hitler. The two governments agreed at the outset of
the conference that they would each respect the other's sensitive
areas, which included negotiating with Germany, sending material aid into Europe for persecuted civilians (through the
blockade), anything that might inflame Arab opinion on Palestine, and tight domestic immigration regulations. The delegates
and their governments kept the deliberations and recommendations confidential even after the meetings ended, cloaking the
fact that they had agreed only on very small measures.[39]

On May 2, 1943, some twenty thousand people filled Boston
Garden in what was called a nonsectarian demonstration

without parallel in Boston's history to demand help for decimated Jews in Europe. Assistant Secretary of State Adolf Berle,
who was ill, responded in a prepared speech read by one of his
assistants to the audience. In the face of Jewish and non-Jewish
calls for more substantial Allied action, Berle wrote that the
Nazis mass killings were not limited to Jews, but they were exterminating Jews in large numbers: "A few stragglers and refugees who have escaped through skill, good fortune, or, more
often, by the corruption of the Nazi officials, may indeed be rescued. . . . But these are so few that they hardly weigh in the
scales." He warned that only a military response would be effective: ". . . the only cure for this hideous mess can come through
Allied Armies when they have cracked the defenses of Western
Europe and are able to maneuver on the European plains. The
cure must depend on them and on the fierce, relentless, and
growing air invasion over Germany, which must continue. . . ."[40]
This was to say publicly that the Bermuda Conference was
hardly worth the effort.

Berle's speech was an attempt to dampen public criticism of
both the US and the UK governments. His views were not
shared by the entire State Department; Under Secretary Welles
had expressed the hope that the Bermuda Conference figure out
ways to save fifty thousand people. Welles, who was far more
liberal than most of his State Department subordinates, had
some experience with trying to place Jews leaving Nazi Germany in the period before World War II. But then again, there
were officials, such as Robert Borden Reams of the Division of
European Affairs, who rejected the evidence that the Nazis were
killing all Jews. And Assistant Secretary Breckinridge Long was
known for his distaste for Jewish refugees.[41]

Some State Department officials had tried to choke off the
flow of information from Switzerland about the Holocaust by
denying Jewish representatives use of the US diplomatic pouch

to send confidential information to Washington. This ban on private use of the pouch was later overturned, but it clearly reflected views among many State Department officials that they should try to prevent any distractions from the war effort. The evidence of their suppression of Holocaust information lay in State Department files.[42]

During the May 1943 Trident Conference, Roosevelt and Churchill tried to reach agreement on new refugee havens in North Africa, one of the Bermuda Conference's recommendations. Their deliberations, partly touching on the future of Palestine, did not reach the point of consensus, let alone action, and their subordinates continued to delay creation of two refugee camps in North Africa until 1944.[43]

Cox concluded that a new organization might well help save more Jews from Nazi executioners. On June 16, Cox discussed his ideas with Treasury Secretary Henry Morgenthau Jr., afterward sending over a rough draft of his plan for a committee of outstanding figures whose work would supplement that of the State Department. The committee would solicit private contributions for the relief and resettlement of all war refugees. It could consult the Treasury, the Lend-Lease Administration, and the State Department, and the Lend-Lease administration might also appropriate some of own its funds. In early July, Cox checked with one of Morgenthau's aides, attorney Charles Kades, to see if the secretary had acted on his idea, which he had not. It turned out that Kades had advised Morgenthau against getting the Treasury involved in the "delicate" refugee problem.[44] One needed element was the support of Under Secretary Sumner Welles.[45]

Hated by Secretary of State Hull and vulnerable because of an attempted homosexual episode on a train, Welles finally submitted his resignation on August 16. Berle called his ouster a tragedy of Greek proportions.[46] Welles's departure gave conservative elements in the State Department greater leverage. Hull himself was frequently in poor health and not in firm control of the State Department bureaucracy. Roosevelt appointed Edward R. Stettinius, Cox's superior and by this time a close family friend of the Coxes, as under secretary.[47] Stettinius knew little of immigration and refugee policy, but Cox helped him get up to speed.

State Department officials in the Visa Division and the Division of European Affairs felt so defensive about criticism from Jewish organizations and liberal voices in the media that they resisted modest reforms and exaggerated what they had already accomplished for refugees. Assistant Secretary Long ultimately carried this misdirection to an extreme point that became obvious to much of Washington.[48]

Another controversy arose over the government's blocking of private aid to keep Jews alive in Europe. In addition to the World Jewish Congress proposal for relief in Romania and France, the same organization wanted to induce Romanian officials into allowing Jews to escape or emigrate. After Romanian losses at Stalingrad and the turn in the war toward the Allies generally, the Romanian government was no longer eager to collaborate with Germany's policy of extermination. The WJC envisioned a work-around with funding of aid: find local, wealthy Jews to supply financing, then reimburse the lenders with money deposited in accounts blocked until war's end.[49] In mid-July, Treasury official John Pehle decided that humanitarian considerations justified funds for emigration, too; by the end of July, Pehle and General Counsel Randolph Paul, two of Morgenthau's top subordinates, supported funds for both emigration and relief. Paul summarized his interaction with the State Department, noting internal disagreement at the State Department but concluding that Treasury ought to go ahead.[50]

Even after Morgenthau got Hull to endorse aid via blocked accounts, the State Department bureaucracy held up a license for the World Jewish Congress.[51] Thus began a months-long battle between the Treasury Department and the dominant forces in the State Department over the use of private funds for the relief and rescue of Jews in Europe. The State Department faction was led by Assistant Secretary Long and backed by the foreign service officer group.[52]

By September, even Berle, who had months earlier defended the policy of just winning the war, now thought that private humanitarian measures would not do much harm: ". . . the blockade has now reached a point at which it probably hurts our friends almost as much as it hurts our enemies. . . ."[53] But the opponents of humanitarian measures had a powerful weapon in bureaucratic delay.

Revisionist Zionist Hillel Kook, who had assumed the name Peter Bergson after coming from Palestine to the United States, had founded an organization called the Emergency Committee to Save the Jewish People of Europe, which arranged splashy publicity and public events, including a pageant written by Ben Hecht called "We Will Never Die." Bergson and the Hecht pageant managed to impress Eleanor Roosevelt. When she passed Bergson's suggestion for a government rescue agency to her husband in mid-August, he indicated that no reply to Bergson was necessary. In September, Pierre van Paassen, another official of the Bergson group, sent the president a long letter urging him to warn Balkan nations against cooperation with German deportations of Jews. He also recommended establishing a new rescue organization, an idea not far removed from what Cox had suggested earlier.[54]

As a Washington insider, Cox did not work openly with Bergson, but he agreed with some of Bergson's goals, and it appears that he at least tacitly approved Bergson's methods. On October 5, Bergson's Emergency Committee published a full-page ad in the *New York Times* entitled "A Report of Failure and a Call to Action." It declared that Allied governments had failed and that it was time for mass action to stop the slaughter and alleviate the torment of five million Jews. The committee appealed to readers to sign their petition and to contribute funds. Bergson sent a copy of this ad to Cox, who responded with thanks and a vague statement that he would do what he could along the lines suggested.[55] For Cox and the Bergson group, public pressure was a potential weapon to budge the bureaucrats and the politicians. They both regarded the State Department as an obstacle, and Cox could not yet tell whether Stettinius would be willing or able to overcome department opposition.

On October 6, more than four hundred "somberly clad" rabbis, organized by the Bergson group and the Orthodox rescue organization Vaad ha-Hatzala, marched to the steps of the Capitol. They delivered a petition to Vice President Henry Wallace calling for the creation of an intergovernmental agency to save "the remnants of Israel" in Europe. The petition called for practical measures such as the immediate entry of Jews into the United States and the United Nations and opening Palestine to Jewish immigrants. Speaker of the House Sam Rayburn and Senate Majority Leader Barkley, accompanied by a handful of other legislators, stood with Wallace to receive the respectful contingent. The vice president said he shared their grief and that "we must work and fight and pray for victory."[56]

Bergson and World Jewish Congress leaders, from different political and ideological backgrounds, had also clashed repeatedly over political tactics in the United States.[57] This stormy history, combined with the extreme caution of White House adviser Samuel Rosenman, probably influenced the president to duck a meeting with the rabbis. Rosenman told Roosevelt that he had "tried to stop the horde from storming Washington" and that the group "did not represent the most thoughtful elements in Jewry."⁵⁸ (This was hyperbole.) Rosenman was hypersensitive to any publicity that might allow enemies of the administration at home and abroad to ignite antisemitic passions. He was aware that some Republican opponents of the administration would likely attack Roosevelt's connections with Jews, particularly during the presidential campaign in 1944. Rosenman reinforced FDR's own reluctance to single out Jewish victims or to get caught up in Jewish organizational disputes.

A week after the rabbis' demonstration, Cox sent Stettinius a revised proposal to establish a new refugee committee to rescue victims from Axis territory, establish safe havens, and raise funds. The committee would coordinate its work with the State Department and the Foreign Economic Administration and seek cooperation with other federal agencies as needed.⁵⁹

Stettinius requested background information on refugee problems, and Reams wrote a long summary of policies toward refugees, concluding that Jewish organizations were pushing unwise, extreme measures. Reams told Stettinius that critics of the State Department inside and outside Congress were either ill-informed or irresponsible. He also claimed that since 1933 the United States had admitted a very large number of refugees for permanent residence: "It is believed that the number of such persons . . . amounts to over a half million." Reams betrayed his own leanings when he wrote: "While in theory any approach to the German Government would have met with a blank[et] refusal [to release Jews], there was always the danger that the German Government might agree to turn over to the United States and to Great Britain a large number of Jewish refugees . . . for immediate transportation to areas under the control of the United Nations [i.e., the Allies]."⁶⁰

In one of his October discussions with FDR, Stettinius raised Cox's idea. Roosevelt was aware of a growing chorus of criticism that the United States should do more to intervene on behalf of persecuted Jews. He said that idea was fine, but that he (Stettinius) should talk to Hull first.[61] Cox later recounted: "Stettinius did talk to Hull, and Long was brought in, and the argument that was given to him was that it [setting up a new refugee organization] would cut across the other international committees and upset the report of the Bermuda Conference, and so forth, and Stettinius did not know enough about the technical stuff to say that it wasn't true at all."[62]

During a November meeting with key subordinates, Stettinius disclosed the president's belief that the government could do more to assist Jews in Europe. FDR had mentioned setting up refugee assistance posts in Algiers, Naples, Madrid, Portugal, and Ankara, as well as an additional camp in North Africa; he thought funds could be appropriated for this purpose. Ray Atherton of the European Division objected, and Stettinius asked Long to discuss details with Hull.[63] Days later, the president left the country for a summit meeting with Churchill and Stalin at Tehran. He was gone for about a month.

Despite the resistance within the State Department, on November 19, Stettinius telephoned Cox that he had made progress with the president on refugee matters and that FDR had agreed in principle to have refugee camps set up in neutral countries. Cox informed Ben Cohen of the president's views.[64] But when Stettinius asked Hull to issue a statement on refugees, the proposed draft was more limited than Cox expected, and Hull decided against making any statement.[65]

Meanwhile, Bergson's supporters in Congress, led by Senator Guy Gillette and Representative Will Rogers Jr., introduced similar resolutions in the House and Senate recommending the establishment of a commission of diplomatic, economic, and military experts to work out plans to save surviving Jews from the Nazis. In a closed session on November 26, Long testified against this Gillette-Rogers resolution before the House Foreign

Affairs Committee. Purportedly, Long could not speak publicly because it would give the Nazis confidential information. Saying that the resolution would repudiate all the fine work done by the State Department and the Intergovernmental Committee on Refugees, he claimed that the United States had admitted 580,000 refugees since 1933. This number expanded even the fanciful estimates made previously by Reams. Although limitations in the data make the exact number of Jewish refugees admitted to the United States hard to calculate,[66] Long's total was inflated by at least 250 percent. He and subordinates in the Visa Division had simply taken the number of visas issued by every US consul in Europe to anyone, not all of which were used or issued to refugees.

Long also told Stettinius's assistant that as a belligerent in the war, the United States should not open offices for refugees anywhere. If it did, Germany might react so strongly that no refugees would be able to escape Axis territory. The proper vehicle for refugee assistance was the Intergovernmental Committee on Refugees, Long said, though he did not mention that it had been mostly dormant for the last couple of years.[67] In short, State Department officials simultaneously opposed US initiatives because Germany might release a flood of refugees and because it might allow none to escape. They posed these contradictory excuses for inaction even though the president had suggested that it was time to take some positive steps.

On December 10, the House Foreign Affairs committee made Long's testimony public to justify its refusal to approve the Gillette-Rogers resolution. Within days, immigration experts shredded Long's data, and Representative Emanuel Celler called for his resignation.[68]

State Department officials continued to stall the issuance of a license to the World Jewish Congress for expenditures to evacuate Jews from Romania and France. After Treasury officials complained about the delay, Secretary Hull signed a memo that thrust responsibility for inaction on Treasury itself. When Treasury officials tried to use US ambassador to the UK John Winant to clear away British opposition to private relief inside Axis territories, Winant wrote back that "the British Foreign Office are concerned with the difficulties of disposing of any considerable numbers of Jews should they be rescued from enemy occupied territory. . . . For this reason they are reluctant to agree to . . . even the preliminary financial arrangements." (They feared that Jews evacuated from Romania would end up going to Palestine, which they did not want.) This shocking statement angered the Treasury staff, making them determined to get action. Morgenthau asked them to apprise Cox of the situation because he could bring the problem to Stettinius. They gave Cox copies of the key documents. Morgenthau then called for an appointment with Hull to thrash out the disagreements among department heads.[69]

On December 16, Stettinius told Hull and Long that the State Department should go along with licensing private relief and rescue funds and with finding asylums for refugees. By the time Morgenthau met with Hull on December 20, Hull had disowned the previous months of State Department obstruction and professed astonishment at British policy as well. When Long tried to blame another State Department official for the delay, suggesting he was antisemitic, Morgenthau riposted that a number of people thought Long himself was antisemitic! Although the Treasury staff and Morgenthau celebrated Hull's about-face as a major victory, they knew that the secretary did not control his bureaucracy. They agreed that a new US refugee organization was still needed. Cox quickly drafted an executive order to establish one and suggested a press release as well. He advised that such action would likely forestall any congressional decision on the Gillette-Rogers resolutions. The congressional resolutions lacked teeth and might not pass, but debate in Congress could embarrass the administration.

By this time, Cox had become general counsel of the Foreign Economic Administration (FEA), which included the Lend-Lease Administration. He called for a high-level supervisory board on refugees, consisting of Morgenthau, Hull or Stettinius (with Stettinius likely to stand in for Hull), and Leo Crowley, the head of FEA. That combination would have permitted an activist approach by a new refugee agency. The Treasury staff and Cox stressed the need for the US government to induce neutral countries to take in refugees on a temporary basis. Cox commented:

> There isn't any question that the German policy has been clearly one of extermination of the Jews, complete and final, and we have talked to people from the Polish underground [i.e., Karski] who also, incidentally, have talked to the President about that first-hand observation. . . . Unless you get effective action in all the countries bordering occupied Europe, a good many of these people are turned back and being turned back means certain death as far as the Germans are concerned. . . . The fact that the job can be done was indicated by the Swedish action on the persecution of Jews in Denmark. . . .

If the US government spoke out in favor of saving the Jews, it might influence other neutrals to give escapees asylum, as Sweden had just done with Danish Jews. Then, the new organization would need to place competent and dedicated people in the key neutral countries. Cox said that the basic idea of setting up a board had already been discussed with the president, who approved it. He thought it would be politically inadvisable to let the Gillette-Rogers resolutions reach the floor of the House or

Senate because key backers were enemies of the administration. Presidential action would forestall that. Ansel Luxford of the Treasury staff summarized: "Oscar has a whale of a good plan, but he has to have an excuse to get it to the President. We [in Treasury] have the excuse to get it to the President . . . The British have taken a dogmatic attitude that we can't solve any of these problems. There is where you marry them."[70]

During the next few weeks, Treasury officials gathered all the documentary evidence of the State Department's suppression of information about the Holocaust and prepared a detailed report to the president. Josiah DuBois Jr. and Ansel Luxford managed to acquire the critical documents from State Department files, and DuBois wrote much of the first draft of the report. Although he wanted to title it "Report to the President on the Acquiescence of this Government in the Murder of the Jews," Morgenthau changed the inflammatory tone to "Personal Report to the President." Even so, the opening paragraph charged that one of the greatest crimes in history was continuing unabated. Moreover, the document laid clear blame on "certain officials in our State Department . . . [who have failed] to take any effective action to prevent the extermination of the Jews in German-controlled Europe."[71]

In the meantime, the State Department bureaucrats tried a new gambit, proposing a three-person internal committee headed by Howard Travers, head of the Visa Division—the section that had obstructed most action on refugees over the past years.[72] This nominal organizational reform would have preserved the State Department's control over policy.

Cox and Cohen, invited to serve as outside advisers to the Treasury, attended the final strategy session at the Treasury on Saturday, January 15. At the start, Morgenthau addressed Cox: "Your record is good on this." Cox, responded simply, "Yes, it isn't bad." Luxford started to read the report aloud, but his voice was weak, so Pehle stepped in to do the job. After considerable discussion, Morgenthau decided that it was time to go directly to FDR. He ended up taking Pehle and Randolph Paul with him to meet with the president the next day. They gathered in the same second-floor office next to the president's bedroom where FDR had met with Karski and Ciechanowski almost six months earlier.[73]

Armed with the staff's memorandum and an executive order drafted by Cox, Morgenthau told the president that he wanted to reveal the most shocking thing he had seen since he came to Washington. He asked Pehle to discuss the State Department's suppression of information regarding the Holocaust and State's attempted cover-up. Pehle reviewed the evidence in some detail, having rehearsed his presentation a day earlier. The president needed no convincing. He must have heard about problems with the State Department earlier in discussions with Stettinius, and he must have known of Cox's suggestion for a new refugee organization. Roosevelt did defend his old crony Breckinridge Long from charges of obstruction, but he admitted that Long had soured on refugees after the FBI had found some spies among them. Morgenthau undercut that excuse, noting that the FBI had discovered only three such cases during the entire war. And after Long's blunder with the data on refugees reached the public, his days were numbered. A State Department reorganization enacted a few days later transferred Long to the handling of congressional relations.[74]

The president read and approved the draft executive order with one change. He wanted Secretary of War Henry Stimson to replace FEA chief Leo Crowley on the supervisory board. Cox's boss Crowley was quite liberal, whereas Stimson was a prominent Republican who agreed with FDR's foreign policy. Stimson would also be useful in scrutinizing any proposals that might have adverse effects on the battlefield. It was a step consistent

with Roosevelt's earlier handling of Jewish issues: he preferred
to have at least the appearance of bipartisan support. He never
read or kept a copy of the Treasury staff's memorandum, "Report to the President." The meeting was an anticlimax, but also
a clear victory for the Treasury and for Cox.[75]

Through the fall of 1943, the Allies lacked effective military
reach and means to interfere with the killing of Jews beyond
what occurred as a natural byproduct of an effective military
strategy, as in North Africa. Despite occasionally denouncing
Nazi Germany's killing of Jews or atrocities in general, none of
the big three powers had found the will and the imagination to
devise nonmilitary remedies to mitigate the Holocaust. None of
the Allies, for example, was willing to offer to reimburse neutral
Sweden, Switzerland, or Turkey for sheltering escaping Jews,
and at war's end, pledge to resettle the refugees to new homes.[76]

Cox perceived the change in the balance of military power
and its repercussions for humanitarian action earlier than most.
He was unusually flexible in pursuing his goals, working at
times with the Treasury, Stettinius, and the Treasury again.
Morgenthau recognized his ability and judgment, inviting him
into Treasury staff meetings and listening carefully to his comments. It took time to convince Roosevelt to undertake a special
effort against the Nazi war against the Jews amidst the general
war effort. From late July 1943 until January 1944, Karski, Cox,
and the Treasury group all played critical roles in guiding him in
a fruitful direction.

On January 17, 1944, having learned of FDR's approval of a
War Refugee Board, Cox wrote to Morgenthau: "Thousands
upon thousands will have the cruel hand of suffering and death
lifted from them by what you have done. To feel with . . . [those]
humans whom you haven't seen in the lands of persecution is
one of the marks of your human depth and human greatness.
Deep in my heart I am warmed. . . ."[77]

The Treasury staff and Cox recognized that Allied military successes could translate into greater influence with neutral countries and perhaps even with some Nazi satellites. During the last phase of the war there might be new opportunities to save thousands, perhaps hundreds of thousands of surviving Jews provided that a capable, committed organization assumed the task with resources and people in place. Too many State Department officials, however, regarded this opportunity and those who wanted to seize it as at best a nuisance and at worst a positive danger for the country. That is why various groups and individuals pressed for a "new deal" in refugee policy. The War Refugee Board approved by the president was close enough.

CHAPTER SEVEN

FDR'S PRESS CONFERENCE AND HUNGARY

J ohn Pehle and his War Refugee Board staff first sought safe havens for Jews in Europe. On January 26, 1944, Pehle told Morgenthau that Jews hiding in occupied Poland near the borders of Slovakia and Hungary might be smuggled into Hungary. That was probably the right initial project to pursue, he said; it might save thousands of lives.[1] Assistant Secretary Adolf Berle, too, believed that the "outstanding place of safety today for the Jews in Europe" was Hungary. The State Department, with refugee matters now in Berle's hands, was willing to cooperate with board efforts to move Jews from Poland and Czechoslovak territory into Hungary.[2]

Nearly two months later, however, Hitler ordered the German occupation of Hungary, putting 760,000–780,000 Hungarian Jews and Jewish refugees within Germany's grasp and forcing the board to try to protect Jews in Hungary.[3] That required good information about German-Hungarian collaboration. At his press conference on March 24, 1944, President Roosevelt called attention to the new German threat to Hungarian Jews as part of the Nazi campaign to destroy the Jews of Europe in an unusual statement he read and gave to the press. It reached the American public and the world through prominent articles by the White House press corps and government broadcasts overseas.

Roosevelt's move occurred amidst behind-the-scenes controversy about whether to threaten or appeal to government officials and the public in Axis countries to save the remaining Jews. The War Refugee Board did not have an easy time dealing with the British Foreign Office or the US Office of War Information on what they called psychological warfare. Those advocating humanitarian efforts clashed with officials who claimed to understand what was best to win the war expeditiously.

BACKGROUND TO THE GERMAN OCCUPATION OF HUNGARY

During the war, Hungary's governments had persecuted Hungarian Jews, but in 1943 Prime Minister Miklos Kállay told Nazi officials that further steps against the Jews would jeopardize war production. He ignored Germany's repeated requests to seize Hungarian Jews. Hitler had pragmatic reasons not to challenge the Hungarian government.[4] Hungarian troops fought alongside German forces in the war against the Soviets, and the output of Hungarian factories and farms benefited the German economy. So, Hungary, a predominantly Catholic country, was the last Axis satellite with a large Jewish population.

In January 1943, the Hungarian expeditionary force under German command suffered a catastrophic defeat at Voronezh in southwestern Russia. Weeks later, some 120,000 Hungarian soldiers were killed, wounded, or captured in the battle of Stalingrad. Afterward, Kállay sought to extricate Hungary from a war that no longer served its interests. The Hungarian government publicly signaled its dissatisfaction with Germany by recognizing Italy's new Badoglio government after Mussolini was overthrown in late July.[5]

Hungary also engaged in secret contacts with the West. Hungarian officials talked with British Special Operations Executive agents in Istanbul as early as March 1943. Then, through intermediaries, the Hungarian General Staff managed to reach US representatives in Istanbul. In early 1944, the Hungarian minister in Stockholm started discussions with an Office of Strategic Services official and a US diplomat. The Hungarian diplomat, claiming to be carrying out the instructions of the prime minister and foreign minister, hoped that they could conduct secret talks with the Western Allies without antagonizing Germany and provoking a German occupation. Hungary would not surrender until Anglo-American troops were near enough to liberate the country, he said.[6] This unrealistic strategy assumed that British and US forces would open a second front in the Balkans, a proposition that Churchill had pushed at times.[7] It also counted on Britain and the United States rescuing Hungary from a Soviet occupation, which Hungarian elites feared above all else.

One of the Hungarians involved in exchanges with the British in Istanbul may have been a German agent. In addition, an Istanbul intelligence network codenamed Dogwood, which worked under the OSS, discussed some details of the Hungarian-US contacts, and "Dogwood" contained at least one German double agent.[8] Germany began to prepare for a Hungarian double-cross.

In late January 1944, the Hungarian government demanded the withdrawal of Hungarian troops from German-occupied Ukraine, supposedly to defend the Hungarian border at the Carpathian Mountains. The chief of the Hungarian general staff, on behalf of Prime Minister Kállay and Regent Miklós Horthy, raised this withdrawal with Hitler on January 24, 1944.

Horthy followed up with a letter to Hitler a few weeks later that infuriated the German dictator, who could no longer blame Hungary's disloyalty exclusively on Kállay. After other secret talks with Hungarians in Switzerland, the United States decided to send a small team to Budapest to discuss the details of Hungary's surrender.[9]

Hitler then decided to occupy the country and, in the process, solve Hungary's "Jewish question." Once again, Hitler demonstrated his belief that the Axis war against the Allies and the war against the Jews were tightly linked. In his March 12, 1944, order to all German army commanders and to Himmler, Hitler declared that the destructive influence of Jews in Hungary and the Kállay government's betrayal of Germany justified a "restricted occupation" of Hungary. SS units would accompany German army and Luftwaffe units into the country.[10] Hitler's move was codenamed Operation Margarethe I.

Historian Randolph L. Braham criticizes Kállay for his foolhardy foreign policy. He encouraged the British and Americans, attempted to avoid a Soviet occupation, and failed to take precautions against a German move into Hungary.[11] That last omission became all the more damaging when Horthy and the chief of the Hungarian general staff left the country to meet with Hitler, allegedly to discuss the withdrawal of Hungarian troops from Ukraine.

Meeting at a palace near Salzburg (Schloss Klessheim) while German forces were quietly deployed on Hungary's border, Hitler declared that Germany was about to occupy Hungary. He cited his duty to the German people to prevent Hungary from following Italy's treachery. Horthy was unable to extract any concessions, although Hitler said that German troops would withdraw from Hungary once an acceptable Hungarian government was in place. By the time Horthy and three accompanying high Hungarian government officials returned to Budapest on the morning of March 19, German troops had taken control. The Hungarian army did not resist, and Horthy chose to accept the situation. The American negotiating team, which had parachuted into Hungary, was quickly arrested.[12] In light of Ukraine's ability to ward off a Russian invasion in 2022, it is tempting to speculate on what would have happened if Horthy and the Hungarian military had chosen to fight the Germans at a time when they were increasingly stretched. But most Hungarians viewed the Germans as better than the Soviets.[13]

At an emergency meeting of the Crown Council in Budapest, Horthy reported that he had tried to deter a German occupation, which, he feared, would provoke Anglo-American bombing raids on Hungarian factories. The regent then stated that he intended to stay in office to prevent a pro-Nazi government of Hungarian radicals that might allow German forces to absorb the Hungarian army and carry out the murder of Hungarian patriots. He did not reveal that he had submitted to the Führer's demand to supply Germany with a considerable number of Jewish workers, initially set at 100,000, allegedly to be used for German war production.[14] He did not regard *them* as Hungarian patriots. An Einsatzkommando of some 500–600 men that included Adolf Eichmann's team of deportation experts had already moved into Hungary as well.[15]

ALLIED PSYCHOLOGICAL WARFARE

The Allies viewed Hungary as having limited strategic importance, and Allied military options to respond to Germany's move were impractical. Soviet troops were on the border of Bessarabia, more than four hundred miles away. Use of British or American bombers against Hungary was delayed because of initial uncertainties: Was Hungary still a collaborator or a victim of German aggression? Could the Allies stimulate anti-German sentiment among Hungarians?

Britain *was* prepared for psychological warfare through radio; British planning of radio broadcasts for Hungary had begun in early 1942. The British Political Warfare Executive (PWE), which controlled BBC broadcasts to Hungary, had developed a plan for Hungary after consulting Oxford professor Carlisle Aylmer Macartney, Britain's foremost academic expert on Hungary. BBC broadcasts aimed to reduce Hungary's military effort to assist Germany, to reduce food and other supplies to Germany, to impede German communications through Hungary, and eventually, to compel Germany to divert troops into Hungary to guard against Hungarian resistance or to occupy the country. The PWE regarded a German occupation of Hungary as a positive development because it would draw German troops away from Western Europe, facilitating the planned Anglo-American invasion in France. Macartney also warned that British broadcasts should never associate its cause in Hungary with large, landed interests, big business, liberalism, democracy, Jews in general, internationalism, communism, or Bolshevism. He specified, "We should not mention the Jews at all except to say that on the one hand we want a national Hungary, on the other hand, a tolerant Hungary—[we should] appeal to Hungary's traditions real or imagined." Macartney wrote the Hungarian sections of the British Weekly Political Intelligence Summary, prepared by the Foreign Office Research Department and distributed to British intelligence, British embassies, and senior figures in government, including the prime minister, king, and queen, but not to a wider audience. The PWE's directives also were sent to the OWI to help coordinate British and American propaganda.[16]

The British Special Operations Executive (SOE) showed more sympathy for left-wing elements in Hungary than Macartney did, but a March 1943 update of SOE policy suggested that right-wing figures were more likely to bring about major political disruption in Hungary timed to coincide with an Allied landing on the continent. The British government "no longer fears a German occupation [of Hungary] which would be a positive advantage by increasing the commitments of the German Army."[17] The net effect of British policy was to welcome a German occupation of Hungary and to avoid any warning to Hungary's Jews.

The United States faced handicaps in trying to use shortwave radio broadcasts to deter Nazi and Axis killing of Jews in Eastern Europe. The Office of War Information had established the Voice of America in February 1942, but it struggled to capture large European audiences. Many Europeans viewed the Voice of America as subordinate or inferior to the long-established BBC. In one self-study, the Voice estimated that it reached about 10 percent of French listeners, whereas about 90 percent tuned in the BBC.[18] There is no reason to believe that this disparity was lower in Eastern Europe.

In 1943, there were 822,000 licensed radios in Hungary, the large majority of which could receive Allied broadcasts, in a country with a population of more than 9.4 million, which included some territory annexed since the end of 1938. A Hungarian government survey indicated that nearly half of radio listeners (43.7 percent) tuned in foreign broadcasts.[19] Hungarian shortwave listeners revered the BBC, which they referred to as "Auntie," as in the saying, "Auntie knows best." One Hungarian Jewish survivor later described BBC broadcasts as "a ray of light piercing the darkness around us."[20]

The Voice initially tried to spread American ideals, essentially offering Europeans New Deal principles. But such propaganda sometimes clashed with American military and diplomatic decisions made on pragmatic grounds. After a number of cases where the Voice broadcasts criticized US decisions, Roosevelt fired or arranged the transfer of high OWI officials. Thereafter, OWI and the Voice of America kept their messaging more closely aligned with US foreign policy. By early 1944, they generally consulted and followed the State Department and the military. In the words of a historian of the Voice of America, for these agencies "what made good propaganda was whatever supported and extended military victory."[21]

Individuals inside and outside OWI occasionally raised the idea of using radio propaganda to "threaten or wheedle German and German-satellite anti-Semites into adopting a milder treatment of the Jews or ceasing the persecution altogether." According to State Department official Robert Pell, OWI's psychological experts rejected such proposals some half a dozen times over two years.[22] Meanwhile, the Moscow Conference in October-November 1943, attended by the Allied foreign ministers, released a statement on atrocities that listed countries where the Nazis had committed atrocities but failed to mention Jews as victims anywhere. These practices conformed to the well-established Anglo-American view that Nazi Propaganda Minister Goebbels would exploit Allied references to the Jews by citing them as proof that the Allies were fighting on behalf of international Jewry.

The World Jewish Congress called for the release of a new Allied statement denouncing Nazi atrocities, one that specifically mentioned the mass killing of Jews. Allied military progress since 1943 raised World Jewish Congress hopes that a specific new warning might significantly deter collaboration by satellite countries with Germany. But the British Foreign Office, contacting the State Department in early 1944, discouraged such a statement, partly on the grounds that the December 1942 Allied statement had not done any good, and that a new one might raise unrealistic expectations. One communication London sent to the British Embassy in Washington suggested that the United States might be tempted to issue such a statement during an election year. Therefore, His Majesty's Government wanted to learn whether the United States would grant the World Jewish Congress request. Pehle called this document as "pretty nasty" because it implied that politics was the primary US motive behind any action dealing with the mass killings of Jews.[23]

Pehle and DuBois decided to challenge the British Foreign Office and, in the process, speak through a megaphone to Nazi satellites. They drafted a sharp statement for the president: "One of the blackest crimes in history, the systematic murder of the Jews of Europe, continues unabated. . . . [We are determined] that none who participate in such acts of savagery shall go unpunished. . . . All who knowingly take part in the deportation of Jews to their death in Poland are equally guilty with the executioner." The draft also threatened postwar punishment of war criminals, which went well beyond the board's mandate and its ability to deliver.[24]

The board also pressured the Office of War Information to cooperate in spreading a message along these lines. In late February, a board representative informed the OWI that they must include strong warnings in US broadcasts to the Axis and satellite countries on their treatment of the Jews, allotting time on all broadcasts, except those to the Soviet Union. According to State Department official Robert Pell, OWI experts on psychological warfare, including some who were Jewish, felt that this step was unwise. The Voice of America included such warnings in all broadcasts during the week of February 24 to March 2. On March 6, Pell wrote that the Voice proposed to taper off this campaign. If they continued these warnings, Pell warned, they would endanger the wartime alliance: "The British have indicated that they will not go along with this propaganda. The Russians have always kept off it. The Germans will exploit the

'divided front.'"[25] Pell surely exaggerated the danger that the
Nazis could exploit a divided front. But the War Refugee Board's
very new priority of saving Jews and other victims of persecution did threaten to create problems with the British.

On March 3, top officials of the Intergovernmental Committee on Refugees (IGCR) joined Pehle and DuBois for a
meeting with Stettinius and several other high State Department officials. Myron Taylor called on the board to consult
the IGCR before it acted and warned against activism that
made "the whole government sore." Pell, who had traveled to
Berlin in early 1939 on behalf of the IGCR, recalled German-
Jewish leaders pleading with him not to call attention to Nazi
persecution for fear of making things worse. Surely, he argued, Jews would still not want the Allies to stress their suffering. Pell did not recognize that those German-Jewish
leaders and most of their constituents were by now dead (or
in some cases, in the concentration camp at Theresienstadt);
he still believed that such propaganda might "boomerang."
He cited as an example US criticism of Germany after
Kristallnacht: in retaliation, he claimed, the radical Nazi element took over, destroyed Jewish property, and killed thousands of Jews, he wrote.[26] Pell overlooked the facts that Hitler
was the foremost radical, that Nazi killing of about one hundred Jews occurred during Kristallnacht, not after US criticism of it, and that thousands of Jews were gassed each day at
Birkenau in 1944. Pell invented facts and cause-and-effect
relationships to underscore his view that silence was the best
policy.

British officials likely encouraged the IGCR to challenge the
board. According to historian Louise London, officials in the
Refugee Department of the Foreign Office viewed the board as a
rival and tried to "cut it down to size." They recommended that
British ambassadors merely make a show of cooperation with

the board, and they "showed partisan protectiveness" toward the IGCR.[27]

EDITING MATTERS

The War Refugee Board's draft declaration for the president cleared initial hurdles. Morgenthau approved it, Stimson suggested a few edits, and Stettinius okayed it, too. Morgenthau asked Stettinius to deliver it to the White House. The under secretary agreed to give it to White House adviser Sam Rosenman, but Morgenthau hinted that Rosenman was too cautious on this subject and that some other route was better.[28] Stettinius ended up taking it to White House Press Secretary Steven Early. Still, in a postscript to his cover letter, Stettinius added, "We in the State Department feel that in issuing this statement the President is taking a very important step and we hope he will have an opportunity to study it with great care."[29] This comment shone a flashing yellow light on the text.

After meeting with the president on March 8, Stettinius wrote a key memorandum for Early, explaining that the president thought the title inflated—he wanted a statement, not a declaration—and that the content seemed overly centered on the Jews. Moreover, a redrafted statement would have to be cleared with the British, Stettinius wrote.[30] Then he called Morgenthau to tell him that Rosenman and Early would produce a revised draft. The White House intended merely to inform the British, not to give them the opportunity to block it.[31]

Pehle protested: the whole point of it was to highlight Nazi policy to exterminate the Jews. After listening to Rosenman's objections, Pehle concluded that Rosenman had advised FDR to dilute the board's draft because Rosenman feared that it would stir up antisemitism in the United States; some Americans might conclude that the United States was fighting the war on behalf of the Jews. Rosenman may have been thinking ahead to the November presidential election. Pehle believed Stettinius when he claimed that he had tried and failed to get the president to accept the board's draft.[32] Perhaps so, but Stettinius had some reservations, too.

Pehle then met with Secretary of War Stimson, who looked at Rosenman's redraft and found it better than the board version. Morgenthau found the second draft acceptable, much better than nothing, and Pehle reluctantly came around to that view. On the morning of March 9, Rosenman gave the president the second draft for him to present at a press conference. Then, after a flurry of activity over several days, nothing happened. Morgenthau and Pehle feared that FDR might not release any such statement.[33] Historian Rebecca Erbelding suggests that the document was simply mislaid until Morgenthau persisted in asking Rosenman about it. After being prodded, Rosenman found it in FDR's bedroom.[34]

One key step was still lacking. Both the State Department and the president wanted to alert Britain. A State Department official wrote so on March 7, FDR told Stettinius so on March 8, and when Morgenthau finally got in to see Roosevelt on March 18, the president repeated the need to send it to London.[35] Roosevelt likely wanted to give Churchill or Eden the opportunity to draft their own related statement or to prepare an explanation for not doing so. This would avoid straining the wartime alliance about which Pell had warned.

But no one had given Early the draft to send to London. In retrospect, it looks like Rosenman's responsibility, but he saw no need to rush FDR's statement. He told Morgenthau on March 10 that if the president did not release the statement at his press conference later that day, which would have been before notifying the British, "the question arises in my mind . . . why it should be issued just now and whether it shouldn't be tied up with some event."[36] It looks as if Rosenman let it sit for a few days.

PALESTINE COMPLICATIONS

A months-long battle in Congress over the Wright-Compton Resolution endorsing unrestricted Jewish immigration to Palestine and the ultimate establishment of a "free and democratic Jewish commonwealth" there overlapped with these events. Morgenthau told the president that he feared that this controversial measure in Congress would impede rescue of Jews in Europe: "I feel the thing is to get out the Jews [of Europe] and get the thirty thousand into Palestine, as permitted under the so-called White Paper, before we raise this whole question of [voiding] the White Paper." FDR responded, "I am so glad to hear you say that, Henry, because that is the way I feel."[37] Just over thirty thousand places remained for Jewish immigrants under the 1939 British White Paper policy, out of the maximum of seventy-five thousand. After that, under the 1939 policy, further Jewish immigration would require Arab consent, which seemed impossible.

A War Department official asked Pehle and the War Refugee Board not to adopt any public stance on the Palestine resolution in Congress. He said that Secretary Stimson was very concerned that "the Moslem world would start trouble behind our lines." Pehle agreed with the request even though opening Palestine for at least temporary refuge for Jews would have eased the board's work.[38]

Cincinnati Rabbi Abba Hillel Silver, an independent who leaned toward the Republicans, then accused the president of inspiring War Department testimony against the Wright-Compton Resolution in congressional hearings. In a White House meeting with Silver and Stephen Wise on March 9, FDR denied this, calling Silver's behavior reprehensible. But he authorized the two rabbis to state publicly his view that the United States had never endorsed the White Paper and that (because of the thirty thousand vacancies) he was happy that the doors of Palestine were open to Jewish refugees. It was roughly the formula Morgenthau and Roosevelt had agreed on a month earlier.[39]

The War Refugee Board managed to separate the rescue of Jews from the debate over the status of Palestine, but for the British, the escape of any substantial number of European Jews might burst the White Paper quota for Palestine. In the end, the Wright-Compton Resolution and its Senate counterpart were both tabled, thereby avoiding a potentially significant source of tension with the UK.

THE PRESS CONFERENCE

On March 20, Representative Noam M. Mason of Illinois, the ranking Republican on the House Immigration Committee, attacked the administration for creating the War Refugee Board. The president, he charged, had circumvented Congress, violated the Constitution, and opened a path for unrestricted immigration. He claimed that the administration had already allowed 600,000 European refugees to enter the country. He asked, "After the war, who should have first claim on the jobs available, our returned soldiers or several *million* refugees?" Mason used partisan political rhetoric and invented statistics. The same day, William Rosenwald, honorary president of the nongovernmental organization called the National Refugee Service, publicized a life-saving invention by a Jewish refugee and gave a reasonable estimate that 250,000 refugees of all faiths—the large majority Jewish—had come to the United States since 1933.[40]

On the morning of March 21, the *Washington Post* carried the news of the German occupation of Hungary on its front page. Secretary Hull, Assistant Secretary of War John J. Mc-Cloy, Morgenthau, and Pehle all attended a meeting of the War Refugee Board that morning, but none of them indicated that they had heard about the situation in Hungary.

Published information was still sketchy and unreliable. Hungary's leaders, according to an inaccurate Reuters report, were being held prisoner in the Reich, and Hungarian forces were supposedly resisting the Germans. Horthy was said to have rejected a German demand to use troops to resist the advance of Soviet troops in Bessarabia. These reports were based on pro-Hungarian sources, and their claims hardly squared with the AP article's lead, which was that Germany had taken over Hungary lock, stock, and barrel.[41] The article did not mention the threat to Jews in Hungary.

During the board meeting, Hull announced that the British had asked for two days to consider the president's proposed statement.[42] Pehle reported on the board's progress, and the members discussed a range of other issues, including a proposal to allow a small number of refugees into the United States on a temporary basis, which would be forwarded to the president.[43]

That same day, Gerhart Riegner in Geneva telegraphed his World Jewish Congress counterparts in London and New York to express extreme concern about the fate of Hungarian Jewry. He recommended a "worldwide appeal of Anglo-Saxon personalities [both] non-Jews and Jews, including chiefs of Protestant and Catholic churches, to the Hungarian people warning them not to allow application of the policy of extermination by the German butchers or Hungarian quislings. . . ."[44]

On March 22, Morgenthau informed one of the president's private secretaries that Roosevelt had a statement about refugees ready, but that he was waiting for the opportunity to tie it to a specific event. Now, the Germans had taken over Hungary, and a million Jews in Hungary and Romania might be killed. (There were rumors and stories that Germany might take over other Balkan states besides Hungary.) This was the right moment to release the statement, Morgenthau urged. But then he blundered by advocating a joint statement by Roosevelt, Churchill, and Stalin. It would have carried more weight than a presidential statement alone, but reaching agreement on a joint statement would have taken considerable time, and Stalin was unlikely to join in. Pehle also sent Rosenman some changes in the statement to address the German occupation of Hungary.[45]

Later, White House secretary Grace Tully told Morgenthau that FDR was planning to issue the board's prepared statement at his March 24 press conference; he was not going to wait (further) for the British or anyone else. Morgenthau recommended that he also announce John Pehle's appointment as director of the board. Pehle had been acting director, but he had done well and the board itself had just recommended the move. Tully agreed to pass his suggestion on to the president.[46]

Roosevelt chose to issue this statement on March 24 in part because he recognized the dangerous situation in Hungary and believed that the United States might have some leverage. There was likely a second reason: if he was going to highlight the board's work for the public, he wanted to do it soon, because he was not at all well. Between March 6 and March 23, the president saw his physician, Admiral Ross McIntyre, almost every day, except for several days when, under doctor's orders, he stayed in bed the whole day.[47] He had persistent flu complicated by bronchitis, but there were signs of deeper problems, too. He had headaches, abdominal pain, hand tremors, insomnia, and occasional difficulty breathing. When in mid-March, Churchill pressed him to schedule a major staff meeting in Bermuda in early April, Roosevelt declined on doctor's orders: "Ross decided a week ago that it is necessary for me to take a complete rest of about two to three weeks in a suitable climate, which I am definitely planning to do at the end of the month." He did not mention that, under Roosevelt family pressure, McIntyre had agreed to set up a secret physical exam by a Navy cardiologist at the [Bethesda] Naval Hospital before his trip. It took place a few days after his March 24 press conference. But since McIntyre later destroyed FDR's medical records, the extent of his heart and circulatory problems in March 1944 is unknown.[48] He was examined again in May by a team of physicians, and according to historian David Woolner, the two exams revealed that he was suffering from severe hypertension and the early stages of congestive heart failure.[49]

Even if FDR had wanted to give a radio broadcast on this topic—an unlikely option given Rosenman's views—the president was too ill to do so. He got through the press conference by resting beforehand and kept a light schedule afterward (he ate dinner in bed). He planned to decompress over the following weekend at Hyde Park.[50] Along with its report on the press conference, the AP carried a separate story that a head cold had confined the president to the residential quarters of the White House that week. During the press conference his "head cold" weakened his voice and distorted some words, according to the AP reporter.[51]

FDR did not permit recording of press conference discussions, and he declined to give copies of transcripts to Congress because that would have inhibited him from speaking freely and extemporaneously, as he preferred. He said that he did not have the time to prepare biweekly or weekly remarks intended for publication or broadcast.[52] Therefore, we cannot hear how he sounded.

Roosevelt often used press conferences to convey executive actions and to address the country with greater flexibility than other options such as a fireside chat.[53] The White House press corps constituted a favorable audience as well as a means of reaching a broad public. Later presidents, with the possible exception of John Kennedy, might have wondered at Roosevelt's ability throughout his entire twelve-year presidency to maintain mostly pleasant relations with the press corps and to be widely respected by them. Most of his regular twice-weekly press conferences were held in his office, where the president affected a free-and-easy style.[54] It was as if he played the supreme newspaperman doling out the leads and raw materials for stories to colleagues and entertaining everyone in the process. He did not require questions in advance, and he often made jokes or engaged in light exchanges. On March 17, 1944, for example, a reporter asked the president why geographer Isaiah Bowman had just accompanied Under Secretary Stettinius on a trip to London for official discussions. Roosevelt said that Bowman knew more about geography than anyone in this room, including himself. The reporter responded, "does that mean they are going to talk about territorial questions in London?" Roosevelt said, "no, but they might talk about bananas, and he knows where bananas grow." Laughter cut off any possibly awkward follow-ups; the other reporters knew to move on.[55]

At his March 24 press conference, Roosevelt first read a statement highlighting the tenth anniversary of the passage of the act promising independence to the Philippines. He declared to the people of the Philippines, currently suffering under brutal Japanese occupation, that the return of their freedom drew closer with each Allied victory. He promised that the United States would honor its pledge of future independence. This message was not a simple commemoration but a possible means to increase substantial Philippine resistance to the Japanese. Then the president announced some personnel changes with good humor and appropriate recognition, in the process also recognizing the work of the Foreign Economic Administration.

Then he moved to what he called the "interdepartmental refugee committee," saying that he had prepared a statement about it last week and he was releasing it now; Press Secretary Early would distribute copies to the reporters. He declared that the United States was keeping in close touch with Churchill and Stalin, and that refugee work was done with their full knowledge and approval. He *had* given both the British and the Soviets an alert about the prepared statement, but there had been no responses yet.[56] As Morgenthau had suggested, the president also announced that he was appointing John Pehle as permanent director of the War Refugee Board, and he complimented it on getting some refugees out already. Then he began to read, with impromptu elaborations (here in italics):

The United Nations are fighting to make a world in which tyranny and aggression can not exist; a world based upon freedom, equality and justice; a world in which all persons regardless of race, color or creed may live in peace, honor and dignity.

[To the reporters] Some of you people who are wandering around asking the bellhop whether we have a foreign policy or not. I think that's a pretty good paragraph. We have a foreign policy. Some people may not know it, but we really have.

This sarcastic comment was a reference to some Republican congressmen who had just accused the Roosevelt administration of lacking a forceful and vigorous foreign policy, another attack line for the presidential campaign later that year.[57] Roosevelt continued:

In the meantime, in most of Europe and in parts of Asia the systematic torture and murder of civilians—men, women and children—by the Nazis and the Japanese [—] continue unabated. In areas subjugated by the aggressors innocent Poles and Czechs, Norwegians, Dutch, Danes, French, Greeks, Russians, Chinese, Filipinos—many others—are being starved or frozen to death or murdered in cold blood in a campaign of savagery.

Next, Roosevelt referred to the slaughters of Warsaw, Lidice, Kharkov, and Nanking, all names of places that the press had made symbols of Axis atrocities for many Americans. Warsaw could have covered both the German bombing of the Polish capital at the start of the war as well as the crushing of the Warsaw ghetto uprising. FDR added that the Japanese had tortured and murdered American soldiers as well as civilians. Then he read a modified version of the lead from the original War Refugee Board draft:

> In one of the blackest crimes of all history—begun by the Nazis in the day of peace and multiplied by them a hundred times in time of war—the wholesale systematic murder of the Jews of Europe goes on unabated every hour. As a result of the events of the last few days, hundreds of thousands of Jews, who while living under persecution have at least found a haven from death in Hungary and the Balkans, are now threatened with annihilation as Hitler's forces descend more heavily on those lands. That these innocent people, who have already survived a decade of Hitler's fury, should perish on the very eve of triumph over the barbarism which their persecution symbolizes, would be a major tragedy. It is therefore fitting that we should again proclaim our determination that none who participate in these acts of savagery shall go unpunished.

The president encouraged Germans and citizens of satellite countries to separate themselves from the criminal policies and behavior of high officials, and to keep records of the crimes of the perpetrators. He added:

In so far as the necessity of military operations permit[s], this Government will use all means at its command to aid the escape of all intended victims of the Nazi and Jap executioner— regardless of race or religion or color. We call upon the free peoples of Europe and Asia temporarily to open their frontiers to all victims of oppression. We shall find havens of refuge for them, and we shall find the means for their maintenance and support. . . .

When a reporter asked whether the United States planned to open itself up for refugees, Roosevelt mentioned the existing Allied refugee camps in North Africa but said that not enough people were getting out at present for the United States to take them: "No, not yet."[58] That was the sole question from reporters about the president's statement.

The War Refugee Board staff had wanted pinpoint focus on Nazi Germany's policy of exterminating Jews and a sharp warning to individuals and satellite countries not to collaborate with the Nazi effort. The president's revised statement was broader, but Roosevelt, with Morgenthau's and Pehle's assistance, inserted specific language on the vulnerable situation of Jews in Hungary. The president also offered a partly improvised statement that the War Refugee Board's efforts were consistent with broader American foreign policy goals, which was a way to make the American public understand and accept the board's work. In that sense, the statement on the Philippines and the statement on Nazi crimes, partly based on a kind of American idealism, were logically connected. FDR left no doubt that he stood behind the War Refugee Board, which gave it more weight in Washington. All in all, Roosevelt put his own stamp on a prepared board statement, took a shot at Republican critics of his foreign policy in a presidential election year, and related the general problem of Nazi genocide to a specific crisis facing Jews in Hungary in a way that the press and public could understand.

Historian Rebecca Erbelding notes that, in part because of the Hungarian issue, press coverage was much greater than expected. The *New York Times* carried a front-page story and printed the entire text of the statement on page four. It also carried Pehle's picture and called the presidential statement an unusual step.[59] The AP story, carried by many US newspapers, led the article with the threat to hundreds of thousands of Jews in the Balkans. Many foreign newspapers also reported the president's statement, recognizing that it was atypical for the head of an Allied government.[60] Moreover, Secretary Hull immediately reinforced the section on Hungary by urging Hungarians to resist the Germans: only by doing so could they "regain the respect and friendship of free nations and demonstrate . . . right to independence."[61] There were some drawbacks in beginning the presidential statement with broad rhetoric: the United Press story headlined the warning to war criminals and managed to avoid mentioning Jews even once. The *Washington Post* simply printed the text of the statement on page two without commentary.[62]

OWI headquarters in Washington quickly issued guidance to its Voice of America broadcast offices in New York and London, advising they should use this statement wherever it might reach the responsible officials of Germany, Japan, and their puppets. It added: "We should stress the appeals rather than the threats, and should highlight neither his reference to the Jewish problem nor his references to the problem of other refugees and sufferers." This instruction created confusion in New York, so an OWI official phoned additional color—play down threats, and play the Jewish problem and other refugees and sufferers with equal weight.[63]

At first, the BBC used the president's statement in broadcasts in all languages, including Hungarian.[64] Radio Moscow and Radio Kossuth, the latter a station operated by Hungarian communists in the USSR, called upon Hungarians to resist the Germans and told the Hungarian Jews to remain confident in their ultimate liberation. They paid little, if any, attention to Roosevelt's statement, and they did not comment on what the German occupation would mean for the Jews.[65]

On March 30, Sidney Silverman, MP, and president of the British section of the World Jewish Congress, asked the government in the House of Commons about anti-Jewish measures in Hungary. Foreign Minister Eden responded that persecution of Jews had been "of unexampled horror and intensity," and the Allies were determined to bring the perpetrators of these crimes to justice. He followed Roosevelt by appealing to countries collaborating with or subjugated to Nazi Germany not to participate in such crimes and, if possible, to protect and save the innocent.[66]

On March 31, the British Political Warfare Mission in Washington summarized official guidance for the BBC as follows:

H.M.G. [His Majesty's Government] associate themselves wholeheartedly with declaration issued by President of U.S., warning Germany and her satellites of consequences of further persecution in their territories and appeal to men of good will everywhere to assist so far as they are able in protecting victims of oppression, threatened with torture and death. H.M.G. are taking every opportunity of conveying to the countries and governments concerned their full agreement with the President's declaration, and their determination to cooperate in all measures consistent with efficient prosecution of the war designed to give assistance and refuge to all who can find means of escaping the Nazis and Nazi-inspired tyranny.[67]

This support for US policy conspicuously omitted any mention of the Nazi plan to kill all Jews, and it avoided the word Jews, too. It represented a retreat from Eden's statement.

This was not for lack of knowledge. By coincidence, on the same day as the presidential press conference, the British Political Warfare Executive issued to its staff a "Special Annexe on the persecution of the Jews." Under the heading "The Extermination Policy" it discussed ghettos, camps, deportations, and massacres, and it referred to mass killings at Auschwitz. In suggesting what was about to happen, it referred back to Hitler's prophecy of January 30, 1939, regarding the annihilation of the Jews of Europe.[68]

In early April, Archbishop of Canterbury William Temple asked the BBC to appeal to the people of Romania and Hungary to help Jews to safety. This came at a time when German and Hungarian measures to move Jews into ghettos and camps in Hungary had not yet begun. A BBC official responded that the Political Warfare Executive and the Foreign Office agreed on an appeal but wanted it broad enough to cover all victims of Nazi oppression: "They do not think that it is altogether a sound policy to concentrate exclusively on the Jews when so many others are suffering for their political and religious convictions." Temple also learned that the BBC and the Ministry of Information officials expressed concern that an appeal might make things worse for the Jews in the Balkans.[69] Given what these officials knew about Nazi mass extermination, these justifications seem curious. More likely, Anglo-American officials involved in psychological warfare and British foreign policy experts still feared giving support to Nazi propaganda that the Allies were fighting a war on behalf of the Jews; they worried specifically about whether Hungarian (and Romanian) anti-semitism would affect these countries' attitudes toward the Allies in the war; and British officials fretted about pressure to open Palestine for Jewish escapees.

Historian Frank Chalk, who has studied the use of radio propaganda for and against genocide, argues that the BBC could have informed Hungarian Jews in 1943 that most Polish Jews had been killed and that they likely faced the same fate unless they hid or escaped; they could have called upon Hungarians to do everything possible to step ghettoization and deportations of Jews, and they could have informed Hungarians about the crimes of their leaders against the Jews. They could have raised the alarm and warned Hungarian Jews of the step-by-step process of mass extermination.[70]

Roosevelt's press conference statement came relatively late in the Holocaust. For some twenty-first-century observers, this timing robs it of significance and moral credit. But Allied military progress by March 1944 helps to explain why the president was willing to take responsibility for a humanitarian effort. He was the only one of the three Allied leaders willing to do so even then, and Eden would never have raised the subject of the threat to Hungarian Jews if Roosevelt had not done so first.

The War Refugee Board intended to build on the president's statement in its efforts to save some Hungarian Jews, and the modified version was good enough for that purpose. It remained to be seen whether the board would provoke a fight with the British Foreign Office in Eden's hands, or whether the UK would follow the United States' lead. The biggest question was whether Hungarian government officials would recognize the significance of a new US policy and whether it would matter to them.

CHAPTER EIGHT

HUNGARIAN REALITIES

D uring about two months in mid-1944, less than one year before the war in Europe ended, thousands of Hungarian gendarmes and a team of SS officials forced 437,402 Hungarian Jews onto 147 deportation trains at an average of more than 5,800 per day. Nazi authorities in Hungary deported another 11,000–12,000 on their own. Most of these Jews were gassed upon arrival at Auschwitz-Birkenau. Of those selected for work, a few thousand survived the war. From late April to mid-July 1944, the deportations of Jews in Hungary turned Auschwitz into the most destructive of the Nazi extermination camps.[1]

In July 1944, however, shifts within the Hungarian government opened opportunities for the Western Allies and cooperating neutral governments to slow down this genocide. Deportations to Auschwitz stopped. Although about 100,000 Jews were killed after a pro-Nazi coup in Budapest in mid-October, about 119,000 Jews in Budapest survived the war: 69,000 in a main ghetto, 25,000 in housing under international protection, and 25,000 in hiding, mostly with false papers.[2]

How could a large majority of Jews in Hungary have been killed so late in the war? Those with a stake in this wrenching history still examine options for saving more lives; eighty years later, debate continues. But some claims, such as the belief that the Nazis were willing to spare one million Jews if the Allies would take them, or that the United States might easily have prevented the deportations and gassing of Hungarian Jews, are unfounded.

This chapter describes, chronologically, how the Nazi and Hungarian perpetrators carried out the Holocaust in Hungary, and it summarizes how Hungarian Jews reacted based on imperfect and misleading information. Allied governments quickly learned what was happening, and Roosevelt's March 24, 1944, press conference statement became the centerpiece of US efforts to pressure key Hungarian officials against collaboration with SS officials in Hungary. Finally, this chapter analyzes whether the Allies could have saved a larger number of the Jews in Hungary through negotiations and through bombing, emphasizing the contrast between contemporary perceptions and moral judgments decades later.

HUNGARY'S NEW GOVERNMENT

A relatively small number of Nazi officials and SS officers in Hungary benefited from the wholehearted cooperation of the Hungarian government. Randolph Braham, a distinguished historian and a survivor of the Holocaust in Hungary who died in 2018, judges that without major Hungarian assistance, the Nazis would have failed to achieve their objectives in the country, including the elimination of the Jews. Though critical of Allied decisions and policies in his richly detailed study of the Holocaust in Hungary, Braham primarily condemned those

Hungarians inside and outside government who helped Nazi Germany carry out the Holocaust.[3]

Reich Security Main Office (RSHA) chief Ernst Kaltenbrunner and his security detail escorted Regent Miklós Horthy on the train back to Hungary, following Horthy's March 18 meeting with Hitler at Schloss Klessheim in Austria. At a stop at Linz, Kaltenbrunner's phone call to Budapest revealed that Hungarian troops had not resisted the German occupation. It signaled future Hungarian-German collaboration.[4]

Hitler appointed Edmund Veesenmayer as German plenipotentiary and minister to Hungary to oversee events there. Veesenmayer, a Bavarian who held a high SS rank but reported to Foreign Minister Ribbentrop, insisted on observing the form of Hungarian sovereignty because he thought he could accomplish more than if German officials ruled directly. Döme Sztójay, who had long served in Berlin as Hungarian military attaché and then as minister to Germany, became prime minister, replacing Kállay, who was arrested. Still the supreme Hungarian authority, Regent Horthy mostly stayed out of the new government's way until July 1944. His pre-occupation concession to Hitler to supply the Germans with large numbers of Jews for labor served as a cover for the Nazi program of deportation and mass murder of Jews in Hungary. Although Sztójay put together a coalition cabinet, he appointed notorious antisemites to key positions in the Interior Ministry: László Endre for administration, and László Baky as head of the political department. Endre quickly allied himself with Adolf Eichmann, the SS lieutenant colonel in charge of Jewish affairs, who quipped that Endre "wanted to eat the Jews with paprika." Endre and Baky purged and then harnessed the Hungarian civil service, especially the gendarmerie under László Ferenczy, who worked closely with Eichmann. Veesenmayer arranged for German supervision of the Hungarian press and radio, which subsequently followed the German line of Axis victory in the war. Horthy's personal detective, Peter Hain, was a paid, influential German agent.[5] Both Nazi officials and their Hungarian collaborators sought to remove Jews from Hungary whatever the outcome of the war. Eichmann's team compressed its years of experience with deporting Jews from other countries into weeks of application in Hungary. On March 29, the Sztójay government issued anti-Jewish decrees, including one requiring Jews to wear the yellow Star of David. Two days later, in a meeting with members of a Central Jewish Council at his headquarters in the Hotel Majestic in Buda, Eichmann gave mostly reassuring (and false) guidance. His primary objective, he said, was increasing industrial production. If Jews proved to be good workers, they would be treated like non-Jewish workers. If the Jews engaged in violence, Eichmann warned, he would retaliate mercilessly. But he said he would not tolerate attacks on Jews who wore the yellow star. Jewish representatives at the meeting set up a central Jewish organization as he had instructed, unwittingly creating a false sense of security among Hungarian Jewry. On April 6, Jewish leaders appealed for Jews to follow Eichmann's orders and remain calm. The next day Baky conferred with Endre and some of Eichmann's men about establishing the first ghettos in Carpatho-Ruthenia and southeastern Hungary.[6]

American officials expected that Nazi satellites would seek to earn good will among the Western Allies as Germany's military prospects dimmed. However, Sztójay's government implemented Nazi policies and spread Nazi propaganda far more intensively than any previous Hungarian cabinet. Their ideology and loyalty to Nazi Germany trumped pragmatic calculations. The only uncertainty was whether Horthy would go along with them.

On April 2, US bombers attacked the rail yards in Pest, an armament factory, and an aircraft component factory. Similar

British nighttime bombings followed for the next two days, inflicting substantial damage and civilian casualties in an area of the city where few Jews lived. Hungarian propaganda organs responded by charging that "Allied Judaeo-terrorists had spared their local fellow-gangsters." The Allied raids, magnified by pro-Nazi propaganda attacks, intensified antisemitic feeling within Hungary, which Eichmann and Hain exploited. Hungarian officials proposed to execute ten Jews for every Hungarian killed, and the government forcibly evicted Jews from apartments to create shelter for the victims of Allied bombs.[7]

REPERCUSSIONS OF FDR'S PRESS CONFERENCE

At his March 24 press conference, Roosevelt had denounced "one of the blackest crimes of all history—begun by the Nazis in the day of peace and multiplied by them a hundred times in time of war—the wholesale systematic murder of the Jews of Europe." The Voice of America and the BBC broadcast this statement in English and German for the first few days, but their news cycle focused only on the most recent events. Broadcasters also likely feared internal opposition to constant emphasis on a largely Jewish issue. In Romania, Bulgaria, occupied Poland, and Hungary, shortwave listeners heard Roosevelt's statement in their languages only three times.[8]

On April 7, A. Leon Kubowitzki, head of the rescue department of the World Jewish Congress, wrote to the War Refugee Board to request broadcasts warning Hungarian Jews not to wear the Jewish star because a clear symbol of identification would facilitate the deportation and destruction of the Jews. According to Kubowitzki, the board passed his suggestion on to other agencies, OWI presumably among them, but without success.[9] He persisted a couple of weeks later: "We want Hungarian Jews to hide, not to wear the yellow badge, and to destroy all registers."[10]

Kubowitzki was not alone in calling for a warning to Hungary's Jews. On April 11, Gerhart Riegner in Geneva suggested that US and Allied intelligence services advise the Jews in Hungary to evade registration and identification by the Germans—the usual preliminaries to imprisonment for eventual deportations. He recommended that Jews destroy all identity papers and communal lists before dispersing. Two officials of the British Section of the World Jewish Congress passed these very practical suggestions along to State Department Under Secretary Stettinius, then in London, on April 24.[11]

Allied psychological warfare experts preferred to appeal to Hungarians generally, not to craft a message to Hungarian Jews. On Saturday, April 22, representatives from several different agencies reconsidered psychological warfare broadcasts to Hungary. On April 24, both the Voice of America and the BBC (as well as the Free French Radio Algiers) carried a Hungarian-language appeal by "spokesmen" of the United States government to the people of Hungary:

You are living under Nazi occupation. Although your rulers have long collaborated with the Nazis in the past, you are learning at first hand what a Nazi regiment [sic, regimen?] means, what it has meant to millions of people in occupied Europe. You are witnessing in the course of this occupation one of the most terrible Nazi devices in action. This device is the familiar scapegoat device by which the Nazis hope to divide and conquer. In your country, the scapegoat has been made the Hungarian Jew. You are being told today that the Hungarian Jew is responsible for Allied air-raids on your cities, which manufacture weapons for Germany. . . . We know that many of you have already reacted against Nazi brutality. We know that Hungarians are walking publicly in the streets with Jews who wear the Nazi-inspired star of David, that your own Primate, Cardinal Serédi, has appealed to the Nazi authorities to spare the Jewish people, that Hungarians are aiding the Jews to retain their property, that Hungarians continue to trade in Jewish stores. . . . We ask you, however, to go further. We ask you to remember the words of President Roosevelt:

"I ask every man everywhere under Nazi domination to show the world by his action that in his heart he does not share Hitler's insane criminal desires. Let him hide these pursued victims, help them to go over their borders and do what he can to save them from the Nazi hangman. I ask him also to keep watch and to record the evidence that will one day be used to convict the guilty."

These are the words of President Roosevelt spoken on March 24. . . .[12]

On May 7, as intelligence about roundups of Jews in Hungary accumulated, OWI arranged to broadcast in Hungarian a statement by Pennsylvania senator Joseph Guffey, a Democratic member of the Senate Foreign Relations Committee. Guffey warned Hungarians to discontinue their persecution of Jews. He said that the Nazis had passed a death sentence on eight hundred thousand Hungarian Jews, and that the United States would hold the authorities in Hungary responsible if this were carried out. Guffey repeated President Roosevelt's March 24 warning that war criminals would be brought to justice after the war.[13]

On April 23, top Nazi authorities in Hungary including Eichmann reached agreement with Endre, Baky, and Hungarian Interior Minister Jaross on a comprehensive program to deport all Jews.[14] On April 28, the first trainload of Hungarian Jews left the Kistarcsa internment camp for Auschwitz, a joint effort by Hungarian and Nazi officials. By May 22, top OWI officials in Istanbul reported that according to reliable witnesses in Hungary, about one hundred thousand Jews in Hungary had already been deported to "Poland, which translated, means annihilated." At the current rate, the cable continued, the entire Jewish population in Hungary would vanish by the fall of 1944.[15] Another OWI cable the next day stressed that the deportations in Hungary outpaced those everywhere else in Europe.[16] Late in the Holocaust, the RSHA had streamlined its mass killing operations, and it benefited greatly from official Hungarian cooperation.

The staff of the War Refugee Board solicited and received statements from American politicians and citizens with potential influence in Hungary. Former New York governor Al Smith (a Catholic) led a group of prominent Christians who backed a statement denouncing Nazi atrocities. In a recorded service that the BBC broadcast to Hungary, the First Magyar Reformed Church in New York City invited five hundred Protestants, Catholics, and Jews to wear a Star of David and to pray for intercession.[17] On March 24, the board urged Pope Pius XII to wield his influence to stop the mass killings in Hungary. On May 26, the board tried again through US representative to the Vatican Harold Tittmann, but the pontiff abstained for the time being.[18]

WHAT DID HUNGARIAN JEWS KNOW?

Hungarian Jews had numerous sources of information about the Nazi mass murder of Jews in other parts of Europe. Thousands of Slovak Jews had escaped deportations there and fled to Hungary, where they talked about what they knew about Nazi executions of Jews elsewhere. During their visits home, Hungarian soldiers who had served on the Eastern front discussed massacres of Jews with Jewish acquaintances. Jewish Agency representatives in Istanbul regularly sent information to Budapest and other towns about the comprehensive killing of Jews by the Nazis elsewhere. And some Hungarians Jews heard the relevant broadcasts of the BBC and Voice of America.[19] Of course, many other Hungarian Jews did not follow current events closely and were caught unawares by Hungarian roundups.

Most of the Hungarian Jews who heard something about the general European Jewish catastrophe did not upend their lives. They could not join an existing resistance movement, for there was no significant Hungarian resistance to the German occupation or to the Sztójay government. War conditions and border restrictions prevented most from fleeing to Romania or the former Yugoslavia. Some Zionist youth groups distributed forged papers to Hungarian Jews and connected them with smugglers, and somewhere between five thousand and seven thousand Jews reached Romania.[20] Most Hungarian Jews hoped instead that Allied military advances toward Hungary would improve their situation. Some calculated that Regent Horthy still had the power and the will to protect them. In general, Hungarian Jewish leaders concluded that the Final Solution in other countries and territories had limited relevance because of the specific military and political conditions in Hungary, which left a nominally sovereign Hungarian government in power.[21]

Some Hungarian Jewish leaders heard from their Jewish contacts in Slovakia that bribery might serve as a strategy for survival. Eichmann's team had deported fifty-seven thousand Jews from Slovakia to extermination camps in occupied Poland during 1942. Rabbi Michael Dov Weissmandel, one of the leaders of Slovak Jewry, and Gisi Fleischmann, the leader of the Bratislava Working Group, then offered Eichmann's subordinate Dieter Wisliceny a bribe to stop these deportations. Wisliceny claimed that he complied; in reality, Eichmann had told him to extract what assets he could from the Slovak Jews and proceed as usual. Wisliceny also convinced Slovak Jewish leaders that a much larger payment, if they could raise it from outside sources (they could not), might bring a halt to deportations of Jews in Europe outside of Poland. These Slovak negotiations and the bribe achieved nothing: deportations from Slovakia ceased only because the government of Slovakia withdrew its approval. But, misled by the coincidental end of deportations from Slovakia, Weissmandel informed Zionist leaders in Budapest that Wisliceny was trustworthy and that negotiations with him in Budapest might avert the mass killing of Hungarian Jews. Anticipating more bargaining with Jewish representatives in Budapest, Wisliceny picked up a letter of recommendation from Weissmandel before he returned to Budapest in late March 1944.[22]

TWISTED NEGOTIATIONS

Fülöp Freudiger, who represented the Orthodox community on the Relief and Rescue Committee of Budapest, had been the first prominent Hungarian Jew to contact Wisliceny, asking his help for a relative. Two other figures on this committee played more critical roles. Resző Kasztner, a thirty-eight-year-old lawyer and journalist from Kolozsvár who had moved to Budapest in 1940, quickly became prominent in the relatively weak Zionist movement in Hungary. After the war, Kasztner said he had initiated discussions with Wisliceny and then Eichmann. Joel Brand was a thirty-seven-year-old, Hungarian-born, former Communist in Germany turned Hungarian Zionist. He and his wife Hansi had become successful glove manufacturers in Budapest.[23] SS officers in Budapest preferred to deal with the Zionists because of their perceived connections with powerful Jews abroad.[24] So the

major negotiations in Budapest involved Kasztner and the
Brands on the Jewish side, all three of them influenced by
Rabbi Weissmandel's positive assessment of Wisliceny.

On April 5, Kasztner and Joel Brand asked Wisliceny and
three accompanying SS officials what it would take for Eichmann's Einsatzkommando to refrain from its mission against
the Jews. Wisliceny asked them for a two-million-dollar payment to stop all deportations, insisting on a small portion in
Hungarian currency up front as a sign of good faith. The rest of
the money could come later, he said, from their allies outside
Hungary. Their dialogue continued sporadically over the next
few weeks, while the Eichmann's men and the Hungarian gendarmerie moved Jews from Hungarian countryside provinces
into ghettos and camps and separated them from their possessions. Wisliceny directed this process. The Relief and Rescue
Committee of Budapest lacked the resources to comply with
Wisliceny's high demand, and Allied currency restrictions
blocked Western Jewish organizations from paying ransom.[25]

On April 25, Eichmann ordered Joel Brand to convey an astonishing offer to the Western Allies via Istanbul: the Nazis
would sell them one million Jews in return for some ten thousand trucks and certain other goods from the United States and
Britain. The trucks would be used, Eichmann said, for civilian
purposes or only on the Eastern front, not against the West. The
million Jews to be released could not remain in Hungary, and
they would not be permitted to head toward Palestine because
of Nazi promises to Arab leaders. They could go to any other
Allied-controlled territory, Eichmann stated. He would arrange
for Brand to fly to Istanbul, where Brand was ordered to personally present this offer to Allied representatives, or failing that, to
Jewish Agency representatives there. Brand asked Eichmann
to show his good faith by releasing a transport of six hundred to
twelve hundred Jews simultaneously with his arrival in Istanbul.

Eichmann supposedly accepted but chose Portugal as a destination; the Americans would have to take charge of them and send them to the United States. (All of this posed serious logistical and political problems for the Hungarian Jewish negotiators, which stalled any effort toward the release of even small numbers of Jews. Again, Hungarian Jewish leaders lacked the ability to induce Western and neutral governments to cooperate.) Eichmann repeated and elaborated on the overall offer a few days later, saying that he now had received approval from Berlin.[26]

On Brand's May 19 flight from Vienna to Istanbul, another passenger had his own potentially far-reaching Nazi mission. Andor (Bandi) Grosz, a.k.a. Andreas György, was a thirty-nine-year-old native Hungarian Jew who had converted to Catholicism and taken up smuggling and espionage. An agent for the Abwehr, the central German military intelligence organization, he also worked for Hungarian military intelligence, as a courier for the Relief and Rescue Committee of Budapest, as an agent for the Dogwood intelligence network in Istanbul, and many others. After Germany occupied Hungary, Grosz recognized that the SS had taken over most functions of German military intelligence in Hungary, and he managed to contact German officials in the Foreign Intelligence branch of the SS *Sicherheitsdienst* (SD) in Budapest. One of them, Otto Klages, ordered him to go to Istanbul to arrange a meeting for high SD officials with American intelligence officials to negotiate a separate peace with the West. Higher SS and Police Leader Otto Winkelmann, the highest SS officer in Hungary, referred to a secret order from Himmler for the Brand and Grosz missions to Istanbul.[27]

Lacking proper papers, both emissaries struggled with Turkish authorities, who allowed them to meet briefly with local Jewish representatives. Chaim Barlas, the Jewish Agency representative in Istanbul, interviewed Brand first, and Reuben Resnik, an official of the Joint Distribution Committee, sent his later report of Brand's account to the War Refugee Board. Both interviewers thought even a spurious Nazi offer might yield an opening to save some Jews. Brand and Grosz each (separately) tried to reach Palestine to discuss their missions with Jewish Agency and Allied officials but were taken into British custody in Aleppo, ending up later in British detention in Cairo. British and American officials in Cairo were deeply suspicious of Grosz, whose shady background and role in betraying the Dogwood intelligence network had come to light.[28] The British also viewed Brand's mission as Nazi political warfare or blackmail. A British Foreign Office official, A. W. G. Randall, worried that the Roosevelt administration and the War Refugee Board might show interest in the offer beyond its merits.[29]

Brand sincerely believed that he had a chance to save up to a million Jews. He was also convinced that if he did not return to Budapest with a positive answer from the Allies, he and his family would suffer the consequences. Grosz knew mostly what Klages and Brand told him or what he could infer from their comments. He believed that his mission to bring about separate peace negotiations, which he concealed from Brand, was the real one, but he had no insight into the upper reaches of the SS.

A large declassification of US intelligence records in 2000 offered one valuable piece of evidence in the continuing discussion among historians about the real purpose of the Istanbul offers.[30] In November 1944, a German officer named Karl Marcus turned himself in to British forces in France. Formerly an assistant to a key adviser to Walter Schellenberg, head of SD foreign intelligence, Marcus defected to try to convince the British government to moderate its view of Germany in the coming peace settlement. (He thought the United States, the USSR, and France were all irredeemably anti-German.) British authorities dutifully notified the Americans and the Soviets of this feeler. Despite their lack of interest in Marcus's political agenda, British officials valued Marcus's knowledge of German intelligence activities. With Winston Churchill's permission, Marcus was brought to Britain and given various codenames, "Dictionary" among them. In his twenty-fifth interrogation, Marcus revealed that Schellenberg had approved Brand's mission to Istanbul to trade for a million Jews as a device to split the Allied alliance.[31] Schellenberg had no responsibility for the deportation of Jews, so he could not possibly have delivered a million Jews to the Allies, and Eichmann had no interest in sparing them. For high SS officials, Brand and Grosz were both tools to give Nazi Germany a chance to carry on the war only on one front, preferably against the Soviet Union. If the Nazis truly wanted to exchange a million Jews for trucks and commodities, why murder their hostages as rapidly as they could manage? Common sense indicates that the Nazi offer through Brand was spurious.

If the United States had engaged in direct negotiations with Nazi representatives, Nazi propagandists could have "demonstrated" that their *bête noire* Roosevelt cared more about saving Jews than fighting the war. In early July, OSS headquarters requested more information from Cairo about the Brand mission, which they called an incredible Nazi black maneuver. They added: "Obviously the project is meant to cause the Allies embarrassment. Roosevelt is the chief target, for the Nazis claim that he is impeding the war effort by his attempts to rescue Jews."[32]

THE BOARD REACTS TO BRAND

War Refugee Board Director John Pehle needed more evidence to overcome British opposition to any further discussions of Brand's mission. After conferring with Morgenthau and Josiah DuBois on June 6, Pehle concluded that they should try to keep the possibility of negotiations with Nazi officials alive through delay and empty gestures because Nazi officials might release some Jews without any real quid pro quo. To do so, they would first send the board's special envoy, Ira Hirschmann, who had previously succeeded in getting Turkey to allow the transit of hundreds of Jewish children to Palestine, back to the Middle East to interview Brand.[33]

On June 8, two days after the difficult D-Day landings in Normandy and the simultaneous Allied conquest of Rome, Pehle and Morgenthau met with the president. FDR signed a broad authorization letter for Hirschmann to display once he reached the Middle East: "The great task of mercy which the War Refugee Board is successfully undertaking is of paramount importance and I am confident that Ambassador [Lawrence] Steinhardt [in Turkey] and you will receive the support of the governments and individuals whose cooperation we are seeking in the interest of humanity. In this you have our Government's full support and hearty wishes for success."[34] Displaying this expansive language on White House stationary would help Hirschmann clear away obstacles to meeting with Brand in Cairo. Pehle and Morgenthau also discussed Brand's mission with FDR. Pehle commented afterward, "The President was very interested in this development and agreed that we should keep the negotiations open."[35] Pehle then cabled Steinhardt in Turkey that he should pass a message to German officials through intermediaries that the United States was willing to consider genuine proposals for relief and rescue. But he should also notify the Soviet Union about the Brand mission. The Soviet response was blunt: Moscow forbade any discussions with the German government on this subject, that is, any kind of ransom for Jews.[36] Stalin always feared that the West might sell out the Soviet Union in any contacts with Germany.

During the absence of Joel Brand from Budapest, Kasztner and Hansi Brand restarted negotiations with Eichmann and with Himmler's SS procurement specialist Kurt Becher. By June, the pace of deportations indicated the futility of negotiations to save a large part of Hungarian Jewry. Kasztner still hoped, however, that a show of interest by the Western Allies might bring about the release of smaller numbers of Jews. On June 18, he wrote to a Zionist contact, "What can be negotiated is the rescue of a small part of those adults incapable of labor and children . . . [as well as decent treatment of those Jews sent to do labor]."[37] His contacts with Becher and Klages in the second half of June indicated that Himmler might approve one or more trainloads of Jews (four thousand people) for a price of $1,000 to $2,000 per head.[38]

On June 22 in Cairo, Brand told Hirschmann that he recognized the pitfalls of the Nazi offer, including the probability that, one way or another, they would gain something. If the Western Allies turned down the proposal, the Nazis could maintain that because the West did not want these Jews, it was necessary to dispose of them. Still, Brand thought that his mission to Istanbul represented a sign of Germany's military weakness, which meant that negotiations might still be viable. At the least, he believed, the West should keep the door open for future negotiations.[39]

On July 13, the British War Cabinet Committee on Refugees reconsidered its response to Brand after Churchill wrote that the Brand proposals "were not to be taken seriously and that the whole matter was not of a kind which should be dealt with through a Protecting Power [a neutral country such as Switzerland]." The British then decided to inform the United States that they rejected any further secret negotiations. In practice, they first leaked the story to the press, where the *New York Herald Tribune* condemned the notion of ransoming Jews as the most monstrous blackmail in history. The next day, the *Times* of London carried the headline, "A Monstrous Offer— German Blackmail—Bartering Jews for Munitions." This negative publicity, combined with Soviet opposition to negotiations, ended any chance of extracting some benefit for Jews from Brand's mission.[40]

Despite the hold-ups and ultimate failure of Joel Brand's mission, Kasztner and Hansi Brand's parallel negotiations with Eichmann and Becher brought about the release of 1,684 Jews to Switzerland, via Bergen-Belsen and Theresienstadt, and may have been at least partly responsible for the less severe treatment of about 15,000 Jews sent to Strasshof, near Vienna, where they worked as laborers under tolerable conditions. Most of them and their families survived the war.[41] Put into an impossible situation, Kasztner and Hansi Brand managed to save some Hungarian Jews, while the Nazis deported and killed the large majority of Jews outside Budapest.

Brand remained convinced that the Allies had ignored a real opportunity to save a million Jews, that is, that Eichmann's offer was sincere. After the war, he presented his views in books and interviews, and his son has recently updated his charge.[42] But it is apparent today that there was never a chance to save a million Jews through a bargain with the Nazis. Others blamed Kasztner for negotiating with the Nazis, in the process saving some friends and relatives, while keeping silent about what lay ahead for most Hungarian Jews. The culmination of postwar Jewish attacks on Kasztner came in a 1954 libel trial in Israel, where the defense castigated Kasztner, the plaintiff, for failing to communicate to Jews throughout Hungary what he knew about the fate of Jews deported to Auschwitz. Judge Benjamin Halevi concluded that Kasztner had sold his soul to the devil through negotiating with Eichmann and Becher. This verdict toppled the Israeli government, which had supported Kasztner, a civil

servant. Although the Israeli Supreme Court ultimately overturned this judgment of Kasztner's role, he did not live to see
exoneration: a right-wing extremist assassinated him in March
1957, about nine months before the Supreme Court's ruling.[43]

THE AUSCHWITZ REPORTS

During April 1944, five prisoners escaped from Auschwitz to
warn the world about its horrors. Of these, two Slovak Jews, Rudolf Vrba and Alfred Wetzler, supplied by far the most detailed
description of the camp, reconstructing its activities over a two-
year period. They estimated that 1,765,000 Jews had been
gassed during their time there. After their escape they reached
Slovakia, where part of the Jewish Council of Slovakia at Žilina
extensively debriefed and cross-examined them. Once the escapees completed their report, the Working Group of the Jewish
Council translated it and sent it out widely (but with some
delay), particularly to Hungary, to Switzerland, and to the Papal
Legate in Bratislava. Vrba and Wetzler's work has become
known as the Auschwitz Protocols or the Auschwitz Reports.[44]

Hungarian Jewish leaders who received copies of these reports failed to disseminate them among the mass of Hungarian
Jews but did reach Horthy through his son and daughter-in-
law. In Switzerland, the most active distributor of these documents was George Mantello, a native of Transylvania who
served as the first secretary of the consulate of El Salvador in
Geneva and pursued various methods to save Jews in the process. Publication of excerpts and stories about the Auschwitz
Reports in the Swiss press in June soon reached the Western
media.[45]

Decades ago, some historians argued that the Nazis had
managed to keep the gassing operation at Auschwitz secret until
Vrba and Wetzler exposed the killing in their report. Auschwitz

was a large, multipurpose camp, and the SS hid the gassing operation at Birkenau better than other functions.[46] But records in the United States and the UK, declassified over the last twenty-five years, have undermined this interpretation: the Polish underground, British intelligence, and US intelligence learned a good deal about Birkenau's killings even before 1944.[47] Of course, the British and American public and many government officials did not know much about the gassing operation, and some government officials with access to secret intelligence chose not to believe the shocking reports.

Nevertheless, the Auschwitz Reports remain extremely important because of their first-hand sources and extraordinary detail. Roswell McClelland, representative of the War Refugee Board in Switzerland, received these reports at a time when he and officials the board's headquarters in Washington had little information about Auschwitz. McClelland was so shaken by what he read that he sent a sixteen-page summary to Washington.[48] The Auschwitz Reports also influenced political events in Hungary. Regent Horthy now found it untenable to tell his few Jewish contacts and prominent Hungarian acquaintances that the Germans were merely using Hungarian Jews as laborers as he had originally agreed with Hitler.[49]

PRESSURES ON HORTHY

In a move initiated by the War Refugee Board, on June 13 Archbishop Francis Spellman of New York denounced the Hungarian government's alignment with Nazi Germany's ideology, saying, "It seems incredible . . . that a nation which has been so consistently true to the teachings of the Catholic Church should now bow to a false, pagan mysticism of blood and race and disregard those solemn words of Pope Pius XI: 'Abraham is called our patriarch. . . . Anti-Semitism is not compatible with the sublime reality of this text . . . Spiritually we are Semites.'"[50] Members of the Senate Foreign Relations Committee then signed a statement condemning the brutal treatment of Jews in Hungary. On June 21, in what the AP called a highly unusual move, the House Foreign Affairs Committee issued a statement addressed to Hungary, where, it claimed, almost a million Jewish lives hung in the balance: "Let Hungary at this historic moment stem the tide of inhumanity toward the helpless people within her borders." It threatened to punish Hungarian criminals guilty of inhumane conduct. It also praised the activities of the War Refugee Board. Six days later, Secretary of State Hull echoed the House committee's warning to Hungary, adding that there cannot be too many protests against the wholesale murder being practiced by the German Government."[51]

At the War Refugee Board's request, the State Department urged Pope Pius XII to criticize the persecution in Hungary personally by radio and through the clergy in the country. On June 25, the pope addressed a personal appeal to Horthy to do everything possible in favor of "unfortunate persons suffering because of their race or nationality." The pontiff avoided use of the word Jews.[52]

The board and the State Department sent their own warning to Horthy, even if it took several weeks to get it delivered, the United States having no diplomatic presence in an Axis country. On June 6, the board, with the approval of Undersecretary Stettinius, notified Minister Leland Harrison in Switzerland that Hungarian Jews were being forced into ghettos and camps, and then deported, subjecting Jews to mass execution. The United States asked the Swiss government to remind Hungary "of the grave view this Government takes regarding the persecution of Jews and other minorities and the determination . . . to see to it that all those who share the responsibility for such acts are dealt with in accordance with the March 24, 1944, statement of the

President." The board also asked Harrison for suggestions about publicity that might reach the Hungarian people. Harrison reported that broadcasting this warning might be insufficient in view of the small number of radio sets in Hungary. Pamphlets dropped by plane might be a better way to spread information widely to Hungarians. But he requested a delay in all such publicity until after the Swiss had delivered the US message in Budapest. On June 26, the Swiss Foreign Ministry sent this document to the Swiss minister in Budapest through the diplomatic pouch, and he delivered it to Horthy shortly afterwards.[53] Under pressure from the King of Sweden as well, Horthy began to waver on the deportations.[54]

All the American politicians' statements, including Roosevelt's press conference statement, were reproduced in pamphlets dropped by plane over Hungary.[55] This effort was part of an ongoing Allied air campaign of political or psychological warfare against satellite regimes. Each bundle of pamphlets or leaflets was tied up by a cord attached to a barometric mechanism. On the bundle's descent, as the air pressure changed, the device released the papers, which scattered over a wide area.[56]

Bombing missions against Hungary increased at this time. When US Liberator bombers attacked the Rakos rail yard in Budapest on July 2, it was the third strike at this target since June 27. During that July 2 raid, a large group of bombers also hit the Manfréd Weiss rail yards, an airfield southeast of Budapest, and a factory producing Messerschmitt planes. More US bombers returned to these targets the next day.[57] On July 2, US bombs also struck Hungarian government buildings and the homes of senior Hungarian government officials. In an uncoded telegram, British scholar Elizabeth Wiskemann, who worked for Allen Dulles, the OSS chief in Switzerland, and for the British Political Warfare Executive, had suggested bombing such targets as reprisals for Hungarian collaboration in the deportation and mass killing of Jews. Hungarian intelligence officials who read this intercepted message concluded that this American targeting was deliberate.[58] Ironically the bombing raid itself had military and economic objectives, and the hits on government-related buildings were accidental.

The accumulation of US warnings to Hungary about collaboration in the deportations of Jews, combined with the coincidental bombing of government-related buildings, helped push Horthy to abandon the policies of the Sztójay government, including the deportation of Jews to Auschwitz.

State Secretary Baky wanted to dispense with the coalition government, arrest Horthy, and initiate deportations of the Jews in Budapest, who had been left for last. Horthy, however, stymied these efforts: the Hungarian gendarmes cooperating with Eichmann—the likely force for a coup—were sent out of the capital. At a meeting of the Council of Ministers on July 5, Prime Minister Sztójay said that, according to the "Anglo-Saxons," deportation meant extermination, and six thousand Jews were being gassed each day. He commented that since no Jews had been killed in Hungary, the "rumors" of Hungarian atrocities should be rebutted, which meant that he wanted to shift all blame to the Nazis. But Horthy announced the suspension of deportations the next day, the first time he had overruled Sztójay's government since March 19. Nazi officials in Hungary were furious, but without Hungarian government cooperation their reach was limited.[59]

Horthy told German Plenipotentiary Veesenmayer that he wanted the Gestapo removed from Hungary and that he had acted against the gendarmerie implicated in Baky's attempted coup. He also confirmed that he had ordered a stop to deportations of Jews but said that he might allow the deportation of Budapest Jews soon if they were treated better, that is, not sent to Auschwitz. He blamed the Sztójay government for international criticism of Hungary, making it clear that he intended to establish a new cabinet. Veesenmayer recommended to Foreign

Minister Ribbentrop that Germany allow Hungary to accept offers from Switzerland, Sweden, and other neutral and Allied countries to receive what became a total of 7,800 Jews, because such limited emigration might persuade Horthy to accept the resumption of deportations. Eichmann, meanwhile, managed to send off two trainloads of Jews interned in the Kistarcsa and Sárvár camps to Auschwitz—despite Horthy's ban—before he left Hungary with his job incomplete.[60]

On July 16, Ribbentrop sent instructions for Veesenmayer to deliver to Horthy: "The Führer expects that the measures against the Budapest Jews will now be carried out without any further delay by the Hungarian government . . . with no delay of any kind in the execution of overall measures because of these exceptions [permitted by the German government]. . . ." Hitler vehemently challenged the ouster of Sztójay and even threatened Horthy's safety.[61] But Hitler had long believed in allowing small groups of Jews to be exempted from the Final Solution if that resulted in the murder of most.[62]

With Hitler distracted by the nearly successful German conspiracy to assassinate him on July 20, Horthy continued his new course. On August 29, he named General Géza Lakatos as his new prime minister. He appointed several anti-Nazi cabinet members and purged Baky and Endre. Lakatos privately agreed with Horthy to seek an exit from the war and to cease persecution of the Jews.[63] As it turned out, the last deportation of Jews from Hungary to Auschwitz-Birkenau was Eichmann's "unauthorized" one on July 24, but other methods of persecution and mass murder erupted within Hungary in mid-October.[64]

NEUTRAL DIPLOMATS, NON-NEUTRAL TONE

US influence on the neutral governments rose after the successful invasion at Normandy, which shortened the road and timeline for Allied victory. The spread of information in the Auschwitz Reports also cleared away previous hesitations in some neutral capitals about relief and rescue efforts in Hungary. The War Refugee Board asked neutral governments to expand their representation in the Hungarian capital.[65]

On April 26, the Swiss Legation in Budapest had applied for exit permits for the emigration of seven thousand Jews holding Palestinian immigration certificates or British offers of admission. Switzerland represented British interests in Hungary, and Swiss Vice Consul Carl Lutz, a graduate of George Washington University, carried out that function well beyond its normal limits. Lutz met with both Veesenmayer and Eichmann in an unsuccessful effort to arrange the emigration of thousands of Jews. Nevertheless, Lutz was able to offer protective papers in Budapest for those Jews slated to emigrate, and he nominally converted the Budapest office of the Jewish Agency into the Emigration Department of the Swiss Legation.[66] Switzerland, however, declined the War Refugee Board's request to increase its diplomatic presence in Budapest, fearing that the Hungarians and Germans would view this move as pro-Allied activity or a cover for espionage.[67]

The War Refugee Board took advantage of unusually favorable circumstances in Stockholm. Board representative Iver Olsen, of Norwegian birth, was a naturalized American and a trusted friend of Pehle. Olsen worked for the OSS in Stockholm before he took on the job of representing the board, too. He had Swedish contacts inside and outside government. The able US Minister to Sweden, Herschel Johnson, was also eager to assist Jews in Hungary, and both Olsen and Johnson helped to select a Swede to go to Budapest.[68]

Raoul Wallenberg became the board's man in Budapest, as Pehle later told Morgenthau.[69] A thirty-one-year-old Swede who had graduated from the University of Michigan and spoke

fluent English, Wallenberg was a member of the most prominent business family in the country, a family of financiers, industrialists, and some diplomats. He had chosen to enter com-
merce, rather than the family business empire, and he had
joined a partnership with Kálmán Lauer, a Hungarian Jew
living in Sweden who still had relatives in Hungary. Wallenberg
had traveled to Budapest for commercial sales before. Encouraged by Lauer, Olsen, and Johnson, the Foreign Ministry asked
him if he would accept an appointment as legation secretary in
Hungary. On June 28, Johnson wrote the board, "We should
emphasize that the Swedish Foreign Office in making this assignment feels that it has cooperated fully in lending all possible
facilities for the furtherance of an American program."[70]

As a neutral citizen, Wallenberg could and did talk with SS
officials, some of whom he bribed. His funds came from wealthy
Hungarian Jews and from the board. Still, hardly anyone at the
Swedish Legation knew of his American connection. He arrived
too late to do anything about the deportation of Jews from the
Hungarian countryside to Auschwitz, but he had time to prepare for potential actions against the Jews in Budapest. He distributed Swedish protective documents and found Swedish-
supervised housing for thousands of them, practices that Per
Anger of the Swedish Legation had initiated.[71] He also told
Hungarian officials that Sweden would accept Jews with any
Swedish papers or connections. He kept the board informed
about the Hungarian government's fluctuating willingness to
permit the emigration of some Jews.[72]

EMIGRATION FROM HUNGARY?

As the result of American and British warnings to Hungary, the
Hungarian government said in effect, "We will permit Jews to
leave Hungary if the United States and Great Britain will take

care of them." Pehle called it a direct challenge. He then suggested that the United States and the UK pledge to find havens
for all Jews that the Hungarians said they would release, without
limit. He did not anticipate very large numbers of emigrants.
But there were about 200,000 Jews in Budapest, and Pehle's
proposal raised British concerns about where any substantial
portion of them might end up. British officials feared that Palestine might become the preferred outlet.[73]

While in London for Treasury negotiations, Morgenthau, in
his talks with Churchill and Eden, raised the issue of a joint
US-UK statement responding to Hungary's offer. Josiah DuBois
flew in from Washington to assist Morgenthau with board issues.
Upon his return to the United States, the treasury secretary reported that the British would go along with a joint statement
pledging to accept all Hungarian Jews allowed to leave; an un-
spoken corollary, however, was that the United States would not
raise the issue of Palestine, nor would it press Britain to abandon
the White Paper quota for Palestine. Morgenthau said later:

> But Joe [DuBois] was insisting on raising the quota question
> of Palestine, and I took the thing up with Mr. Churchill and
> he would have no part of it. . . . I took it up with Eden the first
> night. . . . Eden said it was a matter of the colonies; they are
> scared to death of the Arab question. So I finally had to tell
> Joe I had to give him a directive not to do it. I wanted an over-
> all agreement . . . a joint guarantee that they would take ev-
> erybody [all the Jews] that came out of Hungary. . . . I am
> sure, after talking with Churchill and Eden, that if we had
> gone in there and put up a fight to break down this quota, we
> would have got nothing, absolutely.[74]

The United States and UK did issue a joint positive statement
about taking all Hungarian refugees but made no specific

commitments about where they would go. British officials privately narrowed the wording of the joint statement, indicating that they could take only limited numbers. In any case, the board had to fall back on the parallel strategy of using neutral intermediaries to try to protect those Jews still in Hungary while awaiting conquest of the country by Soviet troops. As with previous proposals for Jewish emigration from Nazi satellites, Nazi officials used their leverage to block action.[75]

THE ARROW CROSS COUP

Horthy finally realized that he had to negotiate with the rapidly approaching Soviets. After secret negotiations in September, the two sides reached a tentative pre-armistice agreement. Recognizing that German forces and the Arrow Cross movement, Hungary's main right-wing extremist party, might challenge him once he announced an armistice, Horthy arranged for the mobilization of military units and political supporters, including members of Jewish labor battalions nearby. But the Hungarian gendarmerie refused to arrest leaders of the Arrow Cross because they were under the protection of the SS. In late September, Veesenmayer and Arrow Cross leader Ferenc Szálasi reached their own secret understanding to establish a new government willing to continue the war and help resolve the "Jewish question." Rumors of their planned coup led Horthy to abruptly move up the date for announcing an armistice, catching his supporters flatfooted. Nazi officials, well prepared for a clash, sought leverage by kidnapping the Regent's son, Miklás Horthy Jr., a leader of the anti-Nazi elements. On October 15, Regent Horthy issued a proclamation read on Hungarian radio that declared the war lost and denounced Germany's crimes. But when measures to protect his government quickly collapsed, he caved in, allegedly to avoid bloodshed. He even went through the humiliating formality of authorizing Arrow Cross leader Szálasi to form a new government.

In the last phase of the Holocaust in Hungary, Arrow Cross street gangs and SS units killed Jews in the streets and elsewhere. Prime Minister Szálasi refrained from intervention and resisted criticism, telling Papal Nuncio Angelo Rotta that Jews in Hungary would not be deported or exterminated but made to work for Hungary.[76]

By this time, Wallenberg had built an efficient organization of many dozens of people to produce Swedish passports or other protective documents for Jews with real or alleged connections to Sweden.[77] He also had devised methods to exceed the limit of immigrants to Sweden that Horthy had set, something that became obvious enough for Nazi officials to criticize. On September 15, Veesenmayer complained that the number of Swedish passports given to Jews had reached six thousand. Although Wallenberg had hoped to go back to Stockholm shortly, the War Refugee Board warned him that German policy had changed and that new deportations were likely. They asked him to warn German officials again of the United States' determination to apprehend and punish all those who participated in deportations or other forms of persecution. Wallenberg chose to remain in Budapest.[78]

Returning to Hungary on October 17, Eichmann immediately demanded fifty thousand Jewish "laborers," whom he said he would march to Germany. He also called for a range of restrictions on Jews living in Budapest, with no exceptions for exempted and protected Jews. He intended to keep demanding the dispatch of groups of fifty thousand Jews to Germany until none were left in Hungary. Nazi officials again used the strategy of agreeing to the emigration of small numbers of Jews—more than eight thousand holding foreign citizenship or immigration certificates but only four hundred bound for Sweden, provided that they were given control of the rest.[79]

Szálasi at first claimed Hungarian Jews for work to defend Budapest against the approaching Soviet armies. Digging trenches and building fortifications under Arrow Cross supervision was itself exhausting and dangerous, but the situation for thirty-five thousand adult Jewish men and Jewish women worsened on October 23, when Veesenmayer persuaded Szálasi to transfer another twenty-five thousand men for "temporary" labor in the Reich. Call-ups of Jewish women followed. Beginning on November 2, these Jewish laborers were marched toward the Austrian border, while deprived of food. It was in effect a death march, the first march of nearly one hundred miles supervised by brutal Hungarian gendarmes, the second part from Hegyeshalom to Austria, by Eichmann's team.[80] On November 16, Swedish Minister Danielsson reported to Stockholm that Swedish officials had rescued fifteen thousand Jews from forced labor or deportation.[81] Another rescue effort took place en route about a week later. With great difficulty, Wallenberg, Per Anger, Swiss consul Carl Lutz, and several others removed from the marches more of those prisoners with protective documents and others they could remove surreptitiously from the group. In the end, the Arrow Cross gave fifty thousand to sixty thousand Jews to the German authorities.[82] The inhabitants of the main ghetto in Budapest and those in housing with international (Swedish or Swiss) protection, meanwhile, remained in jeopardy until the last days of Hungarian-German control over Budapest.

On December 29, Soviet generals Malinovsky and Tolbukhin each sent an officer to offer favorable treatment if the Axis troops surrendered immediately. But the fighting continued.[83] On January 17-18, Soviet troops completed the conquest of Pest, which contained the international ghetto. And on February 13, they conquered Buda. Unlike Wallenberg, Lutz, and some other neutrals, the Soviet forces were not rescuers of the Jews in any moral sense, but they ended the war in Hungary, and some 119,000 Jews in the capital survived. Wallenberg did, too, only to die in a Moscow prison some years after the war.

Wallenberg never saw the last communication Pehle sent to him via Herschel Johnson in Stockholm on December 6, 1944:

> . . . because of circumstances beyond our control our efforts have not met with complete success. On the other hand, there have been measurable achievements in the face of the obstacles which had to be encountered, and it is our conviction that you have made a very great personal contribution to the success which has been realized in these endeavors. On behalf of the War Refugee Board I wish to express to you our very deep appreciation for your splendid cooperation and for the vigor and ingenuity which you brought to our common humanitarian undertaking.[84]

On December 28, 1944, Solomon Adler-Rudel, one of the Jewish representatives operating in Stockholm, wrote: "The constant intervention of the Swedish Legation, the fact that the Hungarian Government was aware of being watched by the Swedish and Swiss Legations considerably hamp[er]ed and delayed the wholesale deportation of Jews from Budapest, even of those who were not protected by Swedish or Swiss documents."[85]

THE NON-BOMBING OF AUSCHWITZ

Visual evidence seems to suggest that the Allies could have destroyed the gas chambers and crematoria at Auschwitz-Birkenau. Aerial photos taken during an August 25, 1944, raid by the US Fifteenth Air Force on Monowitz by chance captured both the crematorium building II at Birkenau and a line of people on their way to the gas chamber. These photos sat in classified government files for decades. CIA photo analysts Dino Brugioni and Robert Poirier, who discovered these images in 1978, took pains to point out that they had magnified them many times beyond what was possible in 1944. At a February 1979 press conference, Poirier added that today's researchers— he meant those who retrospectively argued that Auschwitz should have been bombed—were "Monday morning quarterbacks." In 1944, US analysts never examined the far less distinct photos for the purpose of potentially targeting Birkenau's facilities. The 1944 military officers were interested only in the main industrial targets in the area, which reflected their assignment and longstanding Anglo-American military strategy.[86]

American planning to use its own bombers began months before Pearl Harbor and Germany's declaration of war. General Henry (Hap) Arnold, chief of the Army Air Forces, visited Britain in April 1941 to assess British air strategy, and came away convinced that a major expansion of production of heavy bombers was necessary. Arnold, Undersecretary of War Robert Patterson, and War Department official Robert Lovett drafted a presidential decree calling for the maximum possible increase in the production of bombers. The president announced publicly that the democracies must control the air.[87]

In private, FDR told the army and navy to develop plans for a war against Germany and Japan. General Arnold ordered a strategy based on defeating Germany first while defending against Japan. Colonel Harold George wanted to place an independent strategic bombing campaign at the center of the plan, but to placate army officials, he and his staff of the Army Air War Plans Division added fighters and lighter bombers to support a ground invasion force in Europe. The plan, called AWPD-1, called for an air force of 2.2 million men and 63,000 planes, including 7,000 heavy bombers for an offensive against Germany. AWPD-1 stated that the production of necessary planes and the training of crew would take eighteen months, and in the words of political scientist Phil Haun, "another six months to conduct the air offensive needed to *independently* win the war [italics added]." On August 30, Army Chief of Staff General George C. Marshall approved the plan, and on September 11, Secretary of War Stimson indicated that he would approve if the nation were at war.[88]

By this time, Britain, too, emphasized bombing of Germany, air force analysts having absorbed the doctrine that bombing could destroy enemy morale.[89] British Bomber Command, relatively free of ties and obligations to other armed services, devised an offensive strategy directed at the enemy's home front, not its armed forces. Although British government officials faced moral and political obstacles to targeting civilians, the German invasion of Western European countries in the spring of 1940, combined with Winston Churchill's replacement of Neville Chamberlain as prime minister, removed most constraints. On May 15, Churchill's cabinet approved the policy of carrying out bombing raids resulting in substantial civilian casualties so long as the targets were suitable military objectives. High officials of the Royal Air Force believed that the distinction between soldiers and civilians had virtually disappeared.[90] Another argument was, in effect, that the ends justified the means: Nazi Germany posed such a danger to Western civilization that all other moral and legal considerations could be set aside.[91]

In late December 1940, key officials of the Polish government-in-exile received a request smuggled out by Polish prisoners at a relatively new concentration camp at Auschwitz (Oswiecim) for British bombing of the electrified barbed wire fence around the camp perimeter. The horribly mistreated prisoners, who according to the report numbered twenty thousand, hoped that the destruction and confusion brought about by bombing might allow many of them to escape. At the time this appeal reached the Polish government-in-exile in London, relatively few Jews were prisoners in the main camp.[92]

Polish Prime Minister and Commander-in-Chief Sikorski had his aide-de-camp pass this request to Air Marshal Richard Peirse of the Royal Air Force, who consulted Air Chief Marshal Charles Portal. Peirse noted that a small force of Wellington bombers (carrying less than a full load of bombs) could reach Auschwitz from the UK, and given moonlight, it could try to hit the fence. But he called it a diversion, and he indicated that other such Polish requests might follow. Portal responded, "I think you will agree that apart from any political considerations, an attack on the Polish [sic: German] concentration camp at Oswiecim is an undesirable diversion for our bomber force and is unlikely to achieve its purpose. The weight of bombs that could be carried to a target at this distance with the limited force available, would be very unlikely to cause enough damage, to enable prisoners to escape." At this stage of the war Portal wanted to mount a concentrated bombing attack on Germany's oil resources.[93]

Similar language resurfaced in response to Jewish requests for bombing of Auschwitz in mid-1944 (although the escape of prisoners was not the main goal then). The direct or indirect destruction of the foundations of German military power remained the overriding goal of Allied strategic bombing throughout the war.

Precision bombing was more intention than reality. Bombers flying in formations designed to hinder attacks by German fighters could not all calculate the right release point to hit a specific target. Only the lead bombardier could do so, with the others releasing bombs on order. The result was to reduce accuracy by about one-third. German anti-aircraft weapons around key facilities also forced bombers to fly at higher altitudes, which further diminished the accuracy of bombing. And while the Norden bombsight on B-17 and B-24 bombers gave American-built bombers a major technological advantage, bad weather often nullified its effect or even forced bombing missions to abort. High altitude precision bombing was possible only for a handful of days during the summer of 1943 and again 1944.[94]

By the spring of 1944, the Mediterranean Allied Air Force (MAAF), which included the US Fifteenth Air Force and various British units, had moved from North Africa to bases near Foggia, Italy, once that region was available and existing Italian airfields were lengthened for long-range bombers. The first MAAF commander, Air Chief Marshal Arthur Tedder, set the MAAF's priorities as assisting Allied armies in Italy, contributing to the combined air offensive, and weakening Germany's hold on the Balkans and the Aegean. In April 1944, the Fifteenth consisted of 1,427 heavy bombers and 632 fighter escorts. Allied officials hoped that long-range bombers based in Foggia could avoid the bad weather in northern Europe, striking targets in southern Germany, southern France, Austria, Hungary, Yugoslavia, Greece, Romania, and Bulgaria.[95]

An Allied Central Intelligence Unit had scoured reconnaissance photos to locate every oil target in Germany and German-dominated territory. This unit collaborated with others in the preparation of weekly target lists for Allied bombers.[96] The MAAF had its own Photo Interpretation Center, and no operations took place without referring to relevant photos there.[97]

The German industrial complex at Blechhammer in Upper Silesia included synthetic oil refineries to produce oil from coal, including aviation fuel. When the first refinery had opened in April 1944, its thirty-two hundred forced laborers were placed under the authority of the Auschwitz-Monowitz concentration camp, like the other industrial sub-camps around Auschwitz.[98] Monowitz was also the location of an I.G. Farben synthetic oil and rubber plant, which was photographed by a reconnaissance flight on April 4 and first listed as another Allied bombing target on July 18.[99] On June 16–20, in good weather, the Fifteenth's heavy bombers raided synthetic oil plants at Blechhammer North and South, inflicting major damage on the refineries.[100]

On August 20, B-17 bombers from the Fifteenth dropped more than thirteen hundred bombs in the area of Monowitz. A German employee at the oil plant, in a letter to her brother, complained about constant danger and noise all day long. Two days later, the Fifteenth began what became a series of at least nine raids against the synthetic refineries at Blechhammer. According to the official history of the US Army Air Force, during the second half of September, the Fifteenth deployed fleets of 100 to 150 bombers that dropped 287 tons of bombs on Blechhammer North and 253 tons on "Oswiecim," which likely meant Auschwitz-Monowitz. An airman with the Fifteenth later described the Blechhammer missions as long, tiring, and always dangerous.[101]

Weather again hindered heavy bombers from September 1944 on. For every hundred bombs aimed at synthetic oil plants, eighty-seven missed entirely, and only two hit buildings and equipment. In heavy clouds, 42 percent of bombs fell more than five miles from the target.[102] Despite these problems, for all of August and into mid-September, Allied commanders believed that massive bombing could end the war soon. Germany's oil shortage was part of the reason.[103]

In this context, requests for US bombing missions against non-strategic targets did not receive serious consideration, except at the War Refugee Board. The representative of the War Refugee Board in Switzerland, Roswell McClelland, forwarded to his superiors in Washington a cable from Agudath Israel activist Isaac Sternbuch to the Union of Orthodox Rabbis in New York that called for bombing the rail lines near Munkács, Kaschau, and Prešov, on the route from Hungary to Auschwitz. On June 23, Pehle sent the matter to Assistant Secretary of War John J. McCloy, head of Civil Affairs, who forwarded it to the War Department Operations Division.[104]

The next day Pehle made it clear to McCloy that he had doubts about whether use of military resources was appropriate and whether bombing could damage rail lines long enough to make a difference. But he forwarded additional requests to McCloy as they came in.[105]

On June 29, Benjamin Akzin, a junior staff official of the War Refugee Board, wrote a memo in favor of requesting the bombing of the physical installations of the two extermination camps (by which he meant Auschwitz and Birkenau) as a way of disrupting the assembly-line killing. Akzin knew that Auschwitz lay in the industrial region of Upper Silesia, and he knew that US bombers were active there anyway. He did not sense how close priority industrial targets were to Birkenau. He admitted that such bombing would kill many prisoners but argued that they were doomed anyway. Destroying the gas chambers might save those who arrived subsequently. But on July 1, Leon Kubowitzki, head of the rescue section of the World Jewish Congress, informed Pehle that he opposed the idea of bombing the gas chambers from the air precisely because it would kill prisoners. It would also enable the Nazis to claim that the Allies were responsible for killing the Jews at Auschwitz. He favored the use of Soviet paratroopers or the Polish underground to attack the camp and destroy the killing apparatus.[106] Pehle likely did not think either option politically feasible, and he did not forward Kubowitzki's ideas to McCloy.

On July 4, McCloy put a polite gloss on the firmly negative reaction he received from the War Department's Operations Division, telling Pehle: "The War Department is of the opinion that the suggested air operation is impracticable. It could be executed only by the diversion of considerable air support essential to the success of our forces now engaged in decisive operations and would in any case be of such very doubtful efficacy that it would not amount to a practical project."[107] This turned out to be the template for responses to numerous subsequent requests for bombing of the gas chambers and crematoria, the last one in November.[108]

In retrospect, the phrase "diversion of considerable air support essential to the success of our forces" reflected military attitudes but was prone to misinterpretation. The bombing would *not* have required geographical diversion of planes, since the Fifteenth was already bombing Budapest and would soon bomb Blechhammer and Monowitz, both within a handful of miles of Birkenau. But the bombers would have been diverted from targets selected for the purpose of shortening the war. In that sense, the bombing of Auschwitz-Birkenau had an opportunity cost that the military perceived to be heavy. And the War Department likely feared that acceptance of one humanitarian mission would encourage other such requests.

The planners and pilots of missions targeting Blechhammer and Monowitz could not simply have added the gas chambers and crematoria as targets. The bombing of synthetic oil sites was the product of years of discussion and preparation all along the chain of command. Historian Tami Davis Biddle explains what the addition of Birkenau would have required:

> It would have been necessary, first of all, to make Auschwitz an emergency priority target (following a debate that would win the support of the highest political and military authorities).

It would also have been necessary to make Auschwitz the subject of a dedicated, extensive photo-reconnaissance evalua-
tion. . . . And operational planners would have had to accept
the likelihood of mission failure, large numbers of collateral
casualties among the prisoners or both.[109]

The bombing of Auschwitz received more consideration in
London. After information from the Auschwitz Protocols
reached Foreign Secretary Anthony Eden, he raised the matter
with Churchill, whereas there is no written evidence that it ever
reached Roosevelt. Eden said he was "ready to consider with the
Air Ministry what can be done. We are in fact bombing Budapest already." Eden met personally with Chaim Weizmann and
Moshe Shertok of the Jewish Agency Executive, both of whom
pressed strongly for bombing both rail lines and gas chambers.
Churchill asked Eden to "get anything out of the Air Force you
can and invoke me as necessary. Certainly appeal to Stalin." Still,
the proposal did not move forward, in part because a mission
from the UK of some two thousand miles was considered nearly
impossible. Churchill's friend Sir Archibald Sinclair, secretary
of state for air, responded to Eden that interrupting the rail
lines was impossible for the British and for the Americans, and
that destroying the plant was not feasible for the British, presumably because of inability to hit precise targets. Bombing the
camp and dropping weapons for prisoners at the same time
would be extremely difficult, but the United States might consider it. Even so, an American daytime raid—the distance was
judged too great for a nighttime raid—from Italy would be
costly, hazardous, and likely ineffective; it might not help the
victims even if it succeeded.[110]

British officials asked the United States, but not the Soviets,
to consider this mission, and to prepare, they began to search for
photographic intelligence. But once the Foreign Office learned

that the deportations of Jews from Hungary to Auschwitz had ceased, they decided that the technical difficulties were overwhelming, and they advised the United States not to pursue the matter.[111] Neither military wished to get involved in a difficult mission unrelated to winning the war.

Although Churchill supported the idea of bombing the gas chambers, he did not handle the matter personally, nor did he follow up. It was not a priority for him. Perhaps Churchill the historian wanted a written record of his emotional reaction to Nazi barbarity.

At the end of August and in early September, a request from Hungarian Jews (through the Polish consul in Bern) for the bombing of rail lines in Slovakia on the route from Hungary to Auschwitz reached the US War Department. Officials in Washington forwarded the proposal to Allied Forces Headquarters in the Mediterranean, which sent it to MAAF. MAAF had a category called special requests, that is, those outside the normal priority oil and industrial targets. An MAAF analyst did not fully understand the logistics of the Hungarian Jewish request and probably did not comprehend the Nazi operation at Birkenau either, but he did grasp that it would be very difficult to cut the rail lines to Auschwitz and keep them out of action for an extended period; the Fifteenth Air Force had too many other commitments. MAAF informed the War Department that it could not be done.[112]

The same Hungarian Jewish request had also listed the rail marshaling Vrutsky as a useful target for interrupting traffic to Auschwitz. On September 13, on a mission to Blechhammer, the Fifteenth's Fifth Bombardment Wing found itself hampered by a defensive smokescreen and was unable to see the refinery. It turned to Vrutsky as a target of opportunity, hit the target, and temporarily cut the rail lines.[113] By then, however, the deportations from Hungary to Auschwitz had ceased. The damage at Vrutsky had no effect on Nazi operations at Birkenau.

In this same period the Fifteenth Air Force also tried to destroy the rail line between Athens and Belgrade in the hope of preventing the evacuation of German troops from Greece, but subsequent investigation showed that they only slightly hampered German troop movements. The Fifteenth also tried frequently to cut the rail lines connecting Italy and Germany through the Brenner Pass, but the Germans quickly adapted to any damage, and their war effort did not suffer.[114] These are among numerous examples of unsuccessful bombing of rail lines.

Decades later, some observers blasted what they viewed as the missed opportunity. In his address in the Capitol Rotunda for the first National Day of Remembrance Ceremony in 1979, Elie Wiesel, himself a prisoner at Auschwitz in 1944, said, "When Hungarian Jews began arriving there feeding the flames with ten or twelve thousand persons per day, nothing [military] was done to stop or delay the process. Not one bomb was dropped on the railway tracks to the death camps."[115] He repeated his accusation in his speech at the opening of the United States Holocaust Memorial in 1993, adding, "As long as I live, I will not understand that." Wiesel's advocacy helped to explain how the concept of relatively painless bombing of rail lines to interrupt the Holocaust gained a place in Western discourse, and persuaded President George W. Bush of its feasibility.[116]

David S. Wyman's 1978 *Commentary* article, "Why Auschwitz Was Never Bombed," and books by Martin Gilbert and Wyman in the early 1980s contained the first detailed research and analysis of these appeals to bomb, the United States' and the UK's responses, and alternative scenarios.[117] In 1993, the Smithsonian Air and Space Museum and the United States Holocaust Memorial Museum held a joint conference in Washington, DC. The museums invited many of those who had written on the possibility of bombing Auschwitz. Gerhart Riegner, a contemporary who had appealed for bombing, also took part. Wyman declined an invitation to attend, but Gilbert sent a piece read by another participant. Most of the speakers published their papers in a book, *The Bombing of Auschwitz* (2000), which also reprinted many of the key primary sources and contained excellent introductions.[118] It is still indispensable reading. Its sources and coverage showed a range of well-informed viewpoints with different perspectives and interpretations. (Full disclosure: I was one of the participants.)

By and large, the military experts present were skeptical or cautious about the odds of destroying the gas chambers and the costs of trying. Historian Tami Davis Biddle, for example, notes that during an April 29, 1944, raid aimed at the railway facilities in the Friedrichstrasse area of Berlin, only one of eleven combat groups dropped bombs within five miles of the target. Another military historian, Rondell Rice, a former air force captain who did not attend the conference but submitted an article for the book, argued that the US Fifteenth Air Force could have mounted a serious attempt if the political will to do so had existed. But Rice wrote that it would have required a major daytime effort in clear weather.[119]

None of the participants at the Smithsonian-Holocaust Museum conference argued that such a mission could have succeeded in time to interrupt the gassing of Jews deported from Hungary. The decision-making and operational planning would have taken time, and Horthy stopped the deportations by mid-July. Given that news of the Hungarian deportations had supplied the immediate cause of the appeals for bombing, as historian Michael Neufeld noted, the cessation of deportations from Hungary eliminated any possibility that Roosevelt or Churchill would impose this mission on their air forces.[120]

The gas chambers at Birkenau continued to operate even when Hungarian transports ceased. The SS gassed Jews from labor camps in Upper Silesia and occupied Poland, from Berlin, from Paris, from Trieste, and from the concentration camp at Majdanek in the last two weeks of July.[121] In other words, the moral argument for destroying the gas chambers remained unaffected by the cessation of the trains from Hungary. Historians Gerhard Weinberg and Michael Neufeld were sympathetic to the argument that an attempted Allied bombing of the gas chambers would have made a moral statement.[122]

Since 2000, occasional journal articles about the bombing of Auschwitz have mostly dwelt on hypotheticals. Retrospective advocates of bombing may have aimed for a "quick fix" for genocide and its barbaric use of technology.[123] Opponents sought to explain why precision bombing under wartime constraints and existing technology faced long odds and might not have saved many lives. Authors put more effort and thought into what would or would not have worked to destroy the gas chambers than the military and government officials did at the time. One good scholarly article also dealt with likely SS reaction to a hypothetical bombing attempt at Birkenau. Whenever Allied bombs accidentally fell on Birkenau, historian Joseph White noted, SS guards assumed that the Allies were punishing them because of their treatment of Jews, and they took vengeance on their Jewish prisoners. If all the gas chambers had been put out of action, despite the reinforced concrete buildings with a narrow air profile, the SS still could have killed existing and arriving Jewish prisoners by shooting and other means.[124]

White's line of argument contradicted Wyman, who maintained that Allied destruction of the gas chambers at Birkenau might have induced the Nazi regime to end the mass killing of Jews.[125] Without naming Wyman, historian Gerhard Weinberg commented on this portion of his argument:

The idea that men who were dedicated to the killing program, and who saw their own careers and even their own lives tied to its continuation, were likely to be halted in their tracks by a few line-cuts on the railways or the blowing up of a gas-chamber is preposterous. The notion that people who had by the summer of 1944 . . . [brought about] the deaths of well over four million and quite probably over five million Jews lacked the persistence, ingenuity, and means to kill the majority of Hungary's seven hundred thousand Jews defies all reason.[126]

In my view, Wyman underestimated the reach and depth of Nazi antisemitism and Hitler's determination to kill Jews to the end. Wyman also argued that the Nazis believed that the West did not care what they did with the Jews, and that the West failed to prove otherwise.[127] But Nazi officials as high as Himmler and Schellenberg knew of the activities of the War Refugee Board.

The persistence of controversy about the non-bombing of Auschwitz reflects the emergence of Auschwitz as a symbol of the Holocaust in the late twentieth century. Wyman and others after him turned Allied unwillingness to try to destroy the gas chambers into a microcosm of perceived Allied failures to respond to the Holocaust. At the level of popular discussion, one commonly hears, "they didn't even try to bomb the gas chambers."

This symbolism was skewed in two respects. Vrba and Wetzler's estimate of more than 1.7 million Jews killed at Birkenau over two years was more than half a million high. From the late twentieth century on, scholars have raised the number of Jewish victims killed by mass executions and other means. Allied bombing could not have halted such Nazi actions. In addition, as historian Rebecca Erbelding argued, the War Refugee Board fundamentally changed US policy in January 1944, and its efforts had substantial influence on Horthy's decision to suspend deportations.[128] The absence of deportations from mid-July to mid-October 1944, combined with additional humanitarian efforts by Wallenberg and others in Budapest before and after the Arrow Cross coup in mid-October, resulted in the survival of the majority of Jews in Budapest. Would destroying the gas chambers have saved more?

According to Wyman, destroying the gas chambers in July 1944 would have saved at least 150,000 lives.[129] It *would* have reduced the efficiency of Nazi killing, but Wyman's claim represents false precision. The trade-offs of trying to bomb the gas chambers were complex. How many Jews in wooden barracks would have been killed in Allied bombing of the camp? How many planes and pilots would have been diverted from industrial or military targets with what effect, how many would have been lost, and how much longer might the war have gone on? In a letter to the editor of *Commentary*, in response to Wyman's article there, Milt Groban, a radar navigator bombardier who had participated in the Fifteenth Air Force's raid on Auschwitz-Monowitz (a factory raid) on August 20, 1944, accepted the logic of the War Department's claim that it should not divert planes from war targets. He also pointed out that the Nazis could and did find other ways to kill Jews. If the war in Europe had gone on longer than it did, each day a larger number of malnourished and sick Jewish and non-Jewish prisoners wasting away in camps in Germany would have died.[130] These factors make it impossible to determine how many lives would have been saved by successful bombing, and one would have to discount that estimate by factoring in the probability of success of any bombing mission. Looking at all the issues, historian Michael Neufeld wrote that readers of *The Bombing of Auschwitz* would have to decide for themselves whether bombing the gas

chambers would have been effective.[131] In my view, it would
have been a long-shot attempt.

The only contemporary who belatedly maintained that
Franklin Roosevelt played a role in the decision not to bomb
Auschwitz was Assistant Secretary John J. McCloy, a highly visible member of the postwar US establishment. Late in life Mc-
Cloy found himself under criticism for his rejection of proposals
to bomb the gas chambers and crematoria. In a 1983 interview
about this controversy, McCloy for the first time "remembered"
that the War Department general staff had consulted air force
operational commanders in Europe and reported negative conclusions to him. He also recalled that Judge Rosenman and
Harry Hopkins had asked him to investigate the feasibility of
bombing the death camp. They later allegedly told him that
FDR had rejected the idea.[132] But there are no traces of these
inquiries in the archives. McCloy's 1983 recollections and similar later ones seem to be self-serving inventions.

Wyman severely criticized Franklin Roosevelt for failing to
respond in any significant way to the Holocaust, but Wyman did
not make Roosevelt personally responsible for the decision not
to try to destroy the gas chambers and crematoria at Birkenau.
In fact, Wyman strongly suggested that the issue never reached
the president, although his most explicit statements are buried
in footnotes.[133] Certain subsequent writers have been less cautious, calling the president the decision-maker without any convincing evidence.[134]

Given how Roosevelt operated, without notes or memoranda
of his conversations, one cannot exclude the remote possibility
that he discussed Auschwitz with someone else during the
second half of 1944, but if he did, it did not influence War Department's rejections of appeals for the bombing of the gas
chambers.

CONCLUSION

Scholars of the Holocaust sometimes divide their protago-
nists into fixed moral categories: perpetrators, victims,
bystanders, and rescuers. Observers of a massacre who
could intervene but do not can be called bystanders. Whether
Allied leaders fit this category is not a simple question.

Some moral critics cite the maxim, "The only thing that is
necessary for the triumph of evil is for good men to do nothing."[1]
Those who draw this "lesson" from the Holocaust convert the
Allied leaders into bystanders by separating the Holocaust en-
tirely from the war. But the war effort by the UK, the United
States, and the USSR was doing something indeed.

Churchill, Roosevelt, and Stalin initially viewed the Nazi
campaign against the Jews as one small element of the war.
Only gradually did Roosevelt and Churchill learn that the Holocaust was unprecedented in modern history. Even Stalin, a
practitioner of political murder on a vast scale, saw the Nazi
mass killings of Jews as unusually primitive. Moral critics may
justifiably complain that the three Allied leaders could have
done more to save Jews even while fighting the Axis. For most of
the Holocaust, none of the three was a rescuer. They certainly
could have spoken out more clearly against Nazi genocide; that

might have added credibility to the warnings that Jews in Axis-controlled territories were already receiving.

These failings of Allied leaders do not explain why the Nazis were able to kill six million Jews. The December 5, 1938, prediction by US Consul in Berlin Raymond Geist was prophetic: "They [the Nazis] have embarked on a program of annihilation of the Jews and we shall be allowed to save the remnants if we choose."[2] After the first wave of the Holocaust, characterized by mass shootings in the second half of 1941, Nazi Germany opened an extermination camp (Chełmno) in an annexed part of Poland. Others followed in 1942. For the next two years, the Allies had no military means or diplomatic leverage to interfere with, or stop, massive deportations, gassing, and the continued shooting of Jews. By the time Allied military options and some diplomatic leverage emerged, in 1944, Auschwitz-Birkenau was the only one of the six main extermination camps still operating fully, destroying many thousands of Jews daily in its gas chambers and crematoria; most of the other extermination camps had shut down, having destroyed their assigned Jewish populations.[3]

The historian William Rubinstein has analyzed most of the rescue proposals raised during the Holocaust, seeking to show that the democracies could not have done any more for the Jews than they did.[4] In my view, he exaggerates, because the Western Allies did not make a serious effort until January 1944. Even more responsive US and UK policies, however, could not have saved millions of Jews. Antisemitic elements in Germany and Axis countries (such as Hungary) could kill Jews faster than outsiders could rescue them. On the other hand, if the war in Europe had lasted longer, the Nazis would likely have killed at least hundreds of thousands more Jews—from The Netherlands, Belgium, France, Slovakia, and elsewhere. If the war in North Africa had gone badly for the Allies, we might be talking

today of more than seven million Jewish victims of the
Holocaust.

Franklin Roosevelt most often bears the brunt of moral criticism for alleged Allied passivity before and during the Holocaust, in part because of a US immigration policy laden with
restrictions. The basic immigration law of 1924 established
varying annual national quotas, and during Roosevelt's presidency Congress was hostile to any expansion of these quotas.
Although the quota for Germany was one of the larger ones, ad-
ministrative regulations dating back to the Hoover administration initially prevented much of the quota from being used. Ad-
justments of these regulations accounted for much of the
fluctuation in immigration from Germany during 1933–1941.
Because Nazi Germany made the emigration of European Jews
extraordinarily difficult from the fall of 1941 on, new American
security-based regulations impeded mainly the Jewish refugees
who reached Allied or neutral territory. Despite the small
number of Jews who surmounted all the obstacles to immigrate
in 1942–1945, Jewish immigration was unpopular and remained a politically sensitive issue for Roosevelt.[5]

Eighty years after the end of World War II, too many Americans have forgotten or ignored the context in which Roosevelt
operated before the United States entered the war. Congress
was unsympathetic about intervening in Europe, and public
opinion was sharply divided. Most people today do not know
that, in 1940, the US Army was considerably smaller than Belgium's.[6] The more Roosevelt tried to oppose Nazi Germany's expansion, the more difficult it was for him, politically, to take
public steps on behalf of Jews suffering or dying under Nazi
rule. Aware of antisemitism in Congress and in the electorate,
the president wanted, and needed, strong public support for
what might be an extended war. After the Japanese attack at
Pearl Harbor in December 1941, he chose to emphasize the war

in North Africa and Europe, rather than the war in the Pacific, as discussed in Chapter 2.[7] FDR's military priorities shortened the war in Europe and, in the process, also the Holocaust.

During 1942 and 1943, Roosevelt as war president left most issues related to the Holocaust in the hands of the largely conservative State Department. Neither Under Secretary Welles nor his successor Edward Stettinius, both personally open to refugee initiatives, put in the time or made an aggressive effort to eliminate bureaucratic opposition to assisting European Jews. Mid-level State Department officials judged reports of Nazi extermination policy unsubstantiated and public clamor for Allied rescue efforts detrimental to the war effort. Thus, the United States did not follow up the December 17, 1942, declaration by the Allied governments that Germany was implementing a policy of exterminating the Jews. Switzerland, Turkey, Sweden, Spain, and Portugal might have offered sanctuary or other assistance to more Jewish refugees earlier, had they been given American (or British) encouragement and promises to resettle Jews after the war. Private relief organizations in Switzerland and Sweden managed to get some food parcels to prisoners in some Nazi camps, including Auschwitz, and also to starving Jewish communities, but they struggled to maneuver around Allied blockade restrictions designed to punish Nazi Germany.[8]

Experts in psychological warfare in Washington and London frequently argued against Allied steps that would have appeared to endorse Jewish goals, often citing as justification the high level of existing antisemitism in Germany and other Axis countries, as well as in North Africa and the Middle East. Such considerations probably influenced Roosevelt and Churchill to avoid speaking out publicly for most of the war against the Nazi policy of annihilation of the Jews of Europe and North Africa. In retrospect, psychological warfare experts placed too much weight on their capacity to manipulate opinion in enemy countries or potentially hostile territories. Whatever they did, they could not have driven a wedge between enemy regimes and their subjects. But they did miss an opportunity to underscore the contrast between Western democratic values and Nazi barbarism.

Eventually, Roosevelt decided to establish a War Refugee Board and to praise it at a press conference. On March 24, 1944, he made an explicit statement about the Holocaust, tying it to the need to block the deportation of Jews from Hungary to Auschwitz: it was the only such action by an Allied leader during the war. His action, which did not impair the war effort, supplied a critical weapon in the War Refugee Board's sustained campaign against the deportation of Jews from Hungary to Auschwitz. American warnings, and entreaties by neutral sources, eventually helped persuade Hungary's Regent, Admiral Horthy, in July 1944, to block further deportations. Thus, the majority of the Jews of Budapest managed to survive the war and the Holocaust. One of the implications of the Hungarian experience was that trying to save Jews targeted by the Nazis and their Hungarian collaborators made a difference, even if the War Refugee Board could not tell in advance which measures would work.

Britain, which had no counterpart to the War Refugee Board, cooperated only grudgingly and partially with it. The British Foreign Office was unsympathetic to proposals for rescuing Jews; it also worried that Jews escaping from Nazi control might be sent (or go illegally) to Palestine. Moreover, Foreign Secretary Anthony Eden held pro-Arab views that were more popular than Churchill's in the War Cabinet, which took decisions collectively. Notwithstanding Churchill's reputation as a powerful wartime leader, he did not deal personally with Holocaust issues. Churchill's reputation as a voice of conscience depends largely on several well-crafted expressions of emotion that did not lead to action.

Even so, it is hard to imagine a practical political alternative to Churchill at 10 Downing Street who could have or would have done more about Holocaust-related issues. Churchill's chief Conservative rival in the spring of 1940, Lord Halifax, wanted to pursue a negotiated settlement with Hitler. This would have been a disaster for European Jews and for the world. Churchill was determined to fight Nazi Germany to the end, and he helped inspire his countrymen to bear the costs.

Stalin was uninterested in the rescue of Soviet Jews, except at moments when it might have affected Soviet relations with the West or the flow of Western aid to the USSR when the country was imperiled in 1941–1942. But some of Stalin's moves saved Jews even if that was not his primary intention. When he ordered the evacuation of politically and professionally valuable citizens from western regions of the USSR in late June 1941, large numbers of Soviet Jews were among them. Although this move put them out of immediate Nazi reach, no one considers it as a rescue from the Holocaust.

So, it is hard to force Roosevelt, Churchill, and Stalin into any of the categories of perpetrators, victims, bystanders, and rescuers, even though their war policies and military decisions had substantial repercussions on the Holocaust.

Some twenty-first-century observers overlook the interweaving of the war and the Holocaust. They search for lessons during the Holocaust showing that moral intentions led to positive results and immoral policies to negative ones. Reacting against this tendency, Michael Marrus, a leading Holocaust scholar, once argued that the Holocaust produced no lessons.[9] By this, he did not mean that those living in normal conditions could not grasp the universe of the Holocaust and the suffering of its victims, but that those who see lessons in the catastrophe are interested less in what happened in the past and more in applying them to the present. In doing so, they select historical events that support the present course they wish to follow, and in the process, oversimplify, or distort, the historical record. Marrus cautioned that the phrase "lesson(s) of the Holocaust" should bear a warning label that distortion may follow. If our "lesson" *predetermines* how historical events are selected, or interpreted, it will be useless or even harmful.

In my view, a deep knowledge of historical antecedents offers at least some guidance on current problems. We cannot grapple intellectually, and emotionally, with genocide or ethnic cleansing without understanding and referring to historical precedents: the question is whether we will do it well or poorly. Such guidance rarely yields clear, simple solutions for present problems, but often it helps avoid disastrous mistakes, among them, the drawing of mistaken lessons.

Some bad "lessons" are primarily political. For instance, the American playwright Ben Hecht, in a 1961 book entitled *Perfidy*, examined Joel Brand and Rezső Kasztner's efforts to negotiate with Adolf Eichmann for the release of Jews in Hungary. A supporter of the Revisionist Zionists (the prewar and wartime ancestor of the Likud Party in Israel), Hecht attacked the Zionist establishment and the Allied governments in blistering terms. In a 1962 description by historian Lucy Dawidowicz, Hecht justified Brand's negotiations on Eichmann's offer of "a million Jewish lives for a few thousand trucks," in order to *discredit* Jewish and Allied leaders for not having consummated the deal. Hecht attacked Kasztner for keeping Auschwitz secret from the mass of Hungarian Jewry. Dawidowicz described Hecht's work as a screenplay from history filled with heroes, heroines, villains, and flashbacks, comparing his wild accusations to those made by Senator Joseph McCarthy.[10]

Roosevelt's general reputation as a powerful and successful president served as a red flag to political opponents in his day or in today's rear view. In November 2022, then Israeli Prime Minister Benjamin Netanyahu held a conversation with author Micah Goodman about Netanyahu's new memoir. During their (recorded) talk, Netanyahu said that Roosevelt had responded to Zionist appeals to bomb Nazi extermination camps with the words "over my dead body. Not even one American pilot." As a result of FDR's attitude, the prime minister said, Benjamin Netanyahu's father (Ben Zion Netanyahu, a Revisionist Zionist), allegedly went over to the Republicans.[11] But the conversation with FDR is a fiction.

Others, too, have used Allied decisions not to bomb Auschwitz to intensify moral and political condemnation of Western leaders. Such bombing might not have succeeded and certainly would not have ended the Holocaust.[12] Thus, what the War Refugee Board and the coincidental US bombing of Budapest accomplished in Hungary—helping to save the majority of the Jews of Budapest through warnings and personal diplomacy—measures up well against the failure to bomb the gas chambers often deployed as an example of Allied inaction during the Holocaust.

Other alleged lessons of the Holocaust are moral or ethical in their implications. For example, some critics have argued that, if the Western countries and their colonies had admitted all German Jews at a time when Nazi Germany's Jewish policy was primarily based on Jewish emigration, there would have been no Holocaust. Others have said that Nazi Germany might have halted its extermination factories had the Allies demonstrated greater concern for the Jews during the Holocaust.[13] Such claims shift considerable moral responsibility for the genocide to the Western leaders, and perhaps also, to their citizens. But these are false notions—and not simply because Nazi officials were unwilling to allow all Jews to emigrate, as I showed in Chapter 1.

Hitler and his followers were fixated on the notions of an international Jewish conspiracy and a large German empire in Europe. Forcing out German Jews would not have resolved the basic Jewish problem for these radical antisemites—Germany would gain control of many more Jews as it expanded into Eastern Europe. Once Hitler gained absolute power and momentum, there would have been no easy way to escape a major war to end Hitler's geopolitical and genocidal aspirations. But countries with different interests and different political systems could not coalesce into an alliance until the threats from the Axis powers became pressing. The Allies' industrial mobilization and military expansion took years.

The history of World War II and the Holocaust offers guidance—if not lessons—for how to respond to genocide. If a government or a major political movement carries out genocide amidst a war of expansion or a civil war, it will be extremely difficult for outsiders to limit the killing without directly entering into the conflict. In the worst case, they will be able to save only the "remnants" of the targeted group. Whether major military powers in the future will see military intervention as in their interest remains to be seen; it will likely depend on the identity and geopolitical importance of the victims of aggression and genocide. The historical pattern is discouraging.[14]

THE HISTORY DESCRIBED and analyzed here is not fossilized. It once seemed that World War II and the Holocaust discredited radical antisemitism, but that turned out to be an overly optimistic view. Recent attempts to rehabilitate Hitler have been limited to fringe characters in numerous countries. But the belief that Jews conspire against their countries of residence for their own selfish reasons has found adherents in major political parties in many Western countries, including the United States, and in the Middle East. Many Germans and Westerners doubted the significance of Hitler's ideology before and after he came to power. Today, there are many who ignore antisemitism on the extreme right or on the extreme left, as well as hostility and violence against Jews based on religious extremism.

The white nationalists who organized a rally to "Unite the Right" at Charlottesville, Virginia, in August 2017 chanted, "Jews will not replace us." When the marchers turned violent, it seemed to be a natural extension of their ideology. And when President Trump later commented that there were good people on both sides at Charlottesville, he gave a conscious nod to that ideology.

Some leftist intellectuals have long portrayed Israel as a Western colonial enterprise forced upon a Muslim region—an artificial implant. By the 1960s, the Soviet Union, which had supported the establishment of Israel, promoted in the Third World what it called anti-Zionism. These notions spread in the United States in the wake of protests over the (unrelated) police killing of George Floyd in Minneapolis in 2020.[15] Leftist critics whose empathy for Palestinians leads them to deny the legitimacy of Israel or to insist that Western Jews disavow support for Israel overlook not only the ancient Jewish tie to the land, but also the formal partition of the area between Jewish and Arab dwellers drawn up and approved by the United Nations in 1947. Arab states instead chose to invade and try to destroy Israel militarily.

The organization Hamas, founded in 1987 as the Palestinian branch of the Muslim Brotherhood, believes that Jews, by manipulating and dominating non-Jews in their countries of residence, have been the force behind noxious revolutions throughout history.[16] Hamas promotes the slogan, "From the river to the sea; Palestine will be free." This antisemitic chant is potentially a call for genocide; treating these lines as an innocuous slogan is an example of sympathetic outsiders wishing away the fundamental ideology of a terrorist organization. The founding charter of Hamas calls for its members to kill Jews, not just Israelis. Alvin Rosenfeld, an Indiana University expert on antisemitism, writes, "for Hamas, Islamic Jihad, Hezbollah, and their sponsor, the Islamic Republic of Iran, . . . [this conflict] is primarily religious, and at its heart is the annihilationist fantasy of ending the Jewish state by killing as many Jews as possible. The goal is not a two-state solution but the Final Solution."[17]

On October 7, 2023, Hamas forces based in Gaza slipped into Israel, catching the Israel Defense Forces by surprise. Attacking the large audience at a music festival, Hamas inflicted rape, torture, and the mutilation of bodies. Within days, they slaughtered about 1,200 Israelis as well as some foreigners—the largest massacre of Jews since the Holocaust. Hamas also took some 240 hostages back to Gaza, where they were dispersed and hidden.

At an October 2023 Holocaust conference in Prague, a group of scholars led by University of Toronto Professor Jan Grabowski, an expert on the Holocaust in Poland, formulated and circulated elsewhere a statement, which read in part:

> The global explosion of antisemitism which we witness today is a testimony to the power of forces which seek to threaten not only the Jewish people but, at the same time, to destroy the basic tenets of the democratic system.
>
> Attacks on Jews and Jewish places of worship multiply across our communities and campuses and Holocaust education finds itself increasingly under attack. We cannot allow this situation to continue. Today, more than ever, we need to

reaffirm, without any caveats, the right of Jews to live in Israel and to defend themselves against those who deny Israel
and Jews the right to exist. We deplore the humanitarian catastrophe of the Palestinian people in Gaza and note that it
derives directly from the use of civilians as human shields by
the Hamas. We, the scholars of the Holocaust . . . unequivo-
cally condemn the politics of terror pursued by Hamas and
denounce the forces of global antisemitism. It is our duty to
ensure that the lessons of the past be not unlearned, and that
the legacy of the Shoah be not forgotten.

Grabowski's words captured the immediacy and urgency of Holocaust memory at a critical moment.

Hitler had enough political power and influence over German
culture to try to inculcate a modern industrial, educated nation
into his fantasy world based on an international Jewish enemy.
Many Western politicians and cultural icons today, though
lacking such power, can still spread antisemitic fantasies
whether or not they personally share these fantasies. What is
one to make of a sitting American politician who claims that the
Rothschilds operated a laser from outer space that set off wildfires in California?[18] Not only Donald Trump, but several other
prominent Republican figures have maintained that Jewish
American financier George Soros directly supported Manhattan
District Attorney Alvin Bragg, the first US authority to indict
and try Trump, the implication being that Soros was the mas-
termind behind Bragg.[19] For more than a quarter century, right-
wing extremists have identified Soros, a survivor of the Holocaust in Hungary, as the puppet master responsible for economic
crises, currency fluctuations, immigration problems, and more,
an example of how Jews are the most frequent target for those
who imagine and fear conspiracies.[20]

The level of popular antisemitism has risen in too many Western countries to assume it will quickly fade away under better economic conditions. Outbreaks of this virus, called the world's oldest hatred, have intensified and spread widely enough to inspire extremist violence against Jews and against governments allegedly under Jewish sway.[21] The careful study of history in schools, colleges, and museums in the West (at least, where that is permitted) and the prosecution of those whose incendiary antisemitic speech leads immediately to violence or other hate crimes may counteract some of this extremism. It is necessary to work to prevent a stubborn virus from turning into an epidemic or even a pandemic.

Churchill and Roosevelt usually refrained from denouncing Nazi antisemitism because they likely feared that such "information warfare" could complicate what they viewed as a struggle for the survival of Western civilization. But shortly after the establishment of the War Refugee Board, Roosevelt authorized the reading of the following letter on White House stationery with his signature to a national conference to combat antisemitism: "The attempt by Adolf Hitler and the Nazi party to rule Germany, to rule Europe and then to rule the Western World, was based on two brutal devices: organized terror and organized anti-semitism [FDR's spelling]. . . . Some of the sources of anti-semitism in this country were created to serve Hitler's purpose. . . . Whoever condones or participates in anti-semitism plays Hitler's game. There is no place in the lives or thoughts of true Americans for anti-semitism."[22]

NOTES

INTRODUCTION

1   David I. Kertzer, *The Pope at War: The Secret History of Pius XII, Mussolini, and Hitler* (New York: Random House, 2023), 239–241. Taylor's Memorandum of Conversation, September 25, 1942 . . ., Vatican Myron Taylor folder 1942, President's Secretary's File, Diplomatic, box 51, Franklin D. Roosevelt Library (FDRL). Richard Breitman and Allan J. Lichtman, *FDR and the Jews* (Cambridge, MA: Belknap Press of Harvard University Press, 2013), 203.

2   Easterman to Taylor, October 7, 1942, copy in 740.00116, European War/634, Record Group 59, National Archives and Records Administration (hereafter NARA). Taylor Memorandum for the President and Secretary of State, October 20, 1942, copy in folder 1, Taylor—September-October 1942, box 84, Sumner Welles Papers FDRL.

3   Kertzer, *The Pope at War*, 241–242. Tittmann to Welles, October 16, 1942, 740.00115 E.W. 1939/605 CF, NARA.

4   David Reynolds and Vladimir Pechatnov, eds., *The Kremlin Letters: Stalin's Wartime Correspondence with Churchill and Roosevelt* (New Haven, CT: Yale University Press, 2018). Warren F. Kimball, *Churchill & Roosevelt: The Complete Correspondence*, 3 vols. (Princeton, NJ: Princeton University Press, 1984). Churchill and FDR did exchange letters about the agreements reached at the Bermuda Conference on Refugees (Kimball, *Churchill & Roosevelt*, vol. II, 293, 315–136).

5   Jeffrey Herf, *The Jewish Enemy: Nazi Propaganda during World War II and the Holocaust* (Cambridge, MA: Belknap Press of Harvard University Press, 2008).

6   Political scientist Shlomo Aronson called this situation a trap. Shlomo Aronson, *Hitler, the Allies, and the Jews* (New York: Cambridge University Press, 2004).

7   By the late 1930s Russians were openly favored as first among equals. The Soviets did permit the establishment, in April 1942, of a Jewish Anti-Fascist Committee to serve the foreign policy interests of the USSR and to contact Jews abroad. I am grateful to Zvi Gitelman for these observations.

8   "1944: Should We Bomb Auschwitz?," directed by Tim Dunn, written by Mark Hayhurst, aired September 19, 2019, on BBC Two, https://www.bbc.co.uk/programmes/m00008lj4.

9   Times of Israel Staff, "Netanyahu: Allies could have saved 4 million Jews if they'd bombed death camps in 1942," *Times of Israel*, April 23, 2017, https://www.timesofisrael.com/netanyahu-allies-could-have-saved-4-million-jews-if-theyd-bombed-death-camps-in-1942/.

10   An exception is the work of Michael J. Cohen, especially *Churchill and the Jews, 1900–1948* (London: Routledge, 2016).

1. HITLER'S AUDIENCES

1   Louis P. Lochner Diary, January 30, 1939, box 11, Lochner Papers, Wisconsin Historical Society, Madison, Wisconsin.

2   Geist to Messersmith, January 22, 1939, folder 73, box 10, George S. Messersmith Papers, University of Delaware.

3   Alan E. Steinweis, *Kristallnacht 1938* (Cambridge, MA: Belknap Press of Harvard University Press, 2009), 99–108, 129–133. Saul Friedländer, *Nazi Germany and the Jews, Volume 1: The Years of Persecution 1933–1939* (New York: Harper Perennial, 1998), 280–291.

4   Steinweis, *Kristallnacht 1938*, 132.

5   Daniel Greene and Edward Phillips, eds., *Americans and the Holocaust: A Reader* (New Brunswick, NJ: Rutgers University Press, 2021), 71–74; Deborah E. Lipstadt, *Beyond Belief: The American Press and the Coming of the Holocaust, 1933–1945* (New York: Touchstone, 1993), 99.

6   "Text of the Protests by Leaders in U.S. against Reich Persecution," *New York Times*, November 15, 1938, p. 4.

7   Richard Breitman and Allan J. Lichtman, *FDR and the Jews* (Cambridge, MA: Belknap Press of Harvard University Press, 2014), 114–120. Hand-edited text of Roosevelt's statement reprinted in Greene and Phillips, *Americans and the Holocaust*, 74–75.

8   Richard Breitman, *The Berlin Mission: The American Who Resisted Nazi Germany from Within* (New York: PublicAffairs, 2019), 161–163.

9   Geist to Messersmith, January 22, 1939, folder 73, box 10, Messersmith Papers, University of Delaware. Geist had no authority to threaten to break relations, but Nazi officials thought he did.

10   Franklin D. Roosevelt, State of the Union Address, January 4, 1939, Annual Message to Congress, The American Presidency Project, https://www.presidency.ucsb.edu/node/209128.

11   Translation of Hitler in Ian Kershaw, *Hitler, 1936–1945: Nemesis* (New York: W. W. Norton, 2000), 153. Gilbert to Secretary of State, January 31, 1939, 762.00/230, RG 59, NARA. Gilbert did not name the secretaries who attended, but there were only six men with this title. Geist was one of two first secretaries. Data on the number of secretaries courtesy of David Langbart, archivist at the US National Archives.

12   Friedländer, *Nazi Germany and the Jews*, 1:308. The German original of Hitler's speech available at https://nla.gov.au/nla.obj-52874254/view?partId=nla.obj-109843179#page/n0/mode/1up.

13   Gerhard L. Weinberg, *The Foreign Policy of Hitler's Germany: Starting World War II 1937–1939*, vol. 2 (Chicago: University of Chicago Press, 1980), 432, 462–63. A recent description of Hitler's dissatisfaction with the Munich agreement in Volker Ullrich, *Hitler: Ascent, 1889–1939*, trans. Jefferson Chase, (New York: Vintage, 2017), 744–748.

14   Kershaw, *Hitler: Nemesis*, 36–37; Weinberg, *Foreign Policy of Hitler's Germany*, 2:34n62.

15   Weinberg, *Foreign Policy of Hitler's Germany*, 2:35. Kershaw, *Hitler: Nemesis*, 46–51.

16   Geist to Messersmith, January 4, 1939, folder 72, box 10, Messersmith Papers, University of Delaware. This letter was read by the secretary of state, the undersecretary of state, and probably FDR. On the readers, Messersmith to Geist, February 4, 1939, folder 74. box 10, Messersmith Papers.

17   Jochen Thies, *Hitler's Plans for Global Domination: Nazi Architecture and Ultimate War Aims*, trans. Ian Cooke and Mary-Beth Friedrich (New York: Berghahn Books, 2012), 119. Lochner Diary, May 13, 1939, box 11, Wisconsin Historical Society. Kershaw, *Hitler: Nemesis*, 167–168.

18   Stephen G. Fritz, *The First Soldier: Hitler as Military Leader* (New Haven, CT: Yale University Press, 2018), xii.

19   Andrew Roberts, *Churchill: Walking with Destiny* (New York: Viking, 2018), 434.

20   Tim Bouverie, *Appeasement: Chamberlain, Hitler, Churchill, and the Road to War* (New York: Tim Duggan Books, 2019), 167–169.

21   Roberts, *Churchill*, 440–441.

22   See Fritz, *The First Soldier*, 59.

23   Susan Dunn, *1940: FDR, Willkie, Lindbergh, Hitler—The Election and the Storm* (New Haven, CT: Yale University Press, 2013), 31, 143–144.

24   Breitman, *The Berlin Mission*, 170–171.

25   Breitman and Lichtman, *FDR and the Jews*, 135.

26   Breitman, *The Berlin Mission*, 162.

27   Breitman, *The Berlin Mission*, 173–178.

28   Friedländer, *Nazi Germany and the Jews*, 1:310–311.

29   "Reichstag Speech," January 30, 1939, Holocaust Encyclopedia, United States Holocaust Memorial Museum, https://www.ushmm.org/learn /timeline-of-events/1939-1941/hitler-speech-to-german-parliament.

30   Klaus P. Fischer, *Hitler & America* (Philadelphia: University of Pennsylvania Press, 2011), 32–33, 100.

31   "Bömer is trying hard to get the translated text for us." Lochner Diary, January 30, 1939, box 11, Lochner Papers, Wisconsin Historical Society.

32   *Daily Sentinel*, Grand Junction, Colorado, January 30, 1939, p. 1.

33   "Official Text, Translation Differ as to Hitler's Word," *Oakland Tribune*, January 31, 1939, p. 3.

34   Lochner Diary, January 31, 1939, box 11, Lochner Papers, Wisconsin Historical Society. "Hitler Talk Stirs Hope," *Oakland Tribune*, January 31, 1939, p. 1.

35   "Spade-Work for a Colonial Munich," *The Daily Oklahoman*, February 4, 1939, p. 6.

36   Alexandra Garbarini, Emil Kerenji, Jan Lambertz, and Avinoam Patt, eds., *Jewish Responses to Persecution: 1938–1940* (Lanham, MD: AltaMira Press, 2011), 105–106.

37   James G. McDonald, *Refugees and Rescue: The Diaries and Papers of James G. McDonald, 1935–1945*, ed. Richard Breitman, Barbara McDonald Stewart, and Severin Hochberg (Bloomington: Indiana University Press, 2009), 164.

38   Garbarini, et al., *Jewish Responses to Persecution*, 104.

39   Breitman, *The Berlin Mission*, 178; Lochner Diary, February 2, 1939, box 11, Lochner Papers, Wisconsin Historical Society.

40   "Mass Emigration of German Jews Believed Near," *The Owensboro Messenger* (Owensboro, KY), February 3, 1939, p. 1.

41   Lochner Diary, January 16, 1939, box 11, Lochner Papers, Wisconsin Historical Society.

42   Breitman, *The Berlin Mission*, 179.

43   Breitman, *The Berlin Mission*, 162.

44   See Friedländer, *Nazi Germany and the Jews*, 1:311–312.

45   Ullrich, *Hitler*, 1:680.

46   Zentralverlag der NSDAP, Franz Eher, 1939, https://nla.gov.au/nla.obj-52874254/view?partId=nla.obj-109843179#page/n0/mode/1up.

47   "Nazi Papers Start Chant for Colonies," *The Staunton News-Leader*, February 1, 1939, p. 1.

48   Breitman, *The Berlin Mission*, 180–181, 184.

49   Vicki Caron, *Uneasy Asylum: France and the Jewish Refugee Crisis, 1933–1942* (Stanford: Stanford University Press, 2002), 203, 207–210.

50   Breitman, *The Berlin Mission*, 183.

51   Weinberg, *The Foreign Policy of Hitler's Germany*, 2:467–470.

52   Thies, *Hitler's Plans for Global Domination*, 126–127n30 has a partial list. See also, Fritz, *The First Soldier*, 69.

53   Hildegard von Kotze, ed., *Heeresadjutant bei Hitler, 1938–1943: Aufzeichnungen des Majors Engel* (Stuttgart: Deutsche Verlags-Anstalt, 1974), 44n117. Thies, *Hitler's Plans for Global Domination*, 115–119.

54   Thies, *Hitler's Plans for Global Domination*, 116.

55   On March 8, Hitler held a reception in the New Reich Chancellery for select government officials. Max Domarus, ed., *Hitler: Reden und Proklamationen, 1932–1945*, vol. 2, part 1, *1939–1940* (Munich: 1965), 1089. Himmler's schedule lists an evening event for industrialists on March 8. Himmler's appointments, Microfilm T-581, Roll 37A, Captured German Records, RG 242, NARA. Hitler's appointments, T-84, R 387, frame 471, RG 242, NARA.

56   Bullitt to Roosevelt, September 19, 1939, secret and personal for the president, Confidential File 740.00/684, and 740.00/2138, RG 59, NARA.

57   The first report gives possible dates as March 9 or 10, but places Hitler in Berchtesgaden. The second, more detailed report places the event on Wednesday evening, March 8, at "the Führer's." The second man who went to Vienna is listed as Vogl, which may mean Alfred Vögler, a major figure in German heavy industry and munitions. Bullitt to Hull, March 25,

1939, secret and personal; Bullitt to Roosevelt, September 19, 1939, secret and personal for the president, Confidential File 740.00/684, and 740.00/ 2138, RG 59, NARA.

58   For example, interrogation of Wilhelm Keppler, November 2, 1945, XL 28239, entry 16, RG 226, NARA.

59   "January 30th, 1939," Franklin D. Roosevelt Day by Day, http://www .fdrlibrary.marist.edu/daybyday/daylog/january-30th-1939/.

60   Presidential Press Conference, January 31, 1939, http://www.fdr library.marist.edu/_resources/images/pc/pc0077.pdf; Kenneth S. Davis, *FDR: Into the Storm, 1937–1940* (New York: Random House, 1993), 405. The president interpreted Hitler's interest in expanded ties with Central and South American countries as designs upon them.

61   FDR's schedule in http://www.fdrlibrary.marist.edu/daybyday/daylog /january-31st-1939/; Presidential Press Conference, January 31, 1939, http://www.fdrlibrary.marist.edu/_resources/images/pc/pc0077.pdf; "The Congress: Senators in Distress," *Time*, February 13, 1939. On Lundeen's German tie, see Bradley W. Hart, *Hitler's American Friends: The Third Reich's Supporters in the United States* (New York: Thomas Dunne Books, 2018), 97.

62   Detailed summary of the White House meeting in Davis, *FDR: Into the Storm, 1937–1940*, 399–408. See also, PSF 188, Franklin D. Roosevelt Library, cited by Fischer, *Hitler and America*, 102; Robert Dallek, *Franklin D. Roosevelt and American Foreign Policy, 1932–1945* (New York: Oxford University Press, 1979), 181–182.

63   Davis, *FDR: Into the Storm*, 405–406.

64   Weinberg, *Foreign Policy of Hitler's Germany*, 2:530.

65   Susan Dunn, *Roosevelt's Purge: How FDR Fought to Change the Democratic Party* (Cambridge, MA: Harvard University Press, 2012).

66   Davis, *FDR: Into the Storm*, 406.

67   See Geist to Messersmith, June 12, 1938, folder 64, box 9, Messersmith Papers, summarized briefly in Breitman, *The Berlin Mission*, 140. See also, *The Berlin Mission*, 200, 208–209.

68   Weinberg, *Foreign Policy of Hitler's Germany*, 2:533–534.

69   "Roosevelt Arms Talk Stirs Europe," *Des Moines Tribune*, February 1, 1939, quoting the *Berliner Nachtausgabe* of January 31, which ran the headline "America's Frontier on the Rhine."

70   Presidential Press Conferences, January 31, 1939, and February 3, 1939, http://www.fdrlibrary.marist.edu/resources/images/pc/pc0077.pdf; Davis, *FDR: Into the Storm*, 407–409.

71   Dallek, *Franklin Roosevelt and American Foreign Policy*, 174–175; Tami David Biddle, *Rhetoric and Reality in Air Warfare: The Evolution of British and American Ideas About Strategic Bombing, 1914–1945* (Princeton, NJ: Princeton University Press, 2002), 204.

72   Presidential Press Conferences, January 31, 1939, and February 3, 1939, http://www.fdrlibrary.marist.edu/resources/images/pc/pc0077.pdf.

73   See the account in Dallek, *Franklin D. Roosevelt and American Foreign Policy*, 179–205.

74   Lucy S. Dawidowicz, *The War Against the Jews 1933–1945* (New York: Bantam Books, 1976), 147–148; Jeffrey Herf, *The Jewish Enemy: Nazi Propaganda during World War II and the Holocaust* (Cambridge, MA: Belknap Press of Harvard University Press, 2008), 77, 166–167. For the broad list of Hitler's references to prophecy, Saul Friedländer, *The Years of Extermination: Nazi Germany and the Jews, 1939–1945* (New York: HarperCollins, 2007), 239, 265, 273–274, 279–280, 287, 331–332, 402–404.

75   "Nazi Policy Will Drive Jews from Europe," *Charlotte Observer*, October 28, 1941, p. 14.

2. CHURCHILL'S ALLIES

1   Martin Gilbert, *Churchill and the Jews: A Lifelong Friendship* (New York: Henry Holt, 2007), 186. Andrew Roberts, *Churchill: Walking with Destiny* (New York: Viking, 2018), 678.

2   Speech reprinted in "Mr. Churchill's Message," *Manchester Guardian*, August 25, 1941, p. 5; online version at https://www.jewishvirtuallibrary.org /churchill-broadcast-regarding-his-meeting-with-roosevelt-august-1941. Audio at https://digital.library.unt.edu/ark:/67531/metadc1531966/m1/. Churchill, acting later as historian of World War II, chose not to write at all about his speech of August 24, 1941, and he made no claim to have recognized mass killings of Jews in 1941. He barely touched on the general subject of what was later called the Holocaust. David Reynolds, *In Command of History: Churchill Fighting and Writing the Second World War* (New York: Basic Books, 2005), 260–261, 457–459, 604. Winston S. Churchill, *The Second World War*, vol. 3, *The Grand Alliance* (Boston: Houghton Mifflin, 1950), 433–453.

3   Elizabeth Borgwardt, *A New Deal for the World: America's Vision for Human Rights* (Cambridge, MA: Belknap Press of Harvard University Press, 2005), 33. Discussed further in this chapter's section, "The Grand Alliance."

4   "The Broadcast," *Manchester Guardian* (London edition), August 25, 1941, p. 4.

5   "Churchill Wins Wide U.S. Backing," *New York Times*, August 25, 1941, p. 4.

6   "Next Victim is U.S.—Churchill," *Oakland Tribune*, August 25, 1941, pp. 1–2.

7   Geoffrey Wheatcroft, *Churchill's Shadow: The Life and Afterlife of Winston Churchill* (New York: W. W. Norton, 2021), 69.

8   Roberts, *Churchill*, 269–271.

9   Roberts, *Churchill*, 1–3, 514. Hence Roberts's subtitle, "Walking with Destiny." Also, Wheatcroft, *Churchill's Shadow*, 75.

10   Roberts, *Churchill*, 44.

11   *The Maisky Diaries: Red Ambassador to the Court of St. James's, 1932–1943*, ed. Gabriel Gorodetsky (New Haven, CT: Yale University Press, 2015), 352–353.

12   February 8, 1920, article in the *Illustrated Sunday Herald*, quoted in Roberts, *Churchill*, 278. Article reprinted in https://en.wikisource.org/wiki/Zionism_versus_Bolshevism.

13   Roberts, *Churchill*, 363–364, 415–417, 420; Louise London, *Whitehall and the Jews, 1933–1948: British Immigration Policy, Jewish Refugees and the Holocaust* (Cambridge: Cambridge University Press, 2000), 100.

14   Roberts, *Churchill*, 414, 480, 502, 509, 512.

15   Roberts, *Churchill*, 526–527.

16   Roberts, *Churchill*, 49–50, 552, 580, 585–586.

17   Tim Bouverie, *Appeasement: Chamberlain, Hitler, Churchill, and the Road to War* (New York: Tim Duggan Books, 2019), 404–408; Roberts, *Churchill*, 542–547.

18   James Holland, *The Battle of Britain: Five Months That Changed History, May–October 1940* (New York: St. Martin's Press, 2012); Richard J. Overy, *The Battle of Britain: Myth and Reality* (New York: W. W. Norton, 2002).

19   Gerhard L. Weinberg, *A World at Arms: A Global History of World War II* (New York: Cambridge University Press, 1994), 142.

20   What follows, except where otherwise noted, is a condensed version of Richard Breitman, *Official Secrets: What the Nazis Planned, What the British and Americans Knew* (New York: Hill & Wang, 1998), especially 59, 67–68.

21   Roberts, *Churchill*, 538, 598. For a survey for laymen, see Robert Hanyok, *Eavesdropping on Hell: Historical Guide to Western Communications*

Intelligence and the Holocaust, 1939–1945 (Ft. Meade, MD: Center for Cryptologic History, National Security Agency, 2005).

22   F. H. Hinsley, et al., *British Intelligence in the Second World War: Its Influence on Strategy and Operations*, vol. 2 (Cambridge: Cambridge University Press, 1981), 670; Roberts, *Churchill*, 539; Hanyok, *Eavesdropping on Hell*, 46. More details in Breitman, *Official Secrets*, 56–58, 89–92. Global Command and Control System broke the SS Enigma Code occasionally later, but not in 1941.

23   On Bach-Zelewski, Breitman, *Official Secrets*, 59–60, 92. Summary of German Police Decodes, 275–323, August 21, 1941, part 1, p. 4, HW 16/6, National Archives, UK (NA-UK).

24   Roberts, *Churchill*, 585–586.

25   Weinberg, *A World at Arms*, 62–63, 199–204; Sean McMeekin, *Stalin's War: A New History of World War II* (New York: Basic Books, 2021), 156; Steven Kotkin, *Stalin: Waiting for Hitler* (New York: Penguin Press, 2017), 850–851, 882–884.

26   Kotkin, *Stalin: Waiting for Hitler*, 764; David Reynolds and Vladimir Pechatnov, eds., *The Kremlin Letters: Stalin's Wartime Correspondence with Churchill and Roosevelt* (New Haven, CT: Yale University Press, 2018), 11.

27   Kotkin, *Stalin: Waiting for Hitler*, 882–884; McMeekin, *Stalin's War*, 265, 270–271; Roberts, *Churchill*, 645, 656.

28   *Maisky Diaries*, 354.

29   *Maisky Diaries*, 354.

30   Churchill, *The Grand Alliance*, 370. Roberts, *Churchill*, 659, does not use Churchill's own version. On Churchill's frequent remolding of events, see Reynolds, *In Command of History*.

31   McMeekin, *Stalin's War*, 277, 286–287.

32   Roberts, *Churchill*, 660–661; *Maisky Diaries*, 368–369.

33   Roberts, *Churchill*, 472–473, 659.

34   *Churchill & Roosevelt: The Complete Correspondence*, ed. Warren F. Kimball, vol. 1, *Alliance Emerging, 1933–1942* (Princeton, NJ: Princeton University Press, 1984), 214–216. Cited also by Reynolds, *In Command of History*, 249. On the views of military experts, David Reynolds and V. O. Pechatnov, *The Kremlin Letters: Stalin's Wartime Correspondence with Churchill and Roosevelt* (New Haven, CT: Yale University Press, 2018), 21.

35   Reynolds and Pechatnov, *Kremlin Letters*, 23.

36   Maisky wrote in his diary that the British ruling classes hoped to find additional allies to win the war, or they would be forced to seek a compromise peace with Germany. *Maisky Diaries*, 319.

37   Reynolds and Pechatnov, *Kremlin Letters*, 9–10, 23–26.

38   Reynolds and Pechatnov, *Kremlin Letters*, 26–30; *Maisky Diaries*, 374.

39   Reynolds and Pechatnov, *Kremlin Letters*, 30; *Maisky Diaries*, 380.

40   Reynolds and Pechatnov, *Kremlin Letters*, 31.

41   *Maisky Diaries*, 380–381; Reynolds and Pechatnov, *Kremlin Letters*, 38.

42   David Cesarani, "Secret Churchill Papers Released," *The Journal of Holocaust Education* 4, no. 2 (Winter 1995): 225–226; John P. Fox, "British Intelligence Documents on Einsatzgruppen Operations 1941–1942: Their Historical Significance and Current Status in British and American Archives," paper given at Berlin-Strausberg, intelligence conference, May 2–4, 1997. I am grateful to John Fox for a copy. GPD Report Nos. 324–343, period August 15–31, part 1, p. 1, HW 16/6, NA-UK.

43   September 1 summary in German Police, HW 1/40, NA-UK. I am grateful to Stephen Tyas for a copy of this document and his interpretation of the circle.

44   Breitman, *Official Secrets*, 96.

45   Breitman, *Official Secrets*, 97.

46   Wheatcroft, *Churchill's Shadow*, 239.

47   For accounts of the meeting at Placentia Bay, Churchill, *The Grand Alliance*, 427–447; David Stafford, *Roosevelt and Churchill: Men of Secrets* (New York: Overlook Press, 2011), 66–69; Allen Packwood, *How Churchill Waged War: The Most Challenging Decisions of the Second World War* (Yorkshire, UK: Frontline Books, 2018), 84–94; Jon Meacham, *Franklin and Winston: An Intimate Portrait of an Epic Friendship* (New York: Random House, 2003), 105–121; Nigel Hamilton, *The Mantle of Command: FDR at War, 1941–1942* (Boston: Mariner Books, 2015), 35–40. Good analysis of the Atlantic Charter in Borgwardt, *New Deal for the World*, 22–35.

48   Borgwardt, *New Deal for the World*, 32; Weinberg, *A World at Arms*, 239–243.

49   Weinberg, *A World at Arms*, 260; Hamilton, *Mantle of Command*, 60; Roberts, *Churchill*, 692.

50   Weinberg, *A World at Arms*, 250–253; also, Volker Ullrich, *Hitler: Downfall, 1939–1945*, trans. Jefferson Chase (New York: Vintage, 2021), 221.

51   Weinberg, *A World at Arms*, 240–243, 259–260; Roberts, *Churchill*, 694; Hamilton, *Mantle of Command*, 94, 111.

52   Hamilton, *Mantle of Command*, 111.

53   Harold L. Ickes, *The Secret Diary of Harold L. Ickes: The Lowering Clouds, 1939–1941* (New York: Simon & Schuster, 1954), 665–666.

54   Ickes, *Secret Diary*, 3:664. Hamilton, *Mantle of Command*, 70, 78.

55   Ian Kershaw, *Hitler, 1936–1945: Nemesis* (New York: W. W. Norton, 2000), 442; Stephen G. Fritz, *The First Soldier: Hitler as Military Leader* (New Haven, CT: Yale University Press, 2018), 219.

56   Kershaw, *Hitler: Nemesis*, 444–446.

57   Roberts, *Churchill*, 95–96.

58   *Maisky Diaries*, 330.

59   Churchill Archives Centre, Personal Papers of Winston Churchill, CHAR 9/182/239, cited by Packwood, *How Churchill Waged War*, 95. Contrary to the account in Wheatcroft, *Churchill's Shadow*, Weizmann was not complaining about Churchill's failure to mention that Jews were the primary victims of German police executions.

60   Weizmann to Churchill, September 10, 1941, quoted in Michael J. Cohen, *Britain's Moment in Palestine: Retrospect and Perspectives, 1917–1948* (London: Routledge, 2014), 324. I am grateful to Tuvia Friling for calling the original document to my attention.

61   Cohen, *Britain's Moment*, 325–326.

62   Gilbert, *Churchill and the Jews*, 186.

63   Stafford, *Roosevelt and Churchill*, 37.

64   Roberts, *Churchill*, 678.

65   Michael Smith, "Bletchley Park and the Holocaust," in *Understanding Intelligence in the Twenty-First Century: Journeys in Shadows*, eds. Peter Jackson and L. V. Scott (London: Routledge, 2004), 111–121. This chapter is a direct attack on my 1998 book, *Official Secrets*.

66   Articles dated October 24 and November 7, 1941, cited by Bernard Wasserstein, *Britain and the Jews of Europe, 1939–1945* (Oxford: Clarendon Press, 1979), 167.

67   Quoted in Gilbert, *Churchill and the Jews*, 167; condensed version in Roberts, *Churchill*, 678.

68   For the process of declassifying these records in the 1990s, Breitman, *Official Secrets*, 235–246.

69   Michael Makovsky, *Churchill's Promised Land: Zionism and State-craft* (New Haven, CT: Yale University Press, 2007), 180.

70   Martin Gilbert, "The Most Horrible Crime: Churchill's Prophetic, Passionate and Persistent Response to the Holocaust," *Times Literary Supplement*, June 7, 1996.

3. STALIN'S ANNIVERSARY

1   Joshua Rubenstein and Ilya Altman, eds., *The Unknown Black Book: The Holocaust in the German-Occupied Soviet Territories* (Bloomington: Indiana University Press, 2007), 20; Joshua Rubenstein and Vladimir P. Naumov, *Stalin's Secret Pogrom: The Postwar Inquisition of the Jewish Anti-Fascist Committee* (New Haven, CT: Yale University Press, 2001), 7–9; Joshua Rubenstein, *Tangled Loyalties: The Life and Times of Ilya Ehrenburg* (New York: Basic Books, 1998). On Eisenstein's Jewishness, information from Joshua Rubenstein. An excerpt of the August 24, 1941, presentation is available on YouTube: https://www.youtube.com/watch?v=_WD86czbSAg &ab_channel=kalabusha. I am grateful to Benton Arnovitz for this YouTube reference.

2   "Appeal to World Jewry," Moscow dateline August 24, 1941, *New York Times*, August 25, 1941, p. 3.

3   Joshua Rubenstein and V. P. Naumov, *Stalin's Secret Pogrom: The Postwar Inquisition of the Jewish Anti-Fascist Committee* (New Haven, CT: Yale University Press, 2001), 8. Also, "Appeal to World Jewry," Moscow dateline August 24, 1941, *New York Times*, August 25, 1941, p. 3.

4   I cannot reconstruct the specific sources Mikhoels drew upon.

5   Rodric Braithwaite, *Moscow 1941: A City and Its People at War* (New York: Vintage, 2007), 158–159.

6   Stephen Kotkin, *Stalin: Waiting for Hitler, 1929–1941* (New York: Penguin Press, 2017), 350; Karel C. Berkhoff, *Motherland in Danger: Soviet Propaganda during World War II* (Cambridge, MA: Harvard University Press, 2012), 134–135.

7   Published in *Pravda* on November 30, 1936. Berkhoff, *Motherland in Danger*, 134–135; Simon Sebag Montefiore, *Stalin: The Court of the Red Tsar* (New York: Vintage, 2003), 305, 702n2.

8   And her brother lived in Bridgeport, CT. Information from Joshua Rubenstein, to whom I am grateful.

9   Quoted by Kotkin, *Stalin: Waiting for Hitler*, 354; "Stalin on the Draft Constitution," Seventeen Moments in Soviet History, http://soviet

history.msu.edu/1936-2/stalin-constitution/stalin-constitution-texts/stalin -on-the-draft-constitution/.

10   I am indebted to Zvi Gitelman for this observation.

11   Montefiore, *Stalin*, 304–306.

12   Berkhoff, *Motherland in Danger*, 135; Olga Gershenson, *The Phantom Holocaust: Soviet Cinema and Jewish Catastrophe* (New Brunswick, NJ: Rutgers University Press, 2013), 15–19. On the latitude of filmmakers generally, see Maria Belodubrovskaya, *Filmmaking Under Stalin* (Ithaca, NY: Cornell University Press, 2017).

13   Joshua Rubenstein, "Caught Between Two Evils: Background Paper about the Holocaust in German-Occupied Soviet Territory," unpublished 2011 paper, for which I am grateful.

14   Braithwaite, *Moscow 1941*, 46, 57; Kotkin, *Stalin: Waiting for Hitler*, 376–378, 411–425.

15   Kotkin, *Stalin: Waiting for Hitler*, 433–448.

16   Kotkin, *Stalin: Waiting for Hitler*, 453–454; Michael Gelb, "An Early Soviet Ethnic Deportation: The Far Eastern Koreans," *Russian Review* 54 (July 1995): 389–412; Lynne Viola, "Antisemitism in the 'Jewish NKVD' in Soviet Ukraine on the Eve of World War II," *Holocaust and Genocide Studies* 34, no. 3 (2020): 393–408.

17   For example, Paul Hanebrink, *A Specter Haunting Europe: The Myth of Judeo-Bolshevism* (Cambridge, MA: Belknap Press of Harvard University Press, 2020).

18   Kotkin, *Stalin: Waiting for Hitler*, 621, 625, 628, 637.

19   Dmitri Volkogonov, *Stalin: Triumph and Tragedy*, ed. and trans. Harold Shukman (New York: Grove Weidenfeld, 1991), 352–353. Information about the translations from David Brandenberger and Eric Lohr, to whom I am grateful. On Stalin's reading in general, see Braithwaite, *Moscow 1941*, 33.

20   Volkogonov, *Stalin*, 352–353; Konrad Heiden, *A History of National Socialism* (New York: Knopf, 1935); Dorothy Woodman, *Hitler Rearms: An Exposure of Germany's War Plans* (London: Bodley Head, 1934).

21   "The Text of Premier Stalin's Speech on the Position of the USSR," November 6, 1941, *New York Times*, November 7, 1941, p. 4; Kotkin, *Stalin: Waiting for Hitler*, 157.

22   See Chapter 2 for Churchill; see also Richard Breitman, *The Berlin Mission: The American Who Resisted Nazi Germany from Within* (New York: PublicAffairs, 2019), 51, 209.

288   NOTES TO PAGES 74-77

23   Gerhard L. Weinberg, *The Foreign Policy of Hitler's Germany: Starting World War II 1937-1939*, vol. 2, 601-627. On Hitler's note to Stalin, Volkogonov, *Stalin*, 353-354.

24   Kotkin, *Stalin: Waiting for Hitler*, 671, 699.

25   Rubenstein, *Tangled Loyalties*, 185.

26   I am indebted to Zvi Gitelman for this observation. See also Evgeny Finkel, *Ordinary Jews: Choice and Survival During the Holocaust* (Princeton, NJ: Princeton University Press, 2017), 54.

27   Dov Levin, *Baltic Jews Under the Soviets 1940-1946* (Jerusalem: Centre for Research of East European Jewry, and The Avraham Harman Institute of Contemporary Jewry, Hebrew University, 1994), 100, 116.

28   Harvey Asher, "The Soviet Union, the Holocaust, and Auschwitz," in *The Holocaust in the East: Local Perpetrators and Soviet Responses*, ed. Michael David-Fox, Peter Holquist, Alexander M. Martin (Pittsburgh: University of Pittsburgh Press, 2014), 36-41.

29   Kotkin, *Stalin: Waiting for Hitler*, 817-818; Oleg V. Khlevniuk, *Stalin: New Biography of a Dictator*, trans. Nora Seligman Favorov (New Haven, CT: Yale University Press, 2015), 175.

30   Kotkin, *Stalin: Waiting for Hitler*, 768, 845.

31   Kotkin, *Stalin: Waiting for Hitler*, 871, 890-891; Sean McMeekin, *Stalin's War: A New History of World War II* (New York: Basic Books, 2012), dissents from this view. He has Stalin preparing for an attack and even preparing his own attack.

32   Kotkin, *Stalin: Waiting for Hitler*, 557, 903.

33   Kotkin, *Stalin: Waiting for Hitler*, 341, 376-377.

34   Kotkin, *Stalin: Waiting for Hitler*, 589.

35   Kotkin, *Stalin: Waiting for Hitler*, 841.

36   Among many books on this subject, see Ben McIntyre, *A Spy Among Friends: Kim Philby and the Great Betrayal* (New York: Crown Publishing, 2015), and Yuri Modin, *My 5 Cambridge Friends: Burgess, Maclean, Blunt, Philby, and Cairncross by their KGB Controller* (New York: Farrar, Straus and Giroux, 1995).

37   Later, he predicted between June 22 and 25; Kotkin, *Stalin: Waiting for Hitler*, 837, 883.

38   Braithwaite, *Moscow 1941*, 53, 84-85.

39   Kotkin, *Stalin: Waiting for Hitler*, photo opposite p. 803.

40   Khlevniuk, *Stalin*, 198-199; Montefiore, *Stalin*, 365.

41   Braithwaite, *Moscow 1941*, 69.

42   Braithwaite, *Moscow 1941*, 57.

43   Adam B. Ulam, *Stalin: The Man and His Era* (Boston: Beacon Press, 1989), 492.

44   Rubenstein and Altman, eds., *The Unknown Black Book*, 20. Ponomarenko proposed an organized partisan movement, and in 1942, Stalin put him in charge of leading such a movement in German-held territory.

45   Vadim Dubsin, "Towards a Central Database of Evacuated Soviet Jews' Names for the Study of the Holocaust in the Occupied Soviet Territories," *Holocaust and Genocide Studies* 26, no. 1 (2012): 95–119; Natalie Belsky, "'Am I a Jew?': Soviet Jewish Youth and Antisemitism on the Home Front during the Second World War," *Holocaust and Genocide Studies* 34, no. 2 (2020): 275; in general, *Shelter from the Holocaust: Rethinking Jewish Survival in the Soviet Union*, ed. Mark Edele, Sheila Fitzpatrick, and Atina Grossmann (Detroit: Wayne State University Press, 2017).

46   Braithwaite, *Moscow 1941*, 90–91, 123–124.

47   Braithwaite, *Moscow 1941*, 61–62; Khlevniuk, *Stalin*, 200–205; Montefiore, *Stalin*, 368, 374–377; Volkogonov, *Stalin*, 413.

48   Quoted in Alexander Werth, *Russia at War, 1941–1945* (New York: Carroll & Graf, 1964), 162–167.

49   Braithwaite, *Moscow 1941*, 61, 87–89; Werth, *Russia at War*, 162–166.

50   Ulam, *Stalin*, 457.

51   Khlevniuk, *Stalin*, 208–210; Braithwaite, *Moscow 1941*, 138–139.

52   Braithwaite, *Moscow 1941*, 167–177, 180–185.

53   I am indebted to Zvi Gitelman for information about Smushkevich.

54   Rubenstein and Altman, eds., *The Unknown Black Book*, 20; Rubenstein and Naumov, eds., *Stalin's Secret Pogrom*, 8–9.

55   Rubenstein, *Tangled Loyalties*, 179–186. Additional information from Joshua Rubenstein, to whom I am grateful.

56   Kotkin, *Stalin: Waiting for Hitler*, 635.

57   Rubenstein, *Tangled Loyalties*, 187; Montefiore, *Stalin*, 266, 350.

58   Rubenstein and Naumov, eds., *Stalin's Secret Pogrom*, 9–10, and generally. The Committee was disbanded in 1948 and its surviving members purged and executed in 1952.

59   Albert Kaganovitch, "The Holocaust Propaganda Machine in Soviet Periodicals, 1941–1945," *HGS* 38, no. 2 (Fall 2024): 239; Berkhoff, *Motherland in Danger*, 135, 140.

60   Montefiore, *Stalin*, 380–381; Braithwaite, *Moscow 1941*, 165; Stephen G. Fritz, *The First Soldier: Hitler as Military Leader* (New Haven, CT: Yale University Press, 2018), 201–202.

61   Karel Berkhoff et al., "Basic Historical Narrative of the Babyn Yar Holocaust Memorial Center," Babyn Yar, October 2018, pp. 68–79, https://babynyar.org/en/historical-narrative/1.

62   I thank Zvi Gitelman for the information about Kalinin.

63   Berkhoff, *Motherland in Danger*, 140.

64   Khlevniuk, *Stalin*, 211–212; Nigel Hamilton, *The Mantle of Command: FDR at War, 1941–1942* (Boston: Mariner Books, 2015), 20–21.

65   David Reynolds and Vladimir Pechatnov, eds., *The Kremlin Letters: Stalin's Wartime Correspondence with Churchill and Roosevelt* (New Haven, CT: Yale University Press, 2018), 50; Khlevniuk, *Stalin*, 212.

66   Werth, *Russia at War*, 289.

67   Werth, *Russia at War*, 233–234, but misdating Hitler's speech as October 2. See "The Test of Reichsfuehrer Hitler's Address . . . ," *New York Times*, October 4, 1941, p. 4; Fritz, *The First Soldier*, 205; Braithwaite, *Moscow 1941*, 191–200.

68   Braithwaite, *Moscow 1941*, 191–200.

69   Khlevniuk, *Stalin*, 214–215; Braithwaite, *Moscow 1941*, 202–203, 217–218.

70   Khlevniuk, *Stalin*, 214–215; Braithwaite, *Moscow 1941*, 205–206, 211; Fritz, *The First Soldier*, 206–208.

71   Braithwaite, *Moscow 1941*, 219–226, 250.

72   Montefiore, *Stalin*, 399–403; Braithwaite, *Moscow 1941*, 230, 233, 251; Khlevniuk, *Stalin*, 217; Werth, *Russia at War*, 244. Werth has the Germans forty miles away on November 6.

73   The Bolshevik Revolution of 1917 is known as the October Revolution because it fell on October 25 in the now obsolete Julian calendar.

74   Braithwaite, *Moscow 1941*, 252, 261; Werth, *Russia at War*, 244.

75   Werth, *Russia at War*, 244; Braithwaite, *Moscow 1941*, 253–254; "Russians Pressing Moscow Attacks," *New York Times*, November 8, 1941, p. 2; "Premier Confident," *New York Times*, November 7, 1941, pp. 1, 4.

76   Braithwaite, *Moscow 1941*, 253–254; "Premier Confident," *New York Times*, November 7, 1941, p. 1, 4; "The Text of Premier Stalin's Speech on the Position of the USSR, November 6, 1941," *New York Times*, November 7, 1941, p. 4; Werth, *Russia at War*, 244–247.

77   Berkhoff, *Motherland in Danger*, 141.

78   "The Text of Premier Stalin's Speech on the Position of the USSR, November 6, 1941," *New York Times*, November 7, 1941, p. 4; Werth, *Russia at War*, 246; "Premier Confident," *New York Times*, November 7, 1941, p. 1, 4.

79   "Stalin Calls for Second Front," *Akron Beacon Journal*, November 6, 1941, pp. 1–2; "Stalin Says Hitler Plan Was Failure," *Maryville Journal-Tribune* (Maryville, OH), November 6, 1941, pp. 1, 4.

80   "Stalin Appoints Litvinoff [sic] Ambassador to Washington," *New York Times*, November 7, 1941, p. 1.

81   Berkhoff, *Motherland in Danger*, 141.

82   Walter Laqueur, *The Terrible Secret: Suppression of the Truth about Hitler's "Final Solution"* (Boston: Little, Brown, 1980), 68; Deborah E. Lipstadt, *Beyond Belief: The American Press and the Coming of the Holocaust, 1933–1945* (New York: Touchstone, 1993), 150–151; Laurel Leff, *Buried by the Times: The Holocaust and America's Most Important Newspaper* (New York: Cambridge University Press, 2006), 129.

83   "Kiev, Bombed by Nazis, Fired By Russians, Provides Little Shelter for 300,000 There," *The Record* (Hackensack, NJ), October 23, 1941, p. 3; Larry Heinzerling and Randy Herschaft with Ann Cooper, *Newshawks in Berlin: The Associated Press and Nazi Germany* (New York: Columbia University Press, 2024), 189–191.

84   Berkhoff, *Motherland in Danger*, 141, 336n20.

85   Werth, *Russia at War*, 247–249; "Stalin Says Second Front Will Be Opened," *Los Angeles Daily News* (UP), November 7, 1941, pp. 1, 14; Braithwaite, *Moscow 1941*, 258–261; quote from 259.

86   Yosef Gorny, *The Jewish Press and the Holocaust, 1939–1945: Palestine, Britain, the United States, and the Soviet Union*, trans. Naftali Greenwood (New York: Cambridge University Press, 2012), 35–36, 97–98.

87   "Molotov's Note on German Atrocities in Occupied Soviet Territory," https://www.ibiblio.org/pha/policy/1942/1942-01-06b.html; Berkhoff, *Motherland in Danger*, 119.

88   Reynolds and Pechatnov, *Kremlin Letters*, 81.

89   Berkhoff, *Motherland in Danger*, 142–143.

90   Kaganovitch, "The Holocaust Propaganda Machine," 241.

4. SECRETS PRESERVED

1   Volker Ullrich, *Hitler: Downfall, 1939–1945*, trans. Jefferson Chase (New York: Vintage, 2021), 231–232; Lucy S. Dawidowicz, *The War Against the Jews 1933–1945* (New York: Bantam Books, 1976), 147–148n; "Nazi Sees Victory," *New York Times*, January 31, 1942, p. 1; Ian Kershaw, *Hitler, 1936–1945: Nemesis* (New York: W. W. Norton, 2000), 494.

2   Ullrich, *Hitler: Downfall*, 231; "Nazi Sees Victory," *New York Times*, January 31, 1942, p. 1; Partial text of Hitler's Speech, *New York Times*, January 31, 1942, p. 4.

3   Kershaw, *Hitler: Nemesis*, 450–454. For a good analysis of Hitler's clashes with his generals, see Stephen G. Fritz, *The First Soldier: Hitler as Military Leader* (New Haven, CT: Yale University Press, 2018), 217–223.

4   Partial text of Hitler's Speech, *New York Times*, January 31, 1942, p. 4; Ullrich, *Hitler: Downfall*, 231–232; Gerhard L. Weinberg, *A World at Arms: A Global History of World War II* (New York: Cambridge University Press, 1994), 293–294, 298–299, 348–349.

5   "Hitler's Explanation of his 'Stationary' War," *Manchester Guardian*, January 31, 1942, p. 7; "Hitler Pledges Land and U-Boat Attacks," *Detroit Free Press*, January 31, 1942, p. 2; "Nazi Sees Victory," *New York Times*, January 31, 1942, p. 1.

6   On the connections between euthanasia and the Final Solution, see particularly Henry Friedlander, *The Origins of Nazi Genocide: Euthanasia and the Final Solution* (Chapel Hill: University of North Carolina Press, 1998), especially 39, 62, 111–119, 263; and Leroy Walter, "Paul Braune Confronts the National Socialists' 'Euthanasia' Program," *Holocaust and Genocide Studies* 21 (2007): 454–487. On the specific transfer of gassing specialists to the extermination camps, see Richard Breitman, *The Architect of Genocide: Himmler and the Final Solution* (New York: Knopf, 1991), 199–200.

7   Christopher R. Browning with Jürgen Matthäus, *The Origins of the Final Solution: The Evolution of Nazi Jewish Policy, September 1939–March 1942* (Lincoln: University of Nebraska Press, 2004), 365–366; Saul Friedländer, *The Years of Extermination: Nazi Germany and the Jews, 1939–1945* (New York: Harper Collins, 2007), 283–286.

8   On Chełmno, see Patrick Montague, *Chełmno and the Holocaust: A History of Hitler's First Death Camp* (London: Bloomsbury Academic, 2020).

9   Browning, *Origins of the Final Solution*, 416–419; Friedländer, *The Years of Extermination*, 284.

10   Jeffrey Herf, *The Jewish Enemy: Nazi Propaganda during World War II and the Holocaust* (Cambridge, MA: Belknap Press of Harvard University Press, 2008), 138.

11   Andrew Roberts, *Churchill: Walking with Destiny* (New York: Viking, 2018), 700–703; Weinberg, *A World at Arms*, 352–353.

12   Rick Atkinson, *An Army at Dawn: The War in North Africa, 1942–1943* (New York: Picador, 2002), 12–15; Weinberg, *A World at Arms*, 306, 352.

13   Weinberg, *A World at* Arms, 352–354; Nigel Hamilton, *The Mantle of Command: FDR at War, 1941–1942* (Boston: Mariner Books, 2015), 109, 291, 294, 314, 317; Atkinson, *An Army at Dawn*, 15–16.

14   David Stafford, *Roosevelt and Churchill: Men of Secrets* (New York: Overlook Press, 2011), 131.

15   For this speculation by Michael Smith, see "Bletchley Park and the Holocaust," in *Understanding Intelligence in the Twenty-First Century: Journeys in Shadows*, eds. Peter Jackson and L. V. Scott (London: Routledge, 2004).

16   "Postal And Telegraph Censorship: Volume 396: debated on Wednesday 9 February 1944," House of Commons, UK Parliament, https://hansard .parliament.uk/Commons/1944-02-09/debates/1bc96e9f-465d-4210 -96eb-041b9f521eb1/PostalAndTelegraphCensorship.

17   Editorial, New Secret Series, Postal and Telegraph Censorship, Report on Jewry, no. 3, part 1, January 22, 1942, HO 213/953, NA-UK.

18   More details and quote in Richard Breitman, Norman J. W. Goda, Timothy Naftali, and Robert Wolfe, *U.S. Intelligence and the Nazis* (New York: Cambridge University Press, 2005), 13–18. This document reached the US in March 1942.

19   Morris to Secretary of State, September 30, 1941, and Morris to Secretary of State, October 14, 1941, 862.4016/2204 and 2205, RG 59, NARA.

20   Richard Breitman and Allan J. Lichtman, *FDR and the Jews* (Cambridge, MA: Belknap Press of Harvard University Press, 2013), 195.

21   Larry Heinzerling, Randy Herschaft, and Ann Cooper, *Newshawks in Berlin: The Associated Press and Nazi Germany* (New York: Columbia University Press, 2024), 159–166. On Lochner and censorship, Howard K. Smith, *The Last Train from Berlin* (New York: Knopf, 1942), 88–89, 107.

22   Smith, *Last Train*, 107.

23   The most detailed study of the internment is Charles Burdick, *American Island in Hitler's Reich: The Bad Nauheim Internment* (Mountain

View, CA: Markgraf Publications Group, 1988). I have also drawn on Heinzerling, Herschaft, and Cooper, *Newshawks in Berlin*, 185–187. Lynn Grove, "The American Internee Experience in Nazi Germany," *Traces* [undated, ca.1988] https://usgerrelations.traces.org/americaninternees.html; "The Bittersweet Mementos of War," *Washington Post, February 21, 1981*; Clifton B. Conger, UPI Archives, February 14, 1981.

24   "Back from the Axis," *Time*, June 15, 1942, reproduced by Grove, "American Internees."

25   Heinzerling, Herschaft, and Cooper, *Newshawks in Berlin*, 187.

26   Heinzerling, Herschaft, and Cooper, *Newshawks in Berlin*, 187.

27   Thorsten Noack, "William L. Shirer and International Awareness of Nazi 'Euthanasia' Program," *Holocaust and Genocide Studies* 30, no. 3 (2016): 433–457. On Schultz, David Milne is writing a biography. See https://mosseprogram.wisc.edu/2020/03/04/milne/.

28   Noack, "William L. Shirer," 433–457; "Euthanasia Program and Aktion T4," Holocaust Encyclopedia, https://encyclopedia.ushmm.org/content /en/article/euthanasia-program.

29   "Back from the Axis," *Time*, June 15, 1942, reproduced by Grove, "American Internees"; "Bittersweet Mementos of War," *Washington Post*, February 21, 1981.

30   Military Attaché Report, March 6, 1942, Military Intelligence Division regional file, Germany 2910–2950, entry 77, box 1074, RG 165, NARA.

31   Sub-Annex 8, p. 6, Military Attaché Report, March 6, 1942, Military Intelligence Division regional file, Germany 2910–2950, entry 77, box 1074, RG 165, NARA.

32   Sub-Annex 1, p. 18, to Annex 1, Military Attaché Report, March 6, 1942, Military Intelligence Division regional file, Germany 2910–2950, entry 77, box 1074, RG 165, NARA.

33   Sub-Annex 1 to Annex 1, Military Attaché Report, March 6, 1942, Military Intelligence Division regional file, Germany 2910–2950, entry 77, box 1074, RG 165, NARA.

On the propaganda significance of the Kaufman plan, see Smith, *Last Train from Berlin*, 181–184, where his name is given as Nathan Kaufmann; Herf, *Nazi Propaganda*, 110–115. On the genealogist at the press conference, Smith, *Last Train from Berlin*, 212.

34   More details in Richard Breitman, *Official Secrets: What the Nazis Planned, What the British and Americans Knew* (New York: Hill & Wang, 1998), 125–127.

35   Friedlander, *Origins of Nazi Genocide*, 111.

36   Alfred M. Beck, *Hitler's Ambivalent Attaché: Lt. Gen. Friedrich von Boetticher in America, 1933–1941* (Washington, DC: Potomac Books, 2005), 103, 192.

37   Notes of cabinet, 19 December 1941, cabinet meetings 1941, box 1, Francis Biddle Papers, FDRL. Donovan to FDR, 19 February 1942, microfilm M-1642, reel 22, f 1064ff, entry 180, RG 226, NARA; Beck, *Hitler's Ambivalent Attaché*, 192.

38   Notes of cabinet, 19 December 1941, cabinet meetings 1941, box 1, Biddle Papers, FDRL.

39   Beck, *Hitler's Ambivalent Attaché*, 262n28; "Euthanasia Program and Aktion T4," Holocaust Encyclopedia, https://encyclopedia.ushmm.org/content/en/article/euthanasia-program.

40   "Nazi Firing Squad Toll Put At 400,000, But People Still Defy Reich," *St. Louis Star and Times*, May 18, 1942, p. 2; "Nazis Admit Summer Will Bring Crisis," *St. Louis Star and Times*, May 18, 1942, p. 2; "200,000 Jews Massacred By Nazis in Eastern Europe," *The Pittsburgh Press*, June 1, 1942, p. 1. Also quoted by Laurel Leff, *Buried by the Times: The Holocaust and America's Most Important Newspaper* (New York: Cambridge University Press, 2006), 132.

41   Robert Gerwarth, *Hitler's Hangman: The Life of Heydrich* (New Haven, CT: Yale University Press, 2011), 4.

42   Gerwarth, *Hitler's Hangman*, 4–5.

43   Gerwarth, *Hitler's Hangman*, 279–282, for more details.

44   Roberts, *Churchill*, 736. On the British bombing of Germany, see Richard Overy, *The Bombers and the Bombed: Allied Air War Over Europe, 1940–1945* (New York: Penguin, 2015), 91–101.

45   See Herf, *The Jewish Enemy*, 156–157.

46   For a survey of foreign reaction, Gerwarth, *Hitler's Hangman*, 282–283; Eleanor Roosevelt, "Story of 'My Day'," *Tacoma News-Tribune*, February 14, 1942, p. 9; "Here Was Lidice," editorial in the *Baltimore Evening Sun*, reprinted in the *Akron Beacon Journal*, June 14, 1942, p. 14; "Reprisal for Lidice Urged by Masaryk," *Philadelphia Inquirer*, June 14, 1942, p. 8.

47   "Goebbels Warns More Lidices Yet to Come," *Minneapolis Star Tribune*, June 15, 1942, p. 4. Seymour had served as European director of the AP during the mid-1930s and had plenty of experience dealing with Propaganda Ministry clashes with the AP. "Gideon Seymour, Star and Tribune Editor, Dies at 52," *Minneapolis Star*, May 21, 1954, p. 1.

48   Tuvia Friling, *Arrows in the Dark: David Ben-Gurion, the Yishuv Leadership, and Rescue Attempts during the Holocaust*, trans. Ora Cummings (Madison: Wisconsin University Press, 2005), 1:51–53. "Recent Zionist Activities," June 13, 1942, report of the Foreign Nationalities Branch, Coordinator of Information, OSS, Foreign Politics in the US, box 350, entry 368, RG 208, NARA.

49   Friling, *Arrows in the Dark*, 1:53. "Recent Zionist Activities," June 13, 1942, report of the Foreign Nationalities Branch, Coordinator of Information, OSS, Foreign Politics in the US, box 350, entry 368, RG 208, NARA.

50   See Breitman and Lichtman, *FDR and the Jews*, 239–241.

51   "Recent Zionist Activities," June 13 report of the Foreign Nationalities Branch, Coordinator of Information, Foreign Politics in the US, box 350, entry 368, RG 208, NARA; Caitlin Carenen, "The American Christian Palestine Committee, the Holocaust, and Mainstream Protestant Zionism," *Holocaust and Genocide Studies* 24, no. 2 (2010): 273–296.

52   "Developments in Palestine Are Praised By Roosevelt," *Baltimore Sun*, May 26, 1942, p. 3; "Peril to Palestine Remote, F.D.R. Says," *Philadelphia Inquirer*, May 26, 1942, p. 2.

5. THE ALLIED DECLARATION

1   David Engel, *In the Shadow of Auschwitz: The Polish Government-in-Exile and the Jews, 1939–1942* (Chapel Hill: University of North Carolina Press, 1987), 175–176; Dariusz Stola, "Early News of the Holocaust from Poland," *Holocaust and Genocide Studies* 11, no. 1 (1997): 6; Michael Fleming, *Auschwitz, the Allies and Censorship of the Holocaust* (Cambridge: Cambridge University Press, 2014), 97–103, 331n68. Fleming notes that Bracken, like Churchill, was more sympathetic on this issue than the Foreign Office or the BBC. The *New York Times* picked up the story on July 2.

2   Jon Meacham, *Franklin and Winston: An Intimate Portrait of an Epic Friendship* (New York: Random House, 2003), 180–187. Andrew Roberts, *Churchill: Walking with Destiny* (New York: Viking, 2018), 737–739.

3   Meredith Hindley, *Destination Casablanca: Exile, Espionage, and the Battle for North Africa in World War II* (New York: PublicAffairs, 2017), 161; Roberts, *Churchill*, 738–739.

4   Tuvia Friling, *Arrows in the Dark: David Ben-Gurion, the Yishuv Leadership, and Rescue Attempts during the Holocaust*, trans. Ora Cummings (Madison: Wisconsin University Press, 2005), 1:57–58.

5   "July 7th, 1942," Franklin D. Roosevelt Day by Day, http://www.fdrlibrary.marist.edu/daybyday/daylog/july-7th-1942/; Monty Noam Penkower,

The Jews Were Expendable: Free World Diplomacy and the Holocaust (Detroit: Wayne State University Press, 1988), 14–15.

6   Rick Atkinson, *An Army at Dawn: The War in North Africa, 1942–1943* (New York: Picador, 2002), 16–18.

7   Stephen G. Fritz, *The First Soldier: Hitler as Military Leader* (New Haven, CT: Yale University Press, 2018), 249–253.

8   Dennis Showalter, *Patton and Rommel: Men of War in the Twentieth Century* (New York: Berkley Caliber, 2005), 279.

9   Atkinson, *An Army at Dawn*, 27–29; Hindley, *Destination Casablanca*, 179–182, 191–192; David Reynolds and Vladimir Pechatnov, eds., *The Kremlin Letters: Stalin's Wartime Correspondence with Churchill and Roosevelt* (New Haven, CT: Yale University Press, 2018), 140–149; Roger Hermiston, *All Behind You, Winston: Churchill's Grand Coalition, 1940–1945* (London: Aurum Press, 2016), 228.

10   Engel, *In the Shadow of Auschwitz*, 182, 299n133.

11   "Nazis Deporting 20,000 Jews from Paris," *St. Louis Star and Times*, July 17, 1942, p. 16; "The Jews in France," *Manchester Guardian*, July 23, 1942, p. 4; "Mass Deportations of Dutch Begun," *Wisconsin Jewish Chronicle*, July 31, 1942, p. 7.

12   David Motadel, *Islam and Nazi Germany's War* (Cambridge, MA: Belknap Press of Harvard University Press, 2014), 83–84; Jeffrey Herf, *Nazi Propaganda for the Arab World* (New Haven, CT: Yale University Press, 2009), 132.

13   Roberts, *Churchill*, 740–742, 748–749. Herf, *Nazi Propaganda for the Arab World*, 125–126. Motadel, *Islam and Nazi Germany's War*, 95.

14   Klaus-Michael Mallmann and Martin Cüppers, *Nazi Palestine: The Plans for the Extermination of the Jews in Palestine* (New York: Enigma Books, 2010), 117–118.

15   Rauff's flight is mentioned in a November 23, 1942, British analysis of decoded German messages about Einsatzkommandos. ZIP/IS/I, copy in folder 637, box 25, entry 119A, RG 226, NARA.

16   "Nazi Punishment Seen By Roosevelt," *New York Times*, July 22, 1942, pp. 1, 4. See also, Meacham, *Franklin and Winston*, 188–189.

17   "Nazi Punishment Seen By Roosevelt," *New York Times*, July 22, 1942, pp. 1,4.

18   Wise to Julian W. Mack, Correspondence—Zionism, box 115, Stephen S. Wise Papers, American Jewish Historical Society, Center for Jewish History, NY.

19   "Jews Forced to War Labor," *Minneapolis Star Tribune*, July 22, 1942, p. 5.

20   Sweetser to Davis, July 29, 1942, War Crimes 1942–1944, box 12, entry 3, RG 208, NARA.

21   Minutes of Committee on War Information Policy, September 2, 1942, meetings-4, July-December 1942, box 2, entry 1, RG 208, NARA.

22   This and the following paragraphs, except where noted otherwise, are a condensed version of Walter Laqueur and Richard Breitman, *Breaking the Silence: the German Who Exposed the Final Solution* (Hanover, NH: University Press of New England, 1994), and Richard Breitman and Allan J. Lichtman, *FDR and the Jews* (Cambridge, MA: Belknap Press of Harvard University Press, 2013), 199–206.

23   Quoted by Rebecca Erbelding, *Rescue Board: The Untold Story of America's Efforts to Save the Jews of Europe* (New York: Doubleday, 2018), 20.

24   Both Riegner's telegram to Wise and Silverman's later telegram to Wise are reprinted in facsimile in Daniel Greene and Edward Phillips, eds., *Americans and the Holocaust: A Reader* (New Brunswick, NJ: Rutgers University Press, 2021), 163.

25   Rosenblum to Wertheim, September 8 and 9, 1942, with summaries of the two meetings of Jewish leaders, EXO-29, Poland 1942, Waldman Files, RG 1, American Jewish Committee Archives, quote from September 9. See also, Richard Breitman and Alan M. Kraut, *American Refugee Policy and European Jewry, 1933–1945* (Bloomington: Indiana University Press, 1987), 152–153; Penkower, *The Jews were Expendable*, 68–69.

26   Atkinson, *An Army at Dawn*, 30–32, 58–62, 67.

27   Gerhard L. Weinberg, *A World at Arms: A Global History of World War II* (New York: Cambridge University Press, 1994), 351–352, 359, 361–362; Gerhard L. Weinberg, "The Allies and the Holocaust," in *The Bombing of Auschwitz: Should the Allies Have Attempted It?* ed. Michael J. Neufeld and Michael Berenbaum (New York: St. Martin's Press, 2000), 21; Showalter, *Patton and Rommel*, 284–287; Hindley, *Destination Casablanca*, 138, 156–157, 161–162.

28   Showalter, *Patton and Rommel*, 284–287.

29   Showalter, *Patton and Rommel*, 288–290; Roberts, *Churchill*, 761.

30   White House Press Release, copy in War Crimes, Official File 5152, FDRL.

31   Bernard Wasserstein, *Britain and the Jews of Europe 1939–1945* (Oxford: Clarendon, 1979), 34, 168–170; Fleming, *Auschwitz, the Allies, and Censorship*, 106–108.

32   Minutes of the Executive Committee, December 17, 1942, folder 14, executive committee minutes 1942–1943, box A 78, World Jewish Congress Records, American Jewish Archives, Cincinnati.

33   See Paul C. Squire to Secretary of State, October 29, 1942, strictly confidential, 862.4016/10-4942, RG 59, NARA; Squire's Memorandum of Conversation with Carl J. Burckhardt, November 7, 1942, and Squire to Harrison, November 9, 1942, American Consulate Geneva, Confidential File 800, RG 84, NARA.

34   As discussed in the Introduction.

35   Memorandum of Conversation, September 25, 1942 . . ., Vatican Myron Taylor 1942, President's Secretary's File, Diplomatic, box 51, FDRL. Also, see above, Introduction.

36   Welles to Taylor, October 21, 1942, 740.00116 EW 1939/605, RG 59, NARA; "October 16th, 1942," Franklin D. Roosevelt Day by Day, http://www.fdrlibrary.marist.edu/daybyday/daylog/october-16th-1942/; documents referred to in Taylor's Memorandum for the President and Secretary of State, October 20, 1942, folder 1, Taylor September-October 1942, Office Correspondence 1942, box 84, Sumner Welles Papers, FDRL.

37   Atkinson, *An Army at Dawn*, 31, 69–160. Weinberg, *A World at Arms*, 434–443. Breitman and Lichtman, *FDR and the Jews*, 203.

38   Atkinson, *An Army at Dawn*, 116–160, quote on 184.

39   Atkinson, *An Army at Dawn*, 196–198; Ethan Katz, *The Burdens of Brotherhood: Jews and Muslims from North Africa to France* (Cambridge, MA: Harvard University Press, 2018), 116–131; Raffael Scheck, "Nazi Propaganda Toward French Muslim Prisoners of War," *Holocaust and Genocide Studies* 26, no. 3 (2012): 464–468.

40   Joseph W. Bendersky, *The "Jewish Threat": Anti-Semitic Politics of the U.S. Army* (New York: Basic Books, 2000), 315; Atkinson, *An Army at Dawn*, 43–44.

41   Taylor's Memorandum for the President and Secretary of State re German Atrocities, October 20, 1942, folder 1, Taylor September-October, Office Correspondence 1942, box 84, Welles Papers, FDRL.

42   Hindley, *Destination Casablanca*, 279.

43   Welles to Wise, November 13, 1942, and Wise to Welles, November 17, 1942, Wise folder, Office Correspondence 1942, box 86, Welles Papers, FDRL; David S. Wyman, *The Abandonment of the Jews: America and the Holocaust, 1941–1945* (New York: Pantheon, 1984), 51, 363.

44   Kenneth L. Dixon, "Nazis Seek to Slay Jews in Europe," *Tucson Daily Citizen*, November 25, 1942, p. 1; see also, Larry Heinzlering, Randy

Herschaft, and Ann Cooper, *Newshawks in Berlin: The Associated Press and Nazi Germany* (New York: Columbia University Press, 2024), 227–228;"Two Million Jews Reported Killed by Nazis," *Gettysburg Times*, November 25, 1942, p. 6.

45   "2,000,000 Jews Slain in Hitler's Terror-Ridden Europe, Dr. Wise Learns; Nazis Set Up Price for Each Corpse," *Lincoln Journal-Star*, November 25, 1942, p. 7; "Jewish Extermination Drive Laid to Hitler By Dr. Wise," *Baltimore Sun*, November 25, 1942, p. 3; 213 papers according to the database of newspapers.com (search Stephen Wise AND State Department, November 25, 1942).

46   "How the Nazis Slaughtered 24,000 Jews in Latvia," *PM*, November 26, 1942; Laurel Leff, *Buried by the Times: The Holocaust and America's Most Important Newspaper* (New York: Cambridge University Press, 2006), 155.

47   Wise to Dear Boss, November 2, 1942, and Wise to Niles, December 2, 1942, boxes 68 (microfilm74-47) and 181 (83-9), Stephen S. Wise Papers, American Jewish Historical Society, Center for Jewish History, NY.

48   Breitman and Lichtman, *FDR and the Jews*, 247.

49   Weinberg, *A World at Arms*, 449–452; *Los Angeles Times*, November 25, 1942, p. 4.

50   Sikorski to Welles, December 12, 1942, and Welles to Sikorski, December 18, 1942, 740.00116 EW 1939/739, RG 59, NARA.

51   E. Thomas Wood and Stanislaw M. Jankowski, *Karski: How One Man Tried to Stop the Holocaust* (New York: John Wiley, 1994), 142–143, 147; see also, Fleming, *Auschwitz, the Allies, and Censorship*, 148, 151–152.

52   "The Karski Report," The National Archives, https://www.national archives.gov.uk/education/resources/holocaust/karski-report/.

53   Fleming, *Auschwitz, the Allies, and Censorship*, 151–152. Report on the attacks on the Jewish ghetto in Warsaw, November 26, 1942, but stamped December 1, 1942, C11923/61/18, FO 371/30923, NA-UK.

54   Untitled memorandum, initialed RL, November 26, 1942, C11923/61/18, FO 371/30923, NA-UK.

55   Wood and Jankowski, *Karski*, 151–152.

56   The following quotes are from "The blackest massacre of Jews in all human history: an eyewitness report from Poland," undated [early December 1942], Duker-Dwork Collection, folder 107, box 11, RG 200, NARA. Zygelbojm's thirteen-page account of Karski's experiences and B's message to his colleague went by diplomatic pouch to the Polish Embassy in Washington, which gave it to the Jewish Labor Committee. It is possible that this

was also the document Sikorski gave to Welles. One way or another, OSS got a copy of this document, and it is now found in the US National Archives. This authenticates Karski's experiences independently of his later writings. See also Jan Ciechanowski, "Reports on the Holocaust," in *Intelligence Co-operation between Poland and Great Britain During World War II, vol. I, The Report of the Anglo Polish Historical Committee*, ed. Tessa Stirling, Daria Nalecz, and Tadeusz Dubicki (London: Valentine Mitchell, 2005), 536.

57   Weekly Political Intelligence Summary, No. 165, Foreign Office Political Intelligence Department, December 2, 1942, copy in M982, R 146, RG 59, NARA. It appears to have been written by PWE official Frank Savery, who sent a marked-up draft to F. K. Roberts of the Foreign Office on December 3. Germany 1942 War Crimes.pdf, pp. 5–10, FO 371-30924, NA-UK.

58   Oliver Harvey Memo, December 1, 1942, FO 954/19, NA-UK.

59   Winant to Secretary of State, December 7, 1942, 740.00116 EW1939/660, RG 59, NARA; Wasserstein, *Britain and the Jews*, 170–171; Winant to Secretary of State, December 7, 1942, 740.00116/692, RG 59, NARA; Sikorski to Welles, December 12, 1942, 740.00116 EW 1939/739, RG 59, NARA.

60   Winant to Secretary of State, December 8, 1942, 740.00116 EW 1939/664, RG 59, NARA.

61   Wood and Jankowski, *Karski*, 152.

62   On Temple, see Louise London, *Whitehall and the Jews, 1933–1948: British Immigration Policy, Jewish Refugees, and the Holocaust* (Cambridge: Cambridge University Press, 2000), 124–125, 206; Meier Sompolinsky, *The British Government and the Holocaust: The Failure of Anglo-Jewish Leadership* (Brighton: Sussex Academic Press, 1999), 87, 92.

63   Sompolinsky, *The British Government*, 88, makes Eden the initiator of this strategy.

64   Diary of William Lyon Mackenzie King, 5 December 1942, http://canadaonline.about.com/gi/o.htm?zi=1/XJ&zTi=1&sdn=canadaonline&cdn=newsissues&tm=14&f=10&su=p649.3.336.ip_&tt=2&bt=1&bts=1&zu=http%3A//www.collectionscanada.gc.ca/databases/king/index-e.html.

65   Held's account of the meeting, part 3, section 1, no. 15, Jewish Labor Committee Archives, today available at http://www.jewishvirtuallibrary.org/jsource/Holocaust/fdrmeet.html.

66   Roosevelt's comment on Hitler's psychopathology preceded the substantial, if inconclusive, work on psychoanalyzing Hitler done by individuals associated with OSS. See Daniel Pick, *The Pursuit of the Nazi Mind: Hitler, Hess, and the Analysts* (Oxford: Oxford University Press, 2012), 108–152.

67   Wise to Niles, 9 December 1941, box 181, (M 83-9), Wise Papers, American Jewish Historical Society, Center for Jewish History, NY.

68   See Alexandra Lohse, *Prevail Until the Bitter End: Germans in the Waning Years of World War II* (Ithaca, NY: Cornell University Press, 2021), 92–96.

69   Raczynski to Eden, December 9, 1942, C 12313/61/18, FO 371/30924, NA-UK; Raczynski to Drexel Biddle, Jr., December 9, 1942, attached to Drexel Biddle to Secretary of State, December 18, 1942, 740.00116 EW 1939/712, RG 59, NARA; Wasserstein, *Britain and the Jews of Europe*, 172.

70   Michael Makovsky, *Churchill's Promised Land: Zionism and State-craft* (New Haven, CT: Yale University Press, 2007), 178; Wasserstein, *Britain and the Jews of Europe*, 172.

71   F. K. Roberts memo, December 14, 1942, and reply December 15, p. 125, FO 371-30924 Germany 1942 War Crimes.pdf, NA-UK.

72   Michael J. Cohen, *Churchill and the Jews* (London: Frank Cass, 1985), 269; see also, Sompolinsky, *The British Government*, 88, 90, 234n39.

73   Robert Borden Reams Memorandum to Howard Travers, December 15, 1942, Bermuda Conference Background, box 3, Lot File 52D408, RG 59, NARA; see also, Richard Breitman, *Official Secrets: What the Nazis Planned, What the British and Americans Knew* (New York: Hill & Wang, 1998), 174.

74   Memorandum of Conversation by Hull, December 16, 1942, 740.00116 EW 1939/699, RG 59, NARA.

75   Wasserstein, *Britain and the Jews*, 172–175.

76   Ciechanowski, "Reports on the Holocaust," in *Intelligence Cooperation*, 537–538.

77   Sompolinsky, *The British Government*, 88, suggests that the declaration served as a limiting event.

78   Lohse, *Prevail Until the Bitter End*, 149.

6. TWO INFLUENCERS IN WASHINGTON

1   "July 28th, 1943," Franklin D. Roosevelt Day by Day, http://www.fdrlibrary.marist.edu/daybyday/daylog/july-28th-1943/. In his own memorandum of the meeting, Karski timed it as one and one-quarter hours. At a luncheon in October 1943, Karski, referred to only as Lt. Z, claimed to have spoken with Roosevelt for more than two hours. On Karski's contemporary memorandum, see David Engel, *Facing a Holocaust: The Polish*

Government-in-Exile and the Jews, 1943–1945 (Chapel Hill: University of North Carolina Press, 1993), 90 and 243n67; October 7, 1943, Report on Luncheon with Ambassador Biddle and others, folder 99, Whitney Shepardson, box 8, entry 145, RG 226, NARA. On the second-floor study, E. Thomas Wood and Stanislaw M. Jankowski, *Karski: How One Man Tried to Stop the Holocaust* (New York: John Wiley, 1994), 197; and Rebecca Erbelding, *Rescue Board: The Untold Story of America's Efforts to Save the Jews of Europe* (New York: Doubleday, 2018), 55.

2   Wood and Jankowski, *Karski*, 157–185.

3   Andrew Roberts, *Churchill: Walking with Destiny* (New York: Viking, 2018), 767.

4   Gerhard L. Weinberg, *A World at Arms: A Global History of World War II* (New York: Cambridge University Press, 1994), 433, 438–440.

5   For example, *The Maisky Diaries: Red Ambassador to the Court of St. James's, 1932–1943*, ed. Gabriel Gorodetsky (New Haven, CT: Yale University Press, 2015), 416–417, 463.

6   Stephen G. Fritz, *The First Soldier: Hitler as Military Leader* (New Haven, CT: Yale University Press, 2018), 285. On the full range of Nazi-Soviet contacts, Ingeborg Fleischhauer, *Die Chance des Sonderfriedens: Deutsch-Sowjetische Geheimgespräche, 1941–1945* (Munich: Siedler Verlag, 1986); Vojtech Mastny, *Russia's Road to the Cold War* (New York: Columbia University Press, 1979), 73–85.

7   Stephen Kotkin, *Stalin: Waiting for Hitler, 1929–1941* (New York: Penguin Press, 2017), 744–745; David Reynolds and Vladimir Pechatnov, eds., *The Kremlin Letters: Stalin's Wartime Correspondence with Churchill and Roosevelt* (New Haven, CT: Yale University Press, 2018), 236.

8   Sean McMeekin, *Stalin's War: A New History of World War II* (New York: Basic Books, 2012), 443–444; Timothy Snyder, *Bloodlands: Europe Between Hitler and Stalin* (New York: Basic Books, 2010), 287.

9   Details in Reynolds and Pechatnov, *Kremlin Letters*, 234–244; Roberts, *Churchill*, 755.

10   Copy of pamphlet in C 186/9, World Jewish Congress Collection, American Jewish Archives, Cincinnati; Schwarzbart's March 17, 1943, telegram in M-2-535, Schwarzbart Collection, Yad Vashem, Jerusalem; Schwarzbart Diary quoted in Wood and Jankowski, *Karski*, 177.

11   Wood and Jankowski, *Karski*, 158–159, 267.

12   "Warsaw's Ghetto Fights Deportation," *New York Times*, April 23, 1943, p. 9; "Germans Crushing Remaining Jews in Warsaw Ghetto," *St. Louis Globe-Democrat*, April 23, 1943, p. 15.

13   See Avinoam Patt, *The Jewish Heroes of Warsaw: The Afterlife of the Revolt* (Detroit: Wayne State University Press, 2021).

14   See Wood and Jankowski, *Karski*, 185–187.

15   Although Frankfurter kept a diary, it has a gap after June 1943. It is possible that he scrubbed it before turning it over to the Library of Congress. Wood and Jankowski, *Karski*, 297n188.

16   On Cox and Hopkins, David L. Roll, *The Hopkins Touch: Harry Hopkins and the Forging of the Alliance to Defeat Hitler* (New York: Oxford University Press, 2015), 278; Peter W. Cox, *Journalism Matters* (Gardiner, ME: Tilbury House, 2005), 26.

17   Cox to Hopkins, July 6, 1943, secret, box 75, Oscar Cox Papers, FDRL; also, Cox folder, box 137, Hopkins Papers, FDRL. See also, Wood and Jankowski, *Karski*, 187–188.

18   Cox to Lippmann, July 6, 1943, Lippmann folder, box 29, Cox Papers, FDRL.

19   This is based on a 1992 interview of Karski, summarized in Wood and Jankowski, *Karski*, 187–188; Frankfurter's reaction in Walter Laqueur, *The Terrible Secret: Suppression of the Truth about Hitler's "Final Solution"* (Boston: Little, Brown, 1980), 3.

20   Wood and Jankowski, *Karski*. 188–189.

21   For the July 22 meeting, "July 22nd, 1943," Franklin D. Roosevelt Day by Day, http://www.fdrlibrary.marist.edu/daybyday/daylog/july-22nd-1943/. For the substance, Wise to Roosevelt, July 23, 1943, 840.48 Refugees/4212, RG 59, NARA; FDR to Morgenthau, July 30, 1943, and Morgenthau to Wise, August 11, 1943, PPF 3292, FDRL; Stephen Wise, *Challenging Years: The Autobiography of Stephen Wise* (New York: Putnam's Sons, 1949), 193–194; Rebecca Erbelding, *Rescue Board: The Untold Story of America's Efforts to Save the Jews of Europe* (New York: Doubleday, 2018), 26–29, has a detailed discussion of the early background and the bureaucrats involved.

22   All covered in front-page stories, *New York Times*, July 28, 1943.

23   David Engel was kind enough to share his detailed notes on this long Polish document. The following summary of this meeting is based on this document, except where otherwise noted. Report from conversation during an audience with President Roosevelt, folder 3, box 36, Karski Papers, Hoover Institution, Stanford. I also benefited from Vincent Slatt's help with translation.

24   Irwin F. Gellman, *Secret Affairs: Franklin Roosevelt, Cordell Hull, and Sumner Welles* (Baltimore: Johns Hopkins University Press, 1995),

313–317. Transcript of conversation between Frankfurter and Secretary of War Stimson, June 16, 1943, microfilm roll 127, Henry L. Stimson Papers, Library of Congress.

25   Michael Fleming, "Jan Karski, Auschwitz, and News of the Holocaust," Polish University Abroad in London, *Zeszyty Naokowe*, Seria Trzecia, no. 2 (2014): 96–97.

26   See n. 23 above. Shorter summaries in Wood and Jankowski, *Karski*, 197–199; Engel, *Facing a Holocaust*, 244n69.

27   Jan Ciechanowski, *Defeat in Victory* (Garden City, NY: Doubleday, 1947), 182.

28   Wood and Jankowski, *Karski*, 201.

29   On the August 1942 statement, see Richard Breitman and Allan J. Lichtman, *FDR and the Jews* (Cambridge, MA: Belknap Press of Harvard University Press, 2013), 199. The July 31 press conference is available at http://www.fdrlibrary.marist.edu/_resources/images/pc/pc0151.pdf.

30   October 1978 interview, pp. 55–57, RG 60.5006, United States Holocaust Memorial Museum.

31   Wikipedia, s.v. "Jan Karski," accessed April 11, 2023, https://en.wikipedia.org/wiki/Jan_Karski. Jewish casualties and "stunned" as argued by Jay Winik, *1944 and the Year that Changed History* (New York: Simon & Schuster, 2015), 404–405.

32   Wood and Jankowski, *Karski*, 201.

33   Rebecca Erbelding, *Rescue Board*, 301n54; Cox, *Journalism Matters*, 16, 19; Abraham J. Peck and Jean S. Peck, *Maine's Jewish Heritage* (Charleston, SC: Arcadia Publishing, 2007), 110.

34   Warren F. Kimball, *The Most Unsordid Act: Lend-Lease, 1939–1941* (Baltimore: Johns Hopkins University Press, 1969), 132–133, as cited by W. Raymond Palmer, "The Role of Oscar Cox in the Creation of the War Refugee Board," *Federal History*, no. 9 (April 2017): 28.

35   Kenneth S. Davis, *FDR: The War President, 1940–1943: A History* (New York: Random House, 2000), 71; David Kaiser, *No End Save Victory: How FDR Led the Nation into War* (New York: Basic Books, 2014), 164; Peck and Peck, *Maine's Jewish Heritage*, 110.

36   Erbelding, *Rescue Board*, 301n54; Peter Cox, Oscar Cox's son, reveals that growing up, he did not know he was of Jewish descent. His mother was Presbyterian, and his father occasionally attended church services. (Cox, *Journalism Matters*, 10–19.)

37   Breitman and Lichtman, *FDR and the Jews*, 220–221.

38   Watson to Long, April 1, 1943, 1943 folder, box 3, Official File 3186, FDRL. Celler's account in Minutes of the Joint Emergency Committee on European Jewish Affairs, April 10, 1943, Joint Emergency Committee folder, box 23, EXO-29, YIVO Institute for Jewish Research, Center for Jewish History, NY.

39   Morning Conference, April 20, 1943, Confidential Memorandum for the Chairman, Subject File, box 3, Bermuda Conference Minutes, Lot File 52D408, RG 59, NARA. Summarized in Breitman and Lichtman, *FDR and the Jews*, 224–225.

40   "Invasion Only Way to Save Oppressed Jews, Berle Says," *Boston Globe*, May 3, 1943, pp. 1, 11; "Only Invasion of Europe and Allied Victory Can Save Jews, Berle Tells Boston Meeting," *Jewish Daily Bulletin*, May 3, 1943, https://www.jta.org/archive/only-invasion-of-europe-and-allied-victory -can-save-jews-berle-tells-boston-meeting.

41   On Welles, see Breitman and Lichtman, *FDR and the Jews*, 220. On Long's efforts, see James G. McDonald, *Refugees and Rescue: The Diaries and Papers of James G. McDonald, 1935–1945*, ed. Richard Breitman, Barbara McDonald Stewart, and Severin Hochberg (Bloomington: Indiana University Press, 2009), 200–244.

42   The most recent accounts are Erbelding, *Rescue Board*, 49–53; Andrew Meier, *Morgenthau: Power, Privilege, and the Rise of an American Dynasty* (New York: Random House, 2022), 334–358. See also, Richard Breitman and Alan M. Kraut, *American Refugee Policy and European Jewry 1933-1945* (Bloomington: Indiana University Press, 1987), 182–185.

43   Breitman and Lichtman, *FDR and the Jews*, 249–250.

44   [[Cox] Memorandum], June 16, 1943, book 642, Morgenthau Diaries, FDRL; Cox to Captain Charles Kades, July 3, 1943, chronological correspondence, box 75, Cox Papers, FDRL; Palmer, "Oscar Cox," 33.

45   Representative Sol Bloom and Senator Scott Lucas, both of whom attended the Bermuda Conference, intended to meet with Welles. Cox to Morgenthau, June 16, 1943, book 642, Morgenthau Diaries, FDRL.

46   On the long rivalry between Hull and Welles, see Gellman, *Secret Affairs*, especially 212–222, 302–323. Berle quoted in Breitman and Lichtman, *FDR and the Jews*, 228.

47   See the correspondence in box 32, Cox Papers, Stettinius file, FDRL.

48   Erbelding, *Rescue Board*, 36–48, appropriately titles one of her chapters "State Department Hubris."

49   O'Connell and Pehle to Morgenthau, July 1, 1943, book 646, Morgenthau Diaries, FDRL. On Romanian policy shifts, see Radu Ioanid, *The*

Holocaust in Romania: The Destruction of Jews and Roma under the Antonescu Regime (Chicago: Ivan R. Dee, 2000), 111, 116, 238, 266.

50   O'Connell and Pehle to Morgenthau, July 1, 1943, book 646, Morgenthau Diaries, FDRL. Memorandum of Conversation re Proposal by World Jewish Congress, July 16, 1943, 840.48 Refugees/4074, RG 59, NARA. Quote from Treasury group meeting, August 5, 1943, book 654, Morgenthau Diaries, FDRL.

51   Morgenthau to Hull, August 5, 1943, copy attached to Brandt to Feis, August 3, 1943, 840.48 Refugees/4212, RG 59, NARA. See also Erbelding, *Rescue Board*, 33–34.

52   See Randolph Paul's summary of the conflict, Paul to Morgenthau, August 12, 1943, book 688, Morgenthau Diaries, FDRL.

53   Berle to Hull, September 16, 1943, Hull August-December 1943 file, box 58, Adolf Berle Papers, FDRL.

54   John F. Sears, *Refuge Must Be Given: Eleanor Roosevelt, the Jewish Plight, and the Founding of Israel* (West Lafayette, IN: Purdue University Press, 2021), 130–132.

55   See "A Report of Failure and a Call to Action," *New York Times*, October 5, 1943, p. 29, and Cox to Bergson, October 6, 1943, Bergson file, box 2, Cox Papers, FDRL.

56   "Rabbis Give Wallace Petition to Form U.S. Board to Save Jews," *Washington Evening Star*, October 7, 1943, p. 7; David S. Wyman, *The Abandonment of the Jews: America and the Holocaust, 1941-1945* (New York: Pantheon, 1984), 150–153, has more background and detail. See also Breitman and Lichtman, *FDR and the Jews*, 229–231.

57   On the background of conflict between mainstream Zionists and Revisionist Zionists, see the nuanced discussion in Tuvia Friling, *Arrows in the Dark: David Ben-Gurion, the Yishuv Leadership, and Rescue Attempts during the Holocaust*, trans. Ora Cummings (Madison: Wisconsin University Press, 2005), 1:110–115.

58   Wyman, *Abandonment of the Jews*, 152; Breitman and Lichtman, *FDR and the Jews*, 230–231. Quote from William Hassett, *Off the Record With FDR, 1942-1945* (New York: Enigma Books, 2016), 209.

59   Palmer, "Oscar Cox," 34.

60   Erbelding, *Rescue Board*, 41; Reams to Stettinius, October 8, 1943, 840.48 Refugees/4683 1/5, RG 59, NARA.

61   For Cox's account, Treasury group meeting, January 15, 1944, book 694, p. 93, Morgenthau Diaries, FDRL. Cox dated this meeting as during the Moscow Foreign Minister's Conference.

62   Treasury group meeting, January 15, 1944, book 694, p. 93, Morgenthau Diaries, FDRL.

63   Meeting of the Under Secretary with the Assistant Secretaries, the Political Advisers, and the Geographic Division Heads, November 11, 1943, meetings with assistant secretaries, October 1943 folder, box 732, Edward R. Stettinius Papers, University of Virginia.

64   Palmer, "Oscar Cox," 36.

65   Palmer, "Oscar Cox," 37.

66   Best estimates range around 210,000–220,000. See discussion in Erbelding, *Rescue Board*, 45, 299n45.

67   Raynor to Stettinius re Refugee Problem, November 27, 1943, Refugees folder, box 727, Stettinius Papers, University of Virginia.

68   Breitman and Lichtman, *FDR and the Jews*, 231–232; Erbelding, *Rescue Board*, 44–46.

69   Hull to Morgenthau, December 6, 1943, copy in book 688, Morgenthau Diaries, FDRL; Winant to Secretary of State, December 15, 1943, urgent and for limited distribution, please inform Treasury, copy in Morgenthau Diaries, book 688, FDRL; Jewish Evacuation meetings, December 17, 1943 and December, 20, 1943, book 688, Morgenthau Diaries, FDRL.

70   Jewish Evacuation, December 19, 1943, book 688, part II, Morgenthau Diaries, FDRL.

71   Excellent, detailed discussion in Elberding, *Rescue Board*, 49–54.

72   Jewish Evacuation meeting, January 15, 1944, book 694, Morgenthau Diaries, FDRL.

73   Jewish Evacuation meeting, January 15, 1944, book 694, Morgenthau Diaries, FDRL; Erbelding, *Rescue Board*, 55–56.

74   Erbelding, *Rescue Board*, 56–57.

75   Erbelding, *Rescue Board*, 57.

76   Louise London, *Whitehall and the Jews, 1933–1948: British Immigration Policy, Jewish Refugees, and the Holocaust* (Cambridge: Cambridge University Press, 2000), 227; Bernard Wasserstein, *Britain and the Jews of Europe 1939–1945* (Oxford: Clarendon, 1979), 240–242; Richard Breitman, "American Rescue Activities in Sweden," *Holocaust and Genocide Studies* 7, no. 2 (Fall 1993): 202–215.

77   Cox to Morgenthau, January 17, 1944, copy in book 694, Morgenthau Diaries, FDRL, cited by Erbelding, *Rescue Board*, 302n58. I have trimmed the quote slightly.

7. FDR'S PRESS CONFERENCE AND HUNGARY

1   Jewish Evacuation meeting of January 26, 1944, book 696, Morgenthau Diaries, FDRL. Attached memo, Evacuation of Jewish from Poland to Hungary, ibid.

2   Pehle's Memorandum, January 27, 1944, strictly confidential, book 697, Morgenthau Diaries, FDRL.

3   Data from Zoitán Vági, László Csösz, and Gábor Kádá, *The Holocaust in Hungary: Evolution of a Genocide* (Lanham, MD: AltaMira Press, in Association with the United States Holocaust Memorial Museum, 2013), xlvii.

4   Vági, Csösz, and Kádá, *The Holocaust in Hungary*, xlvi. The prehistory of the Holocaust in Hungary is brilliantly covered by Randolph L. Braham, *The Politics of Genocide: The Holocaust in Hungary*, 3rd ed., 2 vols. (Boulder, CO: Social Science Monographs; Columbia University Press, 2016). The third and final edition of *The Politics of Genocide* has 1654 pages (not including appendices and indexes) in two volumes.

5   For more details, Braham, *The Politics of Genocide*, 1:429–432, 452n9.

6   Independent evidence of SOE contact with influential Hungarian rightists in Istanbul in March 1943 in D/H.70 to S.S.O. (B) 4, March 24, 1943, copy in folder 303, box 74, entry 210, RG 226, NARA; Hungary: Political: Proposed Agreement with Representatives of Hungarian General Staff regarding Intelligence Cooperation, October 4, 1943, folder 160, box 23, entry 137, RG 226, NARA. The key US document from Stockholm is Johnson to Secretary of State, February 28, 1944, strictly confidential, as well as attached Memorandum to the Minister, February 24, 1944, copy in folder 365, box 91, entry 210, RG 226, NARA. It appears that they began contact in late January or early February. The Hungarian minister referred to earlier contacts with the British in Turkey.

7   Gerhard L. Weinberg, *A World at Arms: A Global History of World War II* (New York: Cambridge University Press, 1994), 625–628; Andrew Roberts, *Churchill: Walking with Destiny* (New York: Viking, 2018), 798–799.

8   Braham, *Politics of Genocide*, 1:429, 438–439. The Dogwood double agent was a Hungarian named Andreas Gyorgi aka Bandi Grosz. On the Dogwood network, see Barry Rubin, *Istanbul Intrigues: Espionage, Sabotage, and Diplomatic Treachery in the Spy Capital of World War II* (New York: Pharos Books, 1992), 163–201.

9   Braham, *Politics of Genocide*, 1:432–434, 452n9.

10   Braham, *Politics of Genocide*, 1:435-436.

11   Braham, *Politics of Genocide*, 1:431; Braham with Paul Hanebrink, "The Holocaust in Hungary: A Critical Analysis," *Holocaust and Genocide Studies* 34, no. 1 (Spring 2020): 1-17.

12   Braham, *Politics of Genocide*, 1:452n9.

13   Braham, "The Holocaust in Hungary," 13.

14   Braham, *Politics of Genocide*, 1:438-440, 446-447. Braham allows for the possibility that Horthy revealed this to the Crown Council but that it was not recorded in the minutes of the meeting.

15   Braham, *Politics of Genocide*, 1:437. Vági, Csösz, and Kádáf, *The Holocaust in Hungary*, xlviii. On the Eichmann team of about two hundred men, see generally, Hans Safrian, *Eichmann's Men*, trans. Ute Stargardt (New York: Cambridge University Press, 2009).

16   Frank Chalk, "The BBC Hungarian Service in World War II and the Rescue of the Jews of Hungary, 1940-1945: Explanations and Lessons," in *Resisting Genocide: The Multiple Forms of Rescue*, ed. Jacques Semelin, Claire Andrieu, and Sarah Gensburger (New York: Columbia University Press, 2011), 323-324; Michael Fleming, "British Narratives of the Holocaust in Hungary," *Twentieth Century British History* 27, no. 4 (2016): 558-561.

17   Policy for Hungary, undated, attached to D/H.70 to D.S.O.(B) 4, March 24, 1943, copy in folder 303, box 74, entry 210, RG 226, NARA.

18   Holly Cowan Shulman, *The Voice of America: Propaganda and Democracy, 1941-1945* (Madison: University of Wisconsin Press, 1990), 176.

19   Yehuda Bauer, "Conclusion: The Holocaust in Hungary: Was Rescue Possible," in *Genocide and Rescue: The Holocaust in Hungary*, ed. David Cesarani (Oxford: Berg Publishers, 1997), 208n5.

20   Chalk, "The BBC Hungarian Service," 321-322.

21   See Shulman, *The Voice of America*, quote on 162. On the tendency to project New Deal ideals abroad, see Elizabeth Borgwardt, *A New Deal for the World: America's Vision for Human Rights* (Cambridge, MA: Belknap Press of Harvard University Press, 2005).

22   Pell's Memorandum for the Policy Committee, March 6, 1944, War Refugee Board, miscellaneous, Jan.-June 1944, box 1, Lot File 53D289, RG 59, NARA.

23   Rebecca Erbelding, *Rescue Board: The Untold Story of America's Efforts to Save the Jews of Europe* (New York: Doubleday, 2018), 104; Pehle's statement in Jewish Evacuation meeting, February 13, 1944, 10:30 a.m., book 701, Morgenthau Diaries, FDRL.

24   Partial quote from Erbelding, *Rescue Board*, 105–106.

25   Pell's Memorandum for the Policy Committee, March 6, 1944, folder War Refugee Board, miscellaneous, Jan.-June 1944, box 1. Lot File 53D289, RG 59, NARA.

26   Erbelding, *Rescue Board*, 80–81; Pell's Memorandum for the Policy Committee, March 6, 1944, folder War Refugee Board, miscellaneous, Jan.-June 1944, box 1, Lot File 53D289, RG 59, NARA.

27   Louise London, *Whitehall and the Jews, 1933–1948: British Immigration Policy, Jewish Refugees, and the Holocaust* (Cambridge: Cambridge University Press, 2000), 231,

28   Erbelding, *Rescue Board*, 106.

29   Ed to Dear Steve, March 6, 1944, refugee folder, box 177, President's Secretary File, FDRL

30   Information about appointments from "March 7th, 1944," Franklin D. Roosevelt Day by Day, http://www.fdrlibrary.marist.edu/daybyday /daylog/march-7th-1944/; Stettinius Memorandum for Honorable Stephen Early, March 8, 1944, 12:30 p.m., refugee file, PSF box 177, and Holocaust/ Refugee Collection, box 7, FDRL.

31   Transcripts of Morgenthau's telephone conversations with Grace Tully, Sam Rosenman, and then John Pehle, March 8, 1944, book 707, Morgenthau Diaries, FDRL.

32   Pehle's Memorandum for the Files, March 8, 1944, book 707, Morgenthau Diaries, FDRL. Jewish Evacuation meeting (with Morgenthau, Pehle, Klotz), March 9, 1944, book 708, Morgenthau Diaries, FDRL.

33   Untitled meeting, March 9, 1944, 9:10 a.m., and Jewish Evacuation meeting, March 9, 1944, 3:30 p.m., book 708, Morgenthau Diaries, FDRL; Erbelding, *Rescue Board*, 107–110.

34   Erbelding, *Rescue Board*, 109–110.

35   Memorandum of telephone message from McDermott to Early, March 7, 1944; Stettinius Memorandum for Honorable Stephen Early, March 8, 1944, box 177, PSF, FDRL; Morgenthau's Memorandum of Conversation with the President, March 18, 1944, book 711, Morgenthau Diaries, FDRL.

36   Transcript of Morgenthau-Rosenman phone conversation, March 10, 1944, book 708, Morgenthau Diaries, FDRL.

37   Transcript of Treasury group meeting, February 13, 1944, 4:45 p.m., book 701, Morgenthau Diaries, FDRL. Morgenthau related an earlier conversation, apparently on February 3: "February 3rd, 1944," Franklin D. Roosevelt Day by Day, http://www.fdrlibrary.marist.edu/daybyday/daylog/february -3rd-1944/.

38 Pehle's Strictly Confidential memo, February 10, 1944, book 701, Morgenthau Diaries, FDRL.

39 Jewish Evacuation meeting, February 13, 1944, book 701, Morgenthau Diaries, FDRL.

40 "FDR Assailed in Creating of Refugee Board," *Rochester Democrat and Chronicle*, March 21, 1944, p. 10, italics added; "Jewish Refugee Credited with Sea Aid Device," *Chicago Tribune*, March 21, 1944, p. 26.

41 Minutes of the Third Meeting of the War Refugee Board, War Refugee Board, miscellaneous, January-March 1944, box 1, Lot File 53D289, RG 59, NARA; "Magyar Leaders Declared Held in Reich," *Washington Post*, March 21, 1944, p. 1.

42 Precisely when and how the British received FDR's draft statement are not clear from US records, but Roosevelt had decided to go ahead regardless of British reaction.

43 Minutes of the Third Meeting of the War Refugee Board, War Refugee Board, miscellaneous, January-March 1944, box 1, Lot File 53D289, RG 59, NARA; Erbelding, *Rescue Board*, 110.

44 Quoted by Braham, *Politics of Genocide*, 2:1455–1456.

45 Telephone transcript of Morgenthau's call to Dorothy Brady, March 22, 1944, copy in book 713, Morgenthau Diaries, FDRL. On the new language for Hungary, see also, Erbelding, *Rescue Board*, 111.

46 Pehle's Memorandum for the Secretary's Diary, March 22, 1944, book 713, Morgenthau Diary, FDRL.

47 "March 23rd, 1944," Franklin D. Roosevelt Day by Day, http://www.fdrlibrary.marist.edu/daybyday/daylog/march-23rd-1944/.

48 Nigel Hamilton, *War and Peace: FDR's Final Odyssey, D-Day to Yalta, 1943–1945* (Boston: Houghton Mifflin Harcourt, 2019), 208–210; quote 209.

49 David B. Woolner, *The Last 100 Days: FDR at War and at Peace* (New York: Basic Books, 2017), 4–5.

50 "March 24th, 1944," Franklin D. Roosevelt Day by Day, http://www.fdrlibrary.marist.edu/daybyday/daylog/march-24th-1944/.

51 "Roosevelt's Head Still Stopped Up," *Miami News*, March 24, 1944, p. 1.

52 Roosevelt's Letter to Speaker of the House Joseph W. Byrns on the President's Press Conferences, May 8, 1935, *The Presidential Papers of Franklin D. Roosevelt, 1935, item 63*, (New York: Random House, 1938). I am grateful to archivist Virginia Lewick for this reference.

53   Graham J. White, *FDR and the Press* (Chicago: University of Chicago Press, 1979), 20.

54   White, *FDR and the Press*, 10–13.

55   Press and Radio Conference #943, March 17, 1944, http://www.fdr library.marist.edu/_resources/images/pc/pc0158.pdf.

56   The White House had given both embassies the text in advance; see Erbelding, *Rescue Board*, 111.

57   "Hull Policy Talk Fails to Impress GOP Group," *Washington Post*, March 25, 1944, p. 1.

58   Press and Radio Conference #944, March 24, 1944, http://www .fdrlibrary.marist.edu/_resources/images/pc/pc0158.pdf.

59   Erbelding, *Rescue Board*, 110–112; "Roosevelt Warns Germans on Jews," *New York Times*, March 25, 1944, pp. 1, 4.

60   "Asks Balkans to Hide Jews, Roosevelt Also Urges Free Nations to Open Borders" *Baltimore Sun*, March 25, 1944, p. 2; Erbelding, *Rescue Board*, 110–112.

61   Department of State Bulletin, March 25, 1944, quoted by Braham, *Politics of Genocide*, 2:1456; "Hull Urges Hungary to Resist Germans," *Washington Post*, March 25, 1944, p. 2.

62   "Roosevelt Warns War Criminals, *The Miami News*, March 25, 1944, p. 1; "Text of Pledge to Refugees by President," *Washington Post*, March 25, 1944, p. 2.

63   OWI Dispatch to Control Desk NY and Hamblet London, March 24, 1944, refugees folder, box 116, entry 359, RG 208, NARA. The follow-up to NY is handwritten at the bottom of the page.

64   Erbelding, *Rescue Board*, 112.

65   Braham, *Politics of Genocide*, 2:1474–1475.

66   Quoted by Braham, *Politics of Genocide*, 2:1457.

67   Copy in refugees folder, box 116, entry 359, RG 208, NARA.

68   Fleming," British Narratives of the Holocaust," 562.

69   Fleming, "British Narratives of the Holocaust," 562–563, 568.

70   Chalk, "The BBC Hungarian Service."

8. HUNGARIAN REALITIES

1   David Cesarani, introduction to *Genocide and Rescue: The Holocaust in Hungary 1944*, ed. David Cesarani (Oxford: Berg Publishers, 1997), 5;

Zoitán Vági, László Csösz, and Gábor Kádá,, *The Holocaust in Hungary: Evolution of a Genocide* (Lanham, MD: AltaMira Press, in Association with the United States Holocaust Memorial Museum, 2013), xxviii–xxix, liii.

2   Randolph L. Braham, *The Politics of Genocide: The Holocaust in Hungary*, 3rd ed., 2 vols. (Boulder, CO: Social Science Monographs; Columbia University Press, 2016), 2:1507.

3   Braham, *Politics of Genocide*, 1:443.

4   Interrogation of Carl Berthold Franz Rekowski, September 17 and 19, 1945, XL25105, entry 6, RG 226, NARA.

5   Rekowski claimed that neither Foreign Minister Ribbentrop nor Himmler was happy with Veesenmayer's appointment, even though he was a high SS officer; Interrogation of Carl Berthold Franz Rekowski, September 17 and 19, 1945, XL25105, entry 6, RG 226, NARA; Braham, *Politics of Genocide*, 1:437, 474–490; quote from 477.

6   Braham, *Politics of Genocide*, 1:517–527; 2:1685; Interrogation of Carl Berthold Franz Rekowski, September 17 and 19, 1945, XL25105, entry 6, RG 226, NARA.

7   Braham, *Politics of Genocide*, 1:583; 2:1685.

8   See Chapter 7. On the number of broadcasts, Rebecca Erbelding, *Rescue Board: The Untold Story of America's Efforts to Save the Jews of Europe* (New York: Doubleday, 2018), 114.

9   Braham, *Politics of Genocide*, 1:594.

10   Executive Committee Minutes, April 25, 1944, folder 15, box A 78, World Jewish Congress Records, American Jewish Archives, Cincinnati.

11   Riegner's suggestions discussed in Easterman to Stettinius, April 28, 1944, copy in book 730, Morgenthau Diaries, FDRL.

12   Executive Committee Minutes, April 25, 1944, folder 15, box A 78, World Jewish Congress Records, American Jewish Archives, Cincinnati; OWI Washington to Control Desks New York and London, April 25, 1944, Hungary-Policy folder, box 109, entry 358, RG 208, NARA; Long quote from Records of the War Refugee Board, vol. 4, box 41, FDRL.

13   Appeal by Senator Guffey to People of Hungary, May 7, 1944, War Refugee Board Records, vol. 4, box 41, FDRL.

14   Vági, Csösz, and Kádár, *Holocaust in Hungary*, liii.

15   Britt and Thomas, Istanbul to OWI, Washington, May 22, 1944, Hungary-cables folder, box 109, entry 358, RG 208, NARA. The accuracy and rapidity of this intelligence, probably gathered by Revisionist Zionist Frank Ofner in Istanbul, is still stunning. I am grateful to Tuvia Friling for

the information on Britt, Thomas, and Ofner. Britt recruited Francis Ofner and his wife Ilana, Revisionist Zionists who had outstanding Hungarian contacts. See Friling's study, "Istanbul 1942–1945: The Kollek-Avriel and Berman-Ofner Networks," www.academia.edu.

16   Britt and Thomas to OWI, May 23, 1944, Hungary-cables folder, box 109, entry 358, RG 208, NARA.

17   Erbelding, *Rescue Board*, 165–166.

18   Braham, *Politics of Genocide*, 2:1417.

19   Asher Cohen, "Resistance and Rescue in Hungary," in *Genocide and Rescue*, 126; Braham, *Politics of Genocide*, 1:593; 2:949–954; Yehuda Bauer, conclusion to *Genocide and Rescue*, 196–197.

20   Asher Cohen, "Resistance and Rescue in Hungary," in *Genocide and Rescue*, 129.

21   Braham, *Politics of Genocide*, 2:949–951. Asher Cohen, "Resistance and Rescue in Hungary," in *Genocide and Rescue*, 126, 132.

22   Braham, *Politics of Genocide*, 1:511, 563n22; 2:952–954, 1248–1249.

23   Kasztner's biography in Anna Porter, *Kasztner's Train: The True Story of an Unknown Hero of the Holocaust* (New York: Walker Books, 2007), 9–29; Braham, *Politics of Genocide*, 2:1245–1246. Kasztner was interrogated in Switzerland shortly after the war ended. He claimed credit for initiating the bargaining. Information Group report on SS Organization in Hungary Responsible for Jewish Persecution, May 17, 1945, copy in folder 65-47826-249, entry A1-136-P, box 63, RG 65, NARA. This document does not name Kasztner but describes him in detail. See also, Richard Breitman, "Nazi Jewish Policy in 1944," in *Genocide and Rescue*, 79; Braham, *Politics of Genocide*, 2:1251–1252, accepts this account as well.

24   Randolph L. Braham with Paul Hanebrink, "The Holocaust in Hungary: A Critical Analysis," *Holocaust and Genocide Studies* 34, no. 1 (2020): 14.

25   Braham, *Politics of Genocide*, 2:1252–1254.

26   Braham, *Politics of Genocide*, 2:1254–1258; Andreas Biss, *Der Stopp der Endlösung: Kampf gegen Himmler und Eichmann in Budapest* (Stuttgart-Degerloch: Seewald Verlag, 1966), 53–54; Porter, *Kasztner's Train*, 119–129.

27   Braham, *Politics of Genocide*, 2:1254–1258.

28   See Chapter 7, "Background to the German Occupation of Hungary."

29   Summarized in Braham, *Politics of Genocide*, 2:1458–1463.

30   This occurred because of the 1998 Nazi War Crimes Disclosure Act. See Richard Breitman, Norman J. W. Goda, Timothy Naftali, and Robert Wolfe, *U.S. Intelligence and the Nazis* (New York: Cambridge University Press, 2006).

31   Schellenberg's adviser was Kurt Jahnke, and Jahnke and Marcus became part of a small group of disaffected intelligence men. OSS London Dispatch, Nazi Attempt to Contact British, December 28, 1944; Buxton Memoranda for the Secretary of State, December 28, 1944 and January 16, 1945, all folder 20, box 756, entry 190, RG 226, NARA; Dictionary Interrogation no. 25, April 5, 1945, copy in folder XX11589–XX11599, box 66, entry 109, RG 226, NARA. On Schellenberg's attitudes generally, see Katrin Paehler, *The Third Reich's Intelligence Services: The Career of Walter Schellenberg* (New York: Cambridge University Press, 2017).

32   OSS to Ustravic, London, cc: Cairo, London, Istanbul, folder 1499, box 245, entry 134, RG 226, NARA.

33   Braham, *Politics of Genocide*, 2:1260. See more details on War Refugee Board reactions in Erbelding, *Rescue Board*, 131–137.

34   Roosevelt to Hirschmann, June 8, 1944, copy in book 741, Morgenthau Diaries, FDRL. The main goal of the June 8 meeting was to get the president to approve the establishment of a free port for about 1,000 refugees in the US.

35   Pehle's Memorandum for the File, June 8, 1944, book 741, Morgenthau Diaries, FDRL.

36   Erbelding, *Rescue Board*, 131, 136.

37   Kasztner to ? (probably Nathan Schwalb, Geneva), June 18, 1944, Hagana Archive, Tel-Aviv, Brand/Kasztner files. I am indebted to Shlomo Aronson for a copy of this document.

38   Richard Breitman, "Nazi Jewish Policy in 1944," in *Genocide and Rescue*, 81.

39   Erbelding, *Rescue Board*, 137–138.

40   Martin Gilbert, *Auschwitz and the Allies* (New York: Holt, Rinehart, and Winston, 1981), 270, 277. Churchill's minute is mentioned in an extensive internal British government investigation in 1961 in response to a June 13, 1961, parliamentary inquiry by Arthur Henderson, The Brand Mission and Related Questions, CAB21/SS89, #264838, NA-UK; Erbelding, *Rescue Board*, 138–139; Porter, *Kasztner's Train*, 225.

41   See Porter, *Kasztner's Train*, 176–181, 190–193, for the Strasshof laborers; Braham, *Politics of Genocide*, 2:850–853, 1266–1271.

42   Brand wrote two books published in Hebrew in 1957 and 1960. His version was also conveyed in Alex Weissberg, *Desperate Mission: Joel Brand's Story* (New York: Criterion Books, 1958). The Brands' son Daniel has researched this subject and updated Brand's interpretation: Daniel Brand, *Trapped by Evil and Deceit: The Story of Hansi and Joel Brand* (New York: Cherry Orchard Books-Academic Studies Press, 2021).

43   Porter, *Kasztner's Train*, 324–362; Braham, *Politics of Genocide*, 2:1283–1292, has a balanced summary.

44   A copy of the Auschwitz Protocols is reprinted in Rudolf Vrba, *I Escaped from Auschwitz* (Ft. Lee, NJ: Barricade Books, 2003), 327–363. On Vrba, see also Jonathan Freedland, *The Escape Artist: The Man Who Broke Out of Auschwitz to Warn the World* (New York: Harper, 2022).

45   Braham, *Politics of Genocide*, 2:959–967, traces the path of this document in great detail.

46   This was a major argument in Gilbert, *Auschwitz and the Allies*.

47   For example, Richard Breitman, *Official Secrets: What the Nazis Planned, What the British and Americans Knew* (New York: Hill & Wang, 1998), 110–121; Michael Fleming, *Auschwitz, the Allies, and Censorship of the Holocaust* (Cambridge: Cambridge University Press, 2014), 128–213.

48   Erbelding, *Rescue Board*, 156–158.

49   The internal pressures cannot be covered here, but are available in Braham, *Politics of Genocide*, 2:1006–1018.

50   Spellman to Pehle, June 13, 1944, copy in book 743, Morgenthau Diaries, FDRL.

51   Hull to American Embassy, London and elsewhere, June 24, 1944, copy in War Refugee Board Records, box 41, vol. 3, FDRL; "Protect Jews, Hungary Told," *Pittsburgh Sun-Telegraph*, June 21, 1944, p. 2; "Hull Backs Plea Against Massacre," *Buffalo Evening News*, June 27, 1944, p. 5.

52   Summarized in Pehle to Members of the War Refugee Board, Summary of Steps . . . with Regard to the Jews of Hungary, July 15, 1944, book 754, Morgenthau Diaries, FDRL; Erbelding, *Rescue Board*, 166.

53   Stettinius to American Legation Bern, June 6, 1944; Harrison to Secretary of State, June 16, 1944; Hull to American Legation Bern, June 22, 1944; Harrison to Secretary of State, June 26, 1944; 848.48 Refugees/6271a CF, 6307 CF, /6393 CF, RG 59, NARA; Summary in Memorandum for the Members of the War Refugee Board, July 15, 1944 (re Hungary), book 754, Morgenthau Diaries, FDRL; Braham, *Politics of Genocide*, 2:1019, 1021, but with some inaccuracies. I am grateful to David Langbart for locating the diplomatic documents.

54   Braham, *Politics of Genocide*, 2:1021–1026.

55   Summarized in Pehle to Members of the War Refugee Board, Summary of Steps . . . with Regard to the Jews of Hungary, July 15, 1944, book 754, Morgenthau Diaries, FDRL. The church service covered in Erbelding, *Rescue Board*, 155–156.

56   Richard Overy, *The Bombers and the Bombed: Allied Air War Over Europe, 1940–1945* (New York: Penguin, 2015), 407–408.

57   "Rocket Nests Bombed Anew," *Baltimore Sun*, July 3, 1944, p. 3; "U.S. Bombing Forces Team-Up on Balkans, *Capital Journal* (Salem, Oregon), July 3, 1944, p. 1; "Budapest Raided Again by Yanks' Bombing Forces," *Miami Daily News-Record*, July 3, 1944, p. 1.

58   Martin Gilbert, *Churchill and the Jews* (New York: Henry Holt, 2007), 212–213. Gilbert calls Wiskemann a British diplomat. Additional details in Gilbert, *Auschwitz and the Allies*, 266. On Wiskemann and Dulles, see Neal H. Petersen, ed., *From Hitler's Doorstep: The Wartime Intelligence Reports of Allen Dulles, 1942–1945* (University Park, PA: Pennsylvania State University Press, 1996), 5, 589.

59   Braham, *Politics of Genocide*, 2:1026–1029; Vági, Csősz, and Kádár, *Holocaust in Hungary*, lix.

60   Braham, *Politics of Genocide*, 2:1032–1037, 1040–1043, 1426.

61   Himmler's notes of meeting with Hitler, July 15, 1944, roll 94/frame 2615074, microfilm T-175, RG 242, NARA. Quote from Altenburg's memo to Veesenmayer reprinted in Raul Hilberg, *The Destruction of the European Jews*, 3rd ed. (New Haven, CT: Yale University Press, 2003), 2:912. On Sztójay, Braham, *Politics of Genocide*, 2:1037.

62   Richard Breitman and Shlomo Aronson, "The End of the Final Solution?: Nazi Plans to Ransom Jews in 1944," *Central European History* 25, no. 2 (1992): 181.

63   Braham, *Politics of Genocide*, 2:1071–1073.

64   Braham, *Politics of Genocide*, 2:1043.

65   Erbelding, *Rescue Board*, 166–167.

66   More details in Braham, *Politics of Genocide*, 2:1426–1429, 1431; Theo Tschuy, *Dangerous Diplomacy: The Story of Carl Lutz, Rescuer of 62,000 Hungarian Jews* (Grand Rapids, MI: William B. Erdmann's Publishing, 2000), 42–43, uses the figure 8,000 emigration certificate holders.

67   Erbelding, *Rescue Board*, 170.

68   Ingrid Carlberg, *Raoul Wallenberg: The Incredible Life and Mysterious Disappearance of the Man Who Saved Thousands of Hungarian Jews*

from the Holocaust (London: MacLehose Press, 2017), 183–184, 189–198; Erbelding, *Rescue Board*, 170–172.

69   Group Meeting, August 17, 1944, book 763, Morgenthau Diaries, FDRL.

70   Carlberg, *Raoul Wallenberg*, 196, 207; other biographies in English include Paul A. Levine, *Raoul Wallenberg in Budapest: Myth, History, and Holocaust* (London: Valentine Mitchell, 2010); and Kati Marton, *Wallenberg: The Incredible True Story of the Man Who Saved Thousands of Jews* (New York: Arcade Publishing, 2011).

71   Per Anger, *With Raoul Wallenberg in Budapest: Memories of the War Years in Hungary* (Washington, DC: Holocaust Library, 1996); also, Carlberg, *Raoul Wallenberg*, 176.

72   Erbelding, *Rescue Board*, 171–172; Carlberg, *Raoul Wallenberg*, 175–176.

73   Pehle Memorandum to Stettinius, July 29, 1944, copy in War Refugee Board, June-July 1944, box 2, Lot File 53D289, RG 59, NARA. More details in Erbelding, *Rescue Board*, 172–176; Braham, *Politics of Genocide*, 2:1468–1473.

74   Group meeting, August 17, 1944, book 763, Morgenthau Diaries, FDRL.

75   Hull (War Refugee Board) to American Embassy Ankara (Hirschmann), August 16, 1944, book 763, Morgenthau Diaries, FDRL; Erbelding, *Rescue Board*, 176.

76   Covered in more detail in Braham, *Politics of Genocide*, 2:1101–1114.

77   Carlberg, *Raoul Wallenberg*, 264, estimates that the Jewish "employees" plus their families, all of whom had protective papers, numbered about 250.

78   Carlberg, *Raoul Wallenberg*, 264–271.

79   Braham, *Politics of Genocide*, 2:1115–1117.

80   Braham, *Politics of Genocide*, 2:1118–1128; Carlberg, *Raoul Wallenberg*, 290–295.

81   Carlberg, *Raoul Wallenberg*, 299.

82   Braham, *Politics of Genocide*, 2:1124–1129; Carlberg, *Raoul Wallenberg*, 300–302; Vági, Csősz, and Kádár, *Holocaust in Hungary*, lxiii.

83   Carlberg, *Raoul Wallenberg*, 351.

84   Quoted by Erbelding, *Rescue Board*, 230, and Carlberg, *Raoul Wallenberg*, 320–321.

85   Richard Breitman and Allan J. Lichtman, *FDR and the Jews* (Cambridge, MA: Belknap Press of Harvard University Press, 2013), 292.

86   Dino A. Brugioni and Robert G. Poirier, *The Holocaust Revisited: A Retrospective Analysis of the Auschwitz-Birkenau Extermination Complex*, CIA report no. ST-79-10001 (Washington, DC: February 1979); Dino A. Brugioni, "The Aerial Photos of the Auschwitz-Birkenau Extermination Complex," in *The Bombing of Auschwitz: Should the Allies Have Attempted It?* ed. Michael J. Neufeld and Michael Berenbaum (New York: St. Martin's Press, 2000), 52–53; Poirier at the press conference quoted in "Auschwitz Camp Aerial Photos Found," *St. Louis Post-Dispatch*, February 25, 1979, p. 21.

87   David Kaiser, *No End Save Victory: How FDR Led the Nation into War* (New York: Basic Books, 2014), 211–212.

88   Phil Haun, ed., *Lectures of the Air Corps Tactical School and American Strategic Bombing in World War II* (Lexington: University of Kentucky Press, 2019), 201–202, 232–251: quote on 202; also, Tami Davis Biddle, *Rhetoric and Reality in Air Warfare: The Evolution of British and American Ideas About Strategic Bombing, 1914–1945* (Princeton, NJ: Princeton University Press, 2002), 206–208.

89   Overy, *The Bombers and the Bombed*, 19–20.

90   Overy, *The Bombers and the Bombed*, 36–43.

91   Overy, *The Bombers and the Bombed*, 47.

92   Edward Westermann, "The Royal Air Force and the Bombing of Auschwitz: First Deliberations, January 1941," *Holocaust and Genocide Studies* 15, no. 1 (2001), 70–85. This article reproduces the key documents, and I have drawn on it for the following paragraph. I am also grateful to Westermann for a video conversation on this subject and for his comments on my draft section of this chapter.

93   Westermann, "The Royal Air Force and the Bombing of Auschwitz."

94   Haun, *Lectures*, 205–208.

95   Robert Ehlers, *The Mediterranean Air War: Air Power and Allied Victory in World War II* (Lawrence: University of Kansas Press, 2015), 357.

96   Robert S. Ehlers, Jr., *Targeting the Third Reich: Air Intelligence and the Allied Bombing Campaigns* (Lawrence: University of Kansas Press, 2009), 249.

97   Ehlers, *Mediterranean Air War*, 366.

98   "Blechhammer," Holocaust Encyclopedia, United States Holocaust Memorial Museum, https://encyclopedia.ushmm.org/content/en/article/blechhammer.

99   Tami Davis Biddle, "Allied Air Power: Objectives and Capabilities," in Neufeld and Berenbaum, *The Bombing of Auschwitz*, 51; Richard G. Davis,

"The Bombing of Auschwitz: Comments on a Historical Speculation," in Neufeld and Berenbaum, *The Bombing of Auschwitz*, 216.

100   Ehlers, *Mediterranean Air War*, 372.

101   Breitman and Lichtman, *FDR and the Jews*, 287. Wesley Frank Craven and James Lea Cate, eds., *The Army Air Forces in World War II*, vol. 3, *Europe: Argument to VE-Day, January 1944 to May 1945* (Washington, DC: Office of Air Force History, 1983), 642; Duane L. "Sparky" Bohnstedt, "Blechhammer" (2004), http://15thaf.org/55th_BW/460th_BG/Stories/PDFs/Blechhammer.pdf.

102   This according to the United States Strategic Bombing survey of 57 US missions against three separate synthetic oil plants; Biddle, *Rhetoric and Reality*, 243; Overy, *The Bombers and the Bombed*, 204.

103   Williamson Murray, "Monday-Morning Quarterbacking and the Bombing of Auschwitz," in Neufeld and Berenbaum, *The Bombing of Auschwitz*, 211.

104   Neufeld and Berenbaum, *The Bombing of Auschwitz*, 249–260; Erbelding, *Rescue Board*, 153–158, 215–216.

105   Erbelding, *Rescue Board*, 154–155.

106   Neufeld and Berenbaum, *The Bombing of Auschwitz*, 258–260.

107   Handy Memorandum for the Record, June 23, 1944; McCloy to Pehle, July 4, 1944, reprinted in Neufeld and Berenbaum, *The Bombing of Auschwitz*, 254–255, 260.

108   Documents reprinted in Neufeld and Berenbaum, *The Bombing of Auschwitz*, 271–280.

109   Tami Davis Biddle, "Allied Air Power: Objectives and Capabilities," in Neufeld and Berenbaum, *The Bombing of Auschwitz*, 51.

110   Neufeld and Berenbaum, *The Bombing of Auschwitz*, 262–268; Gilbert, *Auschwitz and the Allies*, 267–273, 284–286.

111   Neufeld and Berenbaum, *The Bombing of Auschwitz*, 269–271.

112   Kevin A. Mahoney, "An American Operational Response to a Request to Bomb Rail Lines to Auschwitz," *Holocaust and Genocide Studies* 25, no. 3 (2011): 439–441.

113   Mahoney, "An American Operational Response," 442.

114   Craven and Cate, *Army Air Forces*, 3:299, 302, 652.

115   Quoted by Michael Berenbaum in Neufeld and Berenbaum, *The Bombing of Auschwitz*, x.

116   "Bush: U.S. Should Have Acted on Auschwitz," January 11, 2008, https://www.nbcnews.com/id/wbna22616187

117   David S. Wyman, "Why Auschwitz Was Never Bombed," *Commentary* 65, no. 5 (May 1978): https://www.commentary.org/articles/david-wyman/why-auschwitz-was-never-bombed/; David S. Wyman, *The Abandonment of the Jews: America and the Holocaust, 1941–1945* (New York: Pantheon, 1984); Gilbert, *Auschwitz and the Allies*.

118   Neufeld and Berenbaum, *The Bombing of Auschwitz*.

119   Neufeld and Berenbaum, *The Bombing of Auschwitz*, 43, 179; Rice's article was added when David Wyman withdrew approval for the republication of his 1978 *Commentary* article. Information about Rice and Wyman from Michael Neufeld.

120   Michael Neufeld makes this point in his introduction to Neufeld and Berenbaum, *The Bombing of Auschwitz*, 6.

121   Gilbert, *Auschwitz and the Allies*, 292.

122   Neufeld and Berenbaum, *The Bombing of Auschwitz*, 8, 25–26.

123   This is Michael Neufeld's term and argument: Neufeld and Berenbaum, *The Bombing of Auschwitz*, 6.

124   Joseph Robert White "Target Auschwitz: Historical and Hypothetical German Responses to Allied Attack," *Holocaust and Genocide Studies* 16, no. 1 (2002): 54–76, especially 63–66.

125   Wyman, *The Abandonment of the Jews*, 304: "Without gas chambers and crematoria the Nazis would have been forced to reassess the extermination program. . . ."

126   Neufeld and Berenbaum, *The Bombing of Auschwitz*, 25.

127   Wyman, *The Abandonment of the Jews*, 334.

128   Erbelding, *Rescue Board*, 57. On Hungary, see Chapter 8, "Pressures on Horthy."

129   Wyman, *The Abandonment of the Jews*, 304; Neufeld and Berenbaum, *The Bombing of Auschwitz*, 7.

130   Cited by Neufeld in Neufeld and Berenbaum, *The Bombing of Auschwitz*, 1–2. Gerhard L. Weinberg has frequently made this argument and does so in Neufeld and Berenbaum, *The Bombing of Auschwitz*, 26.

131   Neufeld and Berenbaum, *The Bombing of Auschwitz*, 10.

132   Edward T. Chase, "Why We Didn't Bomb Auschwitz," *Washington Post*, April 17, 1983, p. 13.

133   Wyman, *The Abandonment of the Jews*, on FDR's general responsibility, 311–313; on the bombing, 307n*, 410n78.

134   Jay Winik, *1944 and the Year that Changed History* (New York: Simon & Schuster, 2015), 471–472. In his acknowledgments, Winik suggests that Elie Wiesel influenced his view of FDR. See Winik, *1944*, 537.

CONCLUSION

1   It is a concise paraphrase of expressions by liberal John Stuart Mill in 1867. It is not a quote from Edmund Burke: "'The only thing necessary for the triumph of evil is for good men to do nothing,' a Quote Falsely Attributed to Edmund Burke," Open Culture, March 13, 2016, https://www.open culture.com/2016/03/edmund-burkeon-in-action.html.

2   Quoted in Richard Breitman, *The Berlin Mission: The American Who Resisted Nazi Germany from Within* (New York: PublicAffairs, 2019), 161.

3   Chełmno operated briefly in June and July 1944.

4   William D. Rubinstein, *The Myth of Rescue: Why the Democracies Could Not Have Saved More Jews from the Holocaust* (London: Routledge, 1997).

5   This is a very brief summary of a very complicated subject I have treated elsewhere. Breitman, *The Berlin Mission*; Richard Breitman and Allan J. Lichtman, *FDR and the Jews* (Cambridge, MA: Belknap Press of Harvard University Press, 2014).

6   Gerhard L. Weinberg, *A World at Arms: A Global History of World War II* (New York: Cambridge University Press, 1994), 154.

7   Chapter 2, "The Grand Alliance."

8   See Jan Láníček and Jan Lambertz, eds., *More Than Parcels: Wartime Aid for Jews in Nazi-Era Camps and Ghettos* (Detroit: Wayne State University Press, 2022), 3, as well as the chapters by Anne Lepper, Jan Láníček, and Pontus Rudberg, on 49–146.

9   Michael R. Marrus, *Lessons of the Holocaust* (Toronto: University of Toronto Press, 2015). Also, book panel presentation at the United States Holocaust Memorial Museum, May 9, 2017.

10   Dawidowicz's March 1962 article in *Commentary* Magazine: "Perfidy, by Ben Hecht," https://www.commentary.org/articles/lucy-dawidowicz/perfidy-by-ben-hecht/.

11   Nadav Eyal, "When Netanyahu Quoted Roosevelt," *Yediot*, December 3, 2022, https://www.yediot.co.il/articles/0,7340,L-6231940,00.html?utm_source=ynet.app.android&utm_medium=social&utm_campaign=general_share&utm_term=6231940&utm_content=Header

This incident, however, does not appear in the English translation of Netanyahu's memoir. Benjamin Netanyahu, *Bibi: My Story* (New York: Threshold Editions, 2022).

12   See Chapter 8, "The Non-Bombing of Auschwitz."

13   I have seen these arguments in sermons and in private correspondence.

14   Samantha Power, *"A Problem from Hell": America and the Age of Genocide* (New York: Basic Books, 2013).

15   For detailed background, see Kenneth S. Stern, *The Conflict Over the Conflict: The Israel-Palestine Campus Debate* (Toronto: New Jewish Press/ University of Toronto Press, 2020), especially 77–148; and Roger Cohen, "History of Colonialism Rears Its Head as Conflicts Rage," *New York Times*, December 15, 2023, p. A4.

16   Jeffrey Herf, "Hamas Terror: Sie machen den Hass zum Weltbild," *Frankfurter Allgemeine Zeitung*, October 20, 2023.

17   Alvin H. Rosenfeld, "The Palestinian Problem is a Religious Problem," *Sapir*, October-November 2023, https://sapirjournal.org/war-in-israel/2023 /11/the-palestinian-problem-is-a-religious-problem/.

18   Jonathan Chait, "Marjorie Taylor Greene Blamed Wildfires on Secret Jewish Space Laser," *New York*, January 28, 2021, https://nymag.com /intelligencer/article/marjorie-taylor-greene-qanon-wildfires-space-laser -rothschild-execute.html

19   Soros did give money to a political action committee that supported Bragg and many others.

20   Jonathan Weisman and Andrew Higgins, "Behind Indictment, Right Wing Sees a Familiar Villain in Soros," *New York Times*, April 25, 2023, p. A17.

21   Robert S. Wistrich, *Antisemitism: The World's Oldest Hatred* (New York: Schocken Books, 1994); Walter Laqueur, *The Changing Face of Anti-Semitism: From Ancient Times to the Present Day* (New York: Oxford University Press, 2008).

22   Roosevelt to Wise, February 9, 1944, microfilm 74–48, Wise Papers, American Jewish Historical Society, Center for Jewish History, NY; "Anti-semitism Aids Hitler, Says F.D.R.," *St. Louis Post-Dispatch*, February 13, 1944, p. 40. It is possible that Wise drafted this letter, and that FDR agreed to sign and release it.

ACKNOWLEDGMENTS

I am grateful to many friends, colleagues, and others who were willing and able to comply with my requests for assistance. The following list is probably incomplete.

My agent, Joe Spieler, helped to sharpen the argument in my book proposal. This book would not have come about without him. He also fine-tuned several chapters.

Kathleen McDermott at Harvard University Press showed strong interest in my subject and carried out work through peer review and acceptance. Emily Silk then took over the remaining editorial and supervisory work at the Press. I am grateful to both of them.

Two of my coauthors on previous books, Allan Lichtman and Norman Goda, gave me valuable critiques of multiple chapters and carried out additional editing. I benefited greatly from their work and skilled judgment.

Benton Arnovitz advised me on publishing issues and read one of my chapters on the Holocaust in Hungary. His extensive experience with Randolph Braham's works served me well.

David Langbart at the National Archives and Records Administration found the key sources that allowed me to fill an important gap in my evidence about US efforts in Hungary. He also carefully read Chapter 5, suggesting a number of valuable improvements.

David Engel generously gave me his detailed notes on Jan Karski's report on his conversation with President Roosevelt. Vincent Slatt translated Polish portions of this report for me. I am very grateful to both.

Randy Herschaft generously alerted me to methods to locate relevant newspaper articles.

Konrad Kwiet and Joe Bendersky read, and encouraged me to improve, an early version of Chapter 1.

Despite COVID-19 problems, Stephen Tyas carried out some essential research for me at the National Archives, Kew (UK). Andrew Silton read my chapter on Churchill's allies and suggested improvements. Tuvia Friling answered my questions about Chaim Weizmann's communications to Churchill and his circle. Kobi Freund called my attention to a good source on Churchill and gave me useful feedback on Chapter 2.

Making available some of his unpublished work, Joshua Rubenstein also answered some of my questions about Stalin and Soviet Jews. Zvi Gitelman and Michael Gelb, formerly my dedicated colleagues at the journal *Holocaust and Genocide Studies*, helped me craft my arguments about Stalin and the Holocaust and commented on a draft of Chapter 3. Eric Lohr and David Brandenberger answered my questions about Stalin's reading.

David Woolner chased down an archival source for me at the Franklin D. Roosevelt Presidential Library and gave me helpful feedback on Chapter 7. Archivist Virginia Lewick helped make my own research visit to the FDR Library efficient, pleasant, and productive. She also found a good source on Roosevelt's handling of press conferences.

Frank Chalk stressed the importance of radio broadcasts before and during the Holocaust in Hungary. He gave me access to some of his work and his secondary readings, and he commented on a key chapter about Hungary.

Michael Neufeld took time out of his work to read Chapter 8. He also added details about the Smithsonian–Holocaust Museum conference on the bombing of Auschwitz. He corrected my recollection of several related issues.

Ed Westermann gave me the benefit of his expertise on the air force and bombing during World War II. He read a draft article of mine about strategic bombing and the Holocaust.

US Holocaust Memorial Museum librarian Ron Coleman tracked down a relevant journal article for me that was not available in local libraries. David Kaiser, a onetime fellow graduate student at Harvard, answered my questions about Lend-Lease.

I am grateful to Malcolm Swanston for his fine work on my two maps.

My longtime friend Marc Alexander helped to mold my conclusion. Marcia Rohrer recommended improvements to Chapter 7.

My wife, Carol, once again put up with many inconveniences, among them my cluttered and steadily expanding workspace at home. She read every chapter and almost always found errors to correct. I am grateful to her most of all.

INDEX

Page numbers followed by *fig* denote an illustration.